Rethi

The Cer ⌐ ociety

Several problems plague contemporary thinking about governance, from the multiple definitions that are often vague and confusing, to the assumption that governance strategies such as networks and markets represent attempts by weakening states to maintain control.

Rethinking Governance questions these assumptions and seeks to clarify how we understand governance. Arguing that it is best understood as 'the strategies used by governments to help govern', the authors counter the view that governments have been decentred. They show that far from receding, states are in fact *enhancing* their capacity to govern by exerting top-down controls and developing closer ties with non-government sectors.

Identifying several 'modes' of governance, Stephen Bell and Andrew Hindmoor use a wide range of practical examples to explore the strengths and limitations of each. In so doing, they demonstrate how modern states are using a mixture of governance modes to address specific policy problems.

This book demonstrates why the argument that states are being 'hollowed out' is overblown. *Rethinking Governance* refocuses our attention on the central role played by governments in devising governance strategies.

Stephen Bell is Professor and former Head of the School of Political Science and International Studies at the University of Queensland.

Andrew Hindmoor is Senior Lecturer in the School of Political Science and International Studies at the University of Queensland.

D1388780

Rethinking Governance

The Centrality of the State in Modern Society

Stephen Bell and Andrew Hindmoor

CAMBRIDGE
UNIVERSITY PRESS

CAMBRIDGE UNIVERSITY PRESS
Cambridge, New York, Melbourne, Madrid, Cape Town, Singapore, São Paulo, Delhi

Cambridge University Press
477 Williamstown Road, Port Melbourne, VIC 3207, Australia

Published in the United States of America by Cambridge University Press, New York

www.cambridge.edu.au
Information on this title: www.cambridge.org/9780521712835

First published 2009

Cover design by Adrian Saunders
Typeset by Aptara Corp.
Printed in Australia by Ligare

A catalogue record for this publication is available from the British Library

National Library of Australia Cataloguing in Publication data
Bell, Stephen.
Rethinking governance : the centrality of the state in modern society / Stephen Bell,
Andrew Hindmoor.
9780521712835 (pbk.).
Bibliography.
Political science.
Hindmoor, Andrew
320

ISBN 978-0-521-71283-5 hardback

Reproduction and communication for educational purposes
The Australian *Copyright Act 1968* (the Act) allows a maximum of
one chapter or 10% of the pages of this work, whichever is the greater,
to be reproduced and/or communicated by any educational institution
for its educational purposes provided that the educational institution
(or the body that administers it) has given a remuneration notice to
Copyright Agency Limited (CAL) under the Act.

For details of the CAL licence for educational institutions contact:

Copyright Agency Limited
Level 15, 233 Castlereagh Street
Sydney NSW 2000
Telephone: (02) 9394 7600
Facsimile: (02) 9394 7601
E-mail: info@copyright.com.au

Reproduction and communication for other purposes
Except as permitted under the Act (for example a fair dealing for the
purposes of study, research, criticism or review) no part of this publication
may be reproduced, stored in a retrieval system, communicated or
transmitted in any form or by any means without prior written permission.
All inquiries should be made to the publisher at the address above.

Cambridge University Press has no responsibility for the persistence or
accuracy of URLs for external or third-party internet websites referred to in
this publication and does not guarantee that any content on such websites is,
or will remain, accurate or appropriate. Information regarding prices, travel
timetables and other factual information given in this work are correct at
the time of first printing but Cambridge University Press does not guarantee
the accuracy of such information thereafter.

For Jo and Hillary,
and Jane, Jordan and Asha

Contents

Figures and tables

FIGURES

TABLES

Preface

THE TERM GOVERNANCE has become a part of day-to-day vocabulary. Politicians talk about the importance of 'good governance' in developing countries and the significance of corporate governance in firms. Journalists write about the governance of charities, football clubs, museums, universities, schools and football clubs. In these cases it appears that governance is an alternative term for management or leadership. In political science, however, governance has a distinct meaning. Here writers talk about a transition from 'government to governance' and even of the exercise of 'governance without government'. At its simplest, the argument is that governments have been 'hollowed out' or 'decentred' and must now work with a range of non-state actors in order to achieve their goals.

In our view these arguments are overblown. In fact, part of the motivation for writing this book was the lack of a sustained alternative account of governance in which the state played a central role in governance arrangements and relationships, but also steered or metagoverned them. Although we point to instances in which governments have been marginalised and collectively valued policy goals are being pursued by non-state actors, such cases are few and far between. In our view governments and the broader set of agencies and public bodies which together constitute the state are and should remain central in governance processes. But while rejecting what we call 'society-centred' arguments about governance, we also express reservations about alternative 'state-centric' accounts in which governments are imagined to operate in splendid isolation from the societies they govern, descending from on high occasionally to impose their policy preferences. Instead, we develop a 'state-centric relational' account of governance, arguing that states have enhanced their capacity to govern by strengthening their own institutional and legal capacities but also by developing closer relations with non-state actors. Ultimately, the choice between society-centred and state-centric approaches to governance or between governance and government is a false one. Our state-centric relational approach emphasises the importance of the state and also the importance of state–society relations in governance.

OUTLINE OF THE BOOK

The first three chapters survey existing debates and arguments about governance and develop our state-centric relational approach to governance. Chapter 1 sets out our aims and emphasises that the state is still central to governance processes. The next chapter critically examines arguments that the state has been undermined by a range of forces, including neoliberal ideology, regulatory failure and globalisation. Chapter 3 looks at the concept of metagovernance, defined as the 'government of governance', and links empirical arguments about how governments govern to normative debates about the role and responsibilities of government within a democratic society.

Chapters 4–8 apply these perspectives to 'governance in action' across the five modes of governance we have identified: via hierarchy, persuasion, markets, community engagement and associations. The wide-ranging survey mixes theoretical discussion with practical examples of governance arrangements, exploring the role that governments and state agencies play in designing and managing various modes of governance. These five chapters develop our state-centric relational account by including perspectives from international relations, economics, development studies and comparative politics. Some studies of governance neglect major developments in political science, but discussions about networks, power, ideas and institutions can illuminate understanding of the forms and limitations of governance.

In challenging society-centred accounts of governance, we do not wish to create the impression that states are omnipotent. Instead, we show how states have augmented their policy capacity by developing closer relations with non-state actors. Governments are not like a modern-day Gulliver tied down by non-state Lilliputians. When there is interdependence in the relations between states and non-state actors, it is often asymmetrical.

Most of our examples are taken from major Western democracies, with a few from other countries. We examine governance beyond as well as within countries. Arguments about the hollowing out of the state and new ways of governing are related to arguments about globalisation and to what some see as the gradual emergence of 'global governance'. We discuss the governance role played by various international institutions, but we do not believe that global governance is a separate category.

All dollar sums are in US$.

ACKNOWLEDGEMENTS

We are extremely grateful to Gerry Stoker and Grace Skogstad who provided us with incisive comments on early drafts and whose endorsements the completed book now carries. Thanks to Brian Head who read and commented on several draft chapters. Thanks to Mike Keating who read some early draft chapters and keenly supported this project. We have also benefited from the comments, suggestions and examples offered to us by the undergraduate and postgraduate students at the University of Queensland upon whom we have piloted various versions of our arguments.

Stephen Bell
Andrew Hindmoor

1 | A state-centric relational approach

THE WORD GOVERNANCE derives from the Classical Greek *kybernan*, meaning to pilot, steer or direct. The term has a long heritage and might be applied to any number of activities. In the Elizabethan Age in England people talked about the governance of the family. These days many use the term corporate governance to refer to the management and control of companies (Kim & Nofsinger, 2007; Maillin, 2007), or more broadly the governance of particular organisations. This book focuses on the increasing use of the term governance to describe the attempts of governments or other actors to steer communities, whole countries, or even groups of countries in the pursuit of collective goals.

A large body of work presents what we call a 'society-centred' focus upon governance. The argument is that the last few decades have resulted in a 'fundamental transformation not just in the scope and scale of government action, but in its basic forms' (Salamon, 2002, 1–2). National governments are said to have been 'hollowed out' by neo-liberal governments intent upon 'rolling back the frontiers of the 'state' (Thatcher, 1993, 744–5), by globalisation, and by the growth of international and occasionally supra-national organisations. The alleged weakening of the state is said to be driven by growing fiscal or legitimacy deficits, by institutional fragmentation, or by pressures from below from social groups wanting more say in policy and governance. As a result of these pressures, it is argued, governments now lack the ability to govern unilaterally and must instead work with interest-groups, private firms, charities, non-governmental organisations (NGOs), supra-national organisations, and a range of other bodies if they are to achieve their objectives.

This book rejects many of these claims. In particular, states have not been hollowed out and the exercise of state authority remains central to

1

most governance strategies. The main problem with many of the current approaches to governance is that the role of the state has either receded from view or remains ambiguous. In our view, governments and the broader set of agencies and public bodies that together constitute the state are, and should remain, central players in governance processes. We thus reject the notion that there has been any general loss of governing capacity and instead agree with Tabatha Wallington, Geoffrey Lawrence and Barton Loechel (2008, 3) who argue that governance is about governments seeking to 'govern better rather than govern less'. We also argue that the scope and scale of governance is actually expanding, and that state-based, hierarchical or top-down forms of governance are doing likewise. States are attempting to expand their governing capacities not only by strengthening central state institutions but by forging new governance partnerships with a range of social actors.

We thus agree that governments have, in recent decades, adopted a broader range of governance strategies. But we disagree that this constitutes a 'fundamental transformation'. This is partly because alternative governance strategies have a far longer pedigree than many of those writing about governance recognise, and also because states generally retain effective control over such arrangements. States are constantly choosing new policy goals and learning to pursue them in different ways. But while much has changed, the state remains a central actor in governance arrangements. We therefore define governance from a state-centric perspective and argue that governance arrangements are largely created and orchestrated by the state to help govern society. Governing can generally be defined as shaping, regulating or attempting to control human behaviour in order to achieve collective ends. Yet effective governance often requires states to build strategic relationships with a range of non-state actors. This is a process of engagement that Donald Kettl (2002, 123) refers to as 'governmentalising' previously non-governmental sectors in attempts to draw in extra governing resources from society, allowing governments to increase their reach without necessarily growing in size. Hence, we argue for a definition of governance from a *state-centric relational* perspective and define governance as *the tools, strategies and relationships used by governments to help govern*. This approach suggests that governance can be seen as an extension of more traditional notions of public policy, except that the rubric of governance implies experimentation with a wide variety of governing strategies and the involvement of a wider range of non-governmental actors.

Our approach is *state-centred* because we argue that governments rely upon hierarchical authority to implement their policies, and because, even when governments *choose* to govern in alternative ways, the state remains the pivotal player in establishing and operating governance strategies and partnerships. We thus see governance and changes in governance arrangements as substantially driven by changes in state preferences and strategy. Our approach to governance is also *relational* because we emphasise the extent to which governments, in establishing and operating governance strategies, develop strategic relationships or partnerships with a range of non-state actors. For this reason, ultimately, the choice between society-centred and state-centric approaches to governance, or between governance and government, is a false one. Our state-centric relational approach emphasises the importance of the state and also the importance of state–society relations in governance. Our state-centric relational approach thus absorbs the *relational* aspects of the society-centred approach, but from a state-centric perspective.

The rest of this chapter elaborates on these claims. We examine the society-centered perspective on governance and ask to what extent changes in governance amount to a fundamental transformation. We then define our state-centred relational approach and outline the range of ways in which governments have deployed different 'modes of governance' in order to govern.

SOCIETY-CENTRED GOVERNANCE

Much of the existing literature on governance is society-centred: it emphasises the proliferation of complex horizontal forms of societal relations and governance networks that are said to have marginalised government or rendered its role ambiguous. As Eva Sorensen and Jacob Torfing (2008a, 3) put it: 'the sovereign state . . . is losing its grip and is being replaced by new ideas about pluricentric government based on interdependence, negotiation and trust'. We begin by critically reviewing this writing as well as the notion that governance represents a 'fundamental transformation' (Salamon, 2002, 1–2) or a 'substantial break from the past' (Stoker, 1998, 26) in the scope, scale and basic forms of government action.

In our view, the society-centred approach consists of two parts. The first is that the alleged shift from government to governance has resulted in the involvement of a wider range of actors within governing processes, and that these actors are held together not by rules, regulations and hierarchy but by informal and relatively egalitarian networks. Hence a major theme within the society-centred approach consists of a focus upon partnerships and networks and the blurring of the boundaries between the public and private sectors. According to Mark Bevir and Rod Rhodes (2003, 55–6), 'networks are the defining characteristics of governance' and offer a 'coordinating mechanism notably different from markets and hierarchies'. Policy network is the name given to the formal and informal links and exchanges that develop between governments and civil society associations, NGOs and interest-groups in specific policy arenas (Marsh & Rhodes, 1992a, b). A major proposition of the society-centred approach is that an increasing number of policy decisions are being taken in and through self-organising policy networks.

Thus Lester Salamon (2002, 2) associates governance with 'an elaborate system of third-party government in which crucial elements of public authority are shared with a host of nongovernmental or other-governmental actors, frequently in complex collaborative systems'. Rod Rhodes (1997, 15) defines governance in terms of 'self-organising inter-organisational networks characterised by interdependence, resource exchange' and a shared acceptance of the 'rules of the game'. In a recent edited work, Sorensen and Torfing (2008a, 3) acknowledge that 'forms of top-down government remain in place', but nevertheless suggest that a major shift in governance has occurred and that 'public management increasingly proceeds in and through pluricentric negotiations among relevant and affected actors on the basis of interdependency, trust and jointly developed rules, norms and discourses. The 'surge in governance networks', they continue, 'is prompted by the persistent critique of traditional forms of governance in terms of hierarchies and markets.' Similarly, Mark Bevir (2007, 2) uses the term governance to describe a 'shift from a hierarchic bureaucracy to a greater use of markets and networks'; while Adrienne Heritier (2002a, 185) concludes that governance entails 'types of political steering in which non-hierarchical modes of guidance . . . are employed'.

The second part of the argument is that the challenges to the state noted above, as well as the involvement of a larger range of actors in the process of governing, have resulted in government being superseded or at least marginalised. As Eerik-Hans Klijn and Joop Koppenjan (2000, 136) argue, a 'broad consensus has developed around the idea that government is not actually the cockpit from which society is governed'. Andrew Jordan, Rüdiger Wurzel, and Anthony Zito (2005, 480) suggest that 'most scholars associate governance with the decline in central government's ability to steer society'. Similarly, for Gerry Stoker (1998, 17), 'the essence of governance is its focus on governing mechanisms which do not rest on recourse to the authority and sanctions of government'. Maarten Hajer (2003) contends that governance has led to a dispersal of power and the emergence of an 'institutional void' in which there are endless negotiations but no clear rules about how policy should be decided. Finally, Rhodes (1997, 52) describes governance networks as operating with 'significant autonomy from the state'.

To be sure, there are some countries in the world where central government has collapsed and non-state actors have stepped in to perform at least some of the functions previously performed by the state. In Somalia the civil war that raged between 1988 and 1992 resulted in the deaths of around a quarter of a million people. In its aftermath, informal coalitions of business leaders, clan elders and Muslim clerics assumed responsibility for constructing a system of local courts and other dispute-resolution mechanisms in the absence of any functioning state (Menkhaus, 2007). As Chapter 7 on community engagement explains, Elinor Ostrom (1990; Dolsak & Ostrom, 2003) has shown that non-state actors are sometimes capable of developing elaborate but informal rules, norms and conventions governing the allocation of natural resources. There are, furthermore, a number of instances in which NGOs have pressed firms to collectively develop and voluntarily agree to abide by codes of conduct in the apparent absence of any state involvement. David Vogel (2008, 262) reports that there are now more than 300 such codes, primarily addressing either labour or environmental practices, on such high-profile political issues as child labour, sweatshops, diamond mining and fair-trade coffee and cocoa production. 'Non-state market-driven' arrangements of this sort (Cashore, 2002) come closest to a model of 'governance without government'. Nevertheless, a later chapter shows that such governance arrangements are limited in scope, are often poorly enforced, and are pursued by NGOs as a second-best alternative to state action.

We acknowledge that not every writer who points to the involvement of a larger range of actors in the process of steering society is willing to discount the state. Janet Newman (2005, 1) suggests that 'governmental power is both retreating – with state institutions being slimmed down, hollowed out, decentred and marketised – and expanding, reaching into more and more citizens' personal lives: for example their decisions about work, health and parenting'. We concur with this latter view. In several of their texts Jon Pierre and Guy Peters (2000; 2005) have offered an avowedly 'state-centric' perspective on governance, proclaiming that, 'despite persistent rumours to the contrary, [the state] remains the key political actor in society and the predominant expression of collective interests' (2000, 25). Yet, even here, changes in, and the limits of, the state's authority are emphasised. Although Pierre and Peters dismiss claims that the state is disappearing, they nevertheless maintain that its role and capacities have been fundamentally changed. The state is no longer the pre-eminent actor whose 'centrality can be taken for granted' and which can 'be employed to enforce the political will of the dominant political constituency' (p. 82).

The society-centred approach to governance also downplays concepts such as political power and authority (Koppenjan, 2008, 133). For Newman (2005, 4), 'governance theory offers an account of the dispersal of power within and beyond the state, undermining the privileged place of representative democracy' (see also Hajer, 2003, 177). Vasudha Chhotray and Gerry Stoker (2009, 12) see governance as a system that is 'not necessarily hierarchical in nature'. Similarly, Sorensen and Torfing (2008a, 10) argue that within governance networks, 'nobody can use their power to exert hierarchical control over anybody else without risking ruin to the network'. In this view, hierarchy, power struggles and conflict seem to get marginalised or replaced by contracts, bargaining, negotiation, networking, mutual dependence, or reciprocity and trust relations. This is a horizontal view of politics in which the state is receding or playing a more marginal role in a system of 'self-organising networks' built on bargaining and negotiation, rather than authority structures. Hence, when writers such as Sorensen and Torfing (2008a) emphasise the centrality of 'non-hierarchical forms of governance', the 'absence of top-down authority' or the 'role of horizontal networks of organised interests in the production of public policy and governance' (pp. 3, 44, 3; see also Borzel & Panke, 2008), this implies that public actors do not have any distinctive role or authority vis-à-vis private actors. Indeed, Tanja Borzel and Diana Panke (2008, 155) argue that 'public and private actors enjoy equal status' in such networks. In other words, the role of government is marginalised or rendered seemingly equivalent to that of private actors amidst processes of horizontal bargaining and negotiation.

A FUNDAMENTAL TRANSFORMATION?

The society-centred account argues that states are being weakened by an array of forces and that, as a result, governments now govern less frequently through the unilateral application of top-down, hierarchical, authority and more frequently in partnership with non-state actors through markets, network associations and other 'new' forms of governance. What are we to make of these empirical claims? We focus in detail on the 'resilience' of the state in the next chapter, but here it is worth exploring the idea that other modes of governance have increasingly marginalised the state.

We do not doubt that governments across the world are more likely than they once were to make use of, in particular, market mechanisms. In some cases – most notably the cap-and-trade provisions found in emissions trading systems – market mechanisms have acquired a high political profile. We accept that faith in market mechanisms is more than a passing policy fad. Neo-liberal governments and international organisations like the World Bank were the first to eulogise the use of markets, but their acceptance has spread beyond this relatively narrow political base. We also recognise that governments have increasingly experimented with strategies to engage the community and governance through partnering with civil society associations. In this sense, the state is certainly experimenting with a wider palette of modes of governance, as we outline below.

Nevertheless, the extent to which there has been a 'fundamental transformation' in the 'basic forms' of governance can be exaggerated (Salamon, 2002, 1–2). In most policy areas in most countries, top-down governance through hierarchy remains the most frequently employed governance strategy. Consider, in this regard, the illuminating study of European environmental policy by Jordan, Wurzel and Zito (2005). They document the extent to which various 'new' environmental policy instruments – eco-taxes, tradable permits, voluntary agreements, eco-labels – have been adopted in seven European countries. They found that, while every country had adopted at least one new policy instrument, 'there has been no wholesale and spatially uniform shift from government to governance' (p. 490).

Hierarchy is not simply holding its own against other governance mechanisms. In many cases it is resurgent, as described in Chapter 4. Governments have increasingly come to rely upon hierarchical solutions to address new policy problems such as:

- *speeding:* heavy fines, surveillance cameras, compulsory educational programs
- *illegal immigration:* fines for lorry drivers or airlines caught intentionally or unintentionally carrying immigrants
- *obesity:* bans on the advertising of junk food during children's television programs, on the sale of junk food within school premises, on the use of certain trans fats in the preparation of food
- *drug abuse:* compulsory drug testing for prisoners and, in some countries, public servants and, in almost every country, longer prison sentences for those caught dealing
- *anti-social behaviour:* court orders in Britain banning people from frequenting a certain area or socialising with certain people
- *smoking:* bans on smoking in public places

- *terrorism:* new legislation making it a criminal offence not simply to plan a terrorist attack but to acquire information likely to be of use to a terrorist.

In some cases the forms of hierarchy employed by governments have changed. Governments are now more likely to employ 'smart' regulatory systems in which the threat of fines and other punishments is accompanied by the promise of self-regulation and extensive consultation. Governments have also devolved more authority to quasi-independent bodies such as central banks, regulatory agencies and courts (Vibert, 2007). Yet such developments do not spell the end of governance through hierarchy. Smart regulatory systems still rely upon the threat of hierarchical intervention to encourage firms and associations to regulate their own activities. Indeed, critics have suggested that smart regulatory systems increase overall government control over society by giving officials the opportunity to intervene in the absence of any clear legislative mandate (Berg, 2008, 45–55). As for the shift toward quasi-autonomous bodies such as independent central banks and regulatory authorities, it should be remembered that they remain a formal part of the state with their authority being parcelled out by government.

Hence, even where governments have embraced alternative governance arrangements, hierarchy remains of central importance. Pierre and Peters (2006, 218) suggest that governments, 'rather than relying on command and control instruments', are now 'utilizing "softer" instruments to achieve their policy goals'. We question this depiction because, although governments are experimenting with different modes of governance, this does not necessarily imply a shift away from hierarchical command and control strategies or from the use of governmental or state authority in structuring a range of governance modes. Instead, the new instruments are running in parallel with command and control strategies because the operation of a wide range of governance mechanisms usually entails hierarchical state oversight; Chapter 3 explores this process further under the rubric of 'metagovernance'.

There are two other reasons why we are sceptical about the notion of a fundamental transformation in the state's role. First, we believe that those writing about governance risk exaggerating not only the extent to which governments now govern through markets, associations and community engagement but also governments' past dependence upon hierarchy. Consider the way in which governments can contract with private firms or voluntary organisations to provide particular services: an important component of governance through the market. There has, undoubtedly, been a dramatic growth in the use of such contract arrangements. The basic principle of contracting-out services is, however, a venerable one. Services provided by private firms under contract to governments in the 17th and 18th centuries included prison management, road maintenance, collection of tax revenue and refuse collection. In that period the British government granted the East India Company monopoly control on overseas trade with the East Indies, India and China and the authority to use armed force to protect its position (Bernstein, 2008, 214–40). Meanwhile, the convict ships that carried prisoners from Britain to Australia were operated by private profit-making firms (Industry Commission, 1996, 74).

Neither can the involvement of organised interests in the policy process be considered novel. In the 1950s President Eisenhower warned of the influence exercised by the military-industrial complex over the United States' defence and procurement policy. In the 1960s social policy innovations such as the Model Cities program saw governments engaging with neighbourhood and religious organisations. And academic work on American democracy in the 1960s pointed to the influence exercised by interest-groups in shaping public policy (Lowi, 1969). In many European countries 'corporatist' power-sharing arrangements between governments and peak associations representing the interests of unions and/or business have been an established feature of the governance landscape for decades. We thus reject the claim by Rod Rhodes (1996, 652) that governance implies 'a change in the meaning of government' or 'a new process of governing' (see also Stoker, 1998, 26).

Our second reason for scepticism is that, even where governments have chosen to cede some of their authority to non-state actors, they always retain the authority to change governance arrangements. The authority the state gives to non-state actors is only ever on loan, and such arrangements are always potentially reversible. Consider, for example, the fate of the United Kingdom's privatised rail network. In 1994 a new profit-making firm, Railtrack, acquired ownership of all track, signalling and stations. Following a fatal rail crash that revealed systemic weaknesses in Railtrack's engineering culture, the rail network ground to a halt in 2000 and, largely as a result of the losses it incurred during this period, Railtrack was bankrupted the following year. A new company, Network Rail, was subsequently established that, in the place of a responsibility to maximise the value of shareholdings, had a board of directors with a responsibility to pursue the public interest. More specifically, Network Rail is required to set policies in a manner consistent with guidelines devised by the Office of Rail Regulation. Nominally, Network Rail is still classified as a private company. In reality, and as ministers have frequently boasted, Network Rail is controlled by the Department of Transport, which sets the overall policy framework within which the Office of Rail Regulation and Network Rail operate.

A STATE-CENTRIC RELATIONAL APPROACH

One of our key arguments then is that governance through hierarchical control imposed by the state is alive and well. In some arenas – defence, security, monetary policy – policies continue to be made and implemented hierarchically by the state and consultation is non-existent or extremely limited. And when governments have *chosen* to govern in alternative ways, we argue that the state usually retains a pre-eminent position. On this basis we argue that states and governments remain critical players in governance *and* that governance is also about state–society relationships, whatever the governance arrangements in place.

Governments and state agencies are attempting to further boost their capacities by employing an expanding array of governance strategies. Governments can choose how they wish to govern and can exercise this choice without necessarily limiting their own powers. As Hans Andersen (2004, 7) writes:

> Many researchers have claimed that the restructuring of governance is a general retreat of government and the state . . . yet there is no reason to assume that the rise of governance necessarily leads to a decline of government . . . the main reason for the rise in state capacity through restructuring is . . . the fact that the state is now able to influence hitherto non-governmental spheres of social life through partnerships, i.e. an enlargement of state competencies [see also Keating, 2004; Pierre & Peters, 2000, 49].

Thus, by building close relationships with non-state actors through alternative governance arrangements, state leaders are attempting to enhance their capacity.

How can this happen? One way of thinking about the relationship between state and non-state actors is in terms of a mutually beneficial exchange. By working with other actors the state can sometimes achieve more than it could by working on its own. The exact nature of these exchanges will vary depending on the type of governance mechanism being employed and the goals being sought. In general terms, however, governments can often acquire greater legitimacy and assistance in implementing their policies by developing relations with interest-groups and community bodies. By working with private firms, governments can purchase expertise and, in the case of controversial decisions, a certain amount of political credibility. Policies that have been endorsed by key stakeholders are more likely to be regarded as legitimate by the media and public. In return, governments must concede to these actors at least some measure of influence in the policy process. Essentially, governing capacity is enhanced or potentially enhanced in such cases because governing relies not only on the state but on a broader array of actors who collectively bring more capabilities to the table than the state alone can.

The existence of exchange relationships between state and non-state actors does not, however, mean that these relations are equal. As we describe more fully in the next chapter, and as Vasudha Chhotray and Gerry Stoker (2009, 22) observe, states are often able to 'dominate the exchange' (also see Pierre & Peters, 2000, 100; Flinders, 2006, 245). Michael Lister and David Marsh (2006, 255) say that 'modern governance involves the state in more complex relationships with other governmental and societal actors, but it doesn't inevitably reduce its role or power'. Similarly, Martin Smith (2006, 32) suggests in a discussion of pluralist theory:

> The problem with [society-centred] governance accounts of state reform and development is that they fall back on the simplistic assumptions of pluralism. They . . . ignore the asymmetries of power that potentially exist even in network relations. Perhaps the main problem is the way in which governance assumes that the central state has lost power when there is a raft of empirical evidence to demonstrate the high level of resources and authority that remains within the central state.

There is a second reason to be wary of assuming that governments have been superseded or marginalised. Even where governments choose to govern through markets, associations and community engagement, they usually retain a responsibility for metagovernance, or the 'government of governance'. As Chapter 3 explains, whatever the governance mechanism employed, the state typically plays (and should play) a key role in overseeing, steering and coordinating governance arrangements; in selecting and supporting the key participants; in mobilising resources; in ensuring that wider systems of governance are operating fairly and efficiently; and in taking responsibility for democracy and accountability issues.

Governments and state agencies thus typically play roles at two levels in governance arrangements. First, they are, with others, players in specific governance arrangements. Second, they also have a metagovernance function, an overall management and oversight role, that transcends specific governance arrangements.

Existing discussions about the role of the state in governance arrangements sometimes encourage us to think about a spectrum of possible positions running from, on the one hand, society-centred governance with minimal governmental presence to, on the other, a state-centric view of governance. Such a typology underpins the work of Jon Pierre and Guy Peters (2005) in *Governing Complex Societies* (see also Chhotray & Stoker, 2009, ch. 1; Jordan, Wurzel & Zito, 2005). Pierre and Peters identify five models of the state and society interactions in governance that are now said to be operating among contemporary democratic systems. These models are distinguished in terms of the actors involved, the nature of the processes and political dynamics at work, and the outcomes of the governing processes; together they constitute a 'continuum ranging from the most dominated by the state to those in which the state plays the least role' (p. 11).

- *The etatiste model:* government is the principal actor for all aspects of governance and can control the manner in which societal actors are involved, if at all, in governance.
- *The liberal-democratic model:* government is influenced by interest-groups but can nevertheless 'have the opportunity to pick and choose . . . [who] it will permit to have influence' (ibid).
- *The state-centric model:* the state 'remains at the centre of the process' but has institutionalised its relationships with social actors in corporatist-type arrangements.
- *The so-called Dutch governance school model:* the state is 'merely one among many actors involved in the process' and 'society may be the most powerful actor' (ibid).
- *The governance without government model:* the state has lost its capacity to govern and is, at best, an arena within which private actors play out their own interests to create more or less self-steering governance arrangements (p. 12).

This typology in which the authority of the state waxes and wanes loses sight of the integral role that governments play in *all* governance arrangements; a role that is the foundation of our state-centric relational approach to governance. Government and governance are not mutually exclusive alternatives between which societies must choose. They are not even the end-points along a spectrum of institutional arrangements. As we argue throughout this book, it is typically the case that government is routinely and authoritatively implicated in the exercise of all forms of governance.

States are central actors because they can bring to bear enormous financial resources to develop and support governance arrangements. In recent decades it has become commonplace to observe that states operate under continuous fiscal stress. Yet as we argue in the following chapter, the financial position of most states remains reasonably robust. In metagoverning its relationships with other actors, a state can deploy not only vast financial resources but large and often highly trained workforces. The US federal government employs around 55 000 physical and biological scientists, 68 000 computer specialists and 33 000 accountants and auditors. More generally, and at a local as well as national level, governments employ large numbers of policy officers trained to identify policy problems, find possible solutions, and negotiate agreements.

Another source of authority states have at their disposal typically sustains their dominance of exchange relationships. Governments do not simply operate within exogenously given sets of governance rules. They also have an authority, not possessed by any other actor, to choose the governance rules. Governments select the mechanisms to address policy problems: they can choose governance partners and can choose whether to govern through hierarchy, markets, persuasion, community engagement or associations. Having chosen which governance mechanism to employ, governments can also choose how to structure governance arrangements. In the case of governance through markets, governments can choose which services to contract-out and the criteria by which contracts are awarded. In the case of governance through community engagement, governments can choose the circumstances in which to engage with community groups and, invariably, how to interpret and respond to the results. Furthermore, governments can always choose to revise the existing governance mechanisms. This is a significant power because, even if governments do not choose to change governance arrangements, the knowledge that they can do so is, in itself, an important resource. Non-state actors will sometimes be deterred from pressing strident demands upon the government if they know that the government can simply change the underlying governance mechanism.

The choices governments make incur opportunity costs. Governing in partnership with other actors often requires governments to make policy concessions. Indeed, governing unilaterally through hierarchy can result in a loss of legitimacy. This is hardly surprising. Every action incurs opportunity costs. In some cases the distribution of resources between state and non-state actors means that states will incur significant costs if they operate unilaterally. Chapter 8 suggests that, if they are to govern effectively, governments must often learn to work constructively with business associations. Yet, even here, governments, in our view, retain a meaningful choice about how to govern. In the first place, governments can still choose how to structure their governance arrangements. In the case of governance through association, governments can set agendas and attribute 'public status' to favoured groups (Offe, 1981). Second, governments can, if they wish, choose to incur considerable short-term costs by governing unilaterally in order to strengthen their long-term position. Upon being elected to office, neo-liberal governments in the United Kingdom, Canada, and Australia chose to dissolve existing corporatist arrangements. In doing so these governments risked considerable political damage. By changing the rules of governance, however, governments can hope to secure a long-term advantage by undermining their opponents.

Governments do not always find themselves in a position to endure these short-term costs. In 2006 the French government, led by Prime Minister Dominique de Villepin, tried to change the prevailing governance rules by excluding the trade union movement from discussions about the introduction of a new employment contract that would have allowed employers to fire employees under the age of 26 during the first two years of their employment. In this case the government underestimated its ability to withstand the resulting political protests. Following a general strike that attracted the support of about two million people, the proposed legislation was eventually abandoned. Governments are not, however, always so constrained. Equipped with an express mandate for reform, President Nicholas Sarkozky more recently managed to oversee a number of similar reforms to French labour markets.

States alone have the capacity to change the rules of the governance game because when operating *within* nation-states they continue to possess legal sovereignty in the sense that they remain the 'final and absolute authority in the political community' (Hinsley, 1986, 26). Governments are constrained by constitutions, parliaments, elections and the media, but they remain authoritative actors who can change the rules of the political game. Governments can, if they wish, impose legal restrictions upon trade unions, side-step pressure groups whose views they oppose, forbid private firms from operating in certain locations or selling certain products, and renege upon the contracts they have signed with private firms.

On what basis does the state's legal sovereignty rest? There are two very different answers to this question, but both of them emphasise the centrality of the state. One theory is that the state's sovereignty rests upon its legitimacy: that is, upon a popular acceptance that the state is entitled to be the final and absolute authority in the political community and has the right to make authoritative decisions, largely because its leaders hold a democratic mandate from the people. In this sense legitimacy is linked directly to notions of democratic authority. Over the last few decades, trust in politicians and willingness to participate in the political process have fallen, in some cases dramatically (Stoker, 2006). A second notion underpinning legitimacy is that the state retains political legitimacy in the sense that people still routinely expect governments to solve policy problems and steer society. In a classic statement of neo-liberal philosophy, Ronald Reagan used his inaugural presidential address in 1980 to argue that, 'in the present crisis, government is not the solution to our problem; government is the problem'. Yet in a secular age it is still government and not God to which people are most likely to turn. When a flood strikes, unemployment increases or an inquiry reveals falling standards of care for the elderly or the mentally ill, it is elected politicians or, occasionally, the executive of a government agency who appear on our television screens to promise swift action. When the American sub-prime mortgage market started to fail in September 2007, placing individual banks and the wider capital market under enormous financial pressure, it was the federal government and the US Federal Reserve which was called upon to inject liquidity into markets and support and even nationalise parts of the banking system.

A second and more brutal argument is that the state's sovereignty rests upon its monopoly on the legitimate use of violence. This might seem dramatic, but the capacity of the state to unilaterally alter governance rules might, ultimately, be thought to depend upon its capacity to force other actors to behave in certain ways. Just as states continue to possess significant financial and bureaucratic resources, so they continue to possess not only an effective monopoly on the *legitimate* use of violence in society but a near-monopoly on the use of all violence. In some countries, well-organised criminal gangs pose a threat not only to public order but to the financial stability of the state. Yet in recent years the Italian judiciary (Della Porta, 2001) and (with a great deal of American assistance) the Colombian army (Bowden, 2001) have shown that they are capable of frustrating the activities of, respectively, the Mafia and the Medellin and Cali drug cartels. Concerns have also been expressed about the legitimacy of, and the dangers posed by, the large and legally protected private security forces employed by Russian energy companies and by large American security firms such as Blackwater (recently renamed Xe for reasons that are discussed in Chapter 6). These concerns need to be placed in context. Blackwater executives have spoken about creating a brigade-sized unit of around 2000 troops capable of being deployed to world trouble-spots at short notice (Scahill, 2007, 348–9). The US Army by contrast consists of around 400 000 enlisted soldiers and 80 000 officers.

MODES OF GOVERNANCE

Far from withering away, states have adapted to new environments and remain the public faces of governance. We therefore remain profoundly sceptical of transformationalist arguments and agree with Graham Wilson (2000, 235) when he says that: 'the popularity of anti-state rhetoric in the 1980s and 1990s [has] led many to confuse changes in the modes of state activity . . . with a decline in the significance of the state'. Our state-centric relational approach to governance recognises that governments have developed new tools, strategies and relationships in order to govern and that governments can therefore choose between different modes of governance. This book distinguishes five modes of governance: hierarchy, persuasion, markets, community engagement, and associative governance.

VIA HIERARCHY

Governance via hierarchy, or top-down governance, occurs when governments or agencies of the state act authoritatively to bring about an outcome. Governments and state agencies directly allocate resources through taxing and spending, or they attempt to impose order, rule and outcomes via direct regulatory, legal and enforcement measures. In this mode of governance state authority is used to foster order, rule and collective capacity. When governments ban smoking in public places (thus directly bringing about an outcome) or raise the taxes on a packet of cigarettes (thus changing the incentives for smokers in order to bring about an outcome), this is an example of governance via hierarchy.

VIA PERSUASION

While an enormous amount has been written about hierarchy and markets as instruments of governance, far less has been said about governance through persuasion – a mode of governance achieved through inculcating modes of 'self-discipline' or 'compliance' in target subjects. Yet attempts by governments to *persuade* people to change their behaviour have become a familiar feature of everyday life. As well as inducing citizens to change their behaviour through laws, taxes or regulations, governments also try to change their attitudes and behaviour by persuading them to smoke less, eat more healthily, drink less alcohol, save water, recycle their rubbish, report suspected terrorists, engage in voluntary work, use public transport, take regular exercise, undertake regular medical examinations, gamble responsibly, eschew drugs, and save for their retirement.

VIA MARKETS

One obvious change in the way in which governments govern is the growing commercialisation of government and the use of markets and contracts in governance processes. Governments across the world have contracted-out services to private firms and encouraged the development of public–private partnerships. Governments have privatised state-owned industries and deregulated other markets. They have also established new markets to tackle policy problems such as climate change. Yet we are sceptical of the claim that markets, any markets, operate independently of government. Rather than 'free markets', we talk about 'managed markets' and suggest that 'the shift to marketisation largely represents an attempt by government to enhance or restore their power to achieve their economic and social objectives, while minimising any loss of efficiency' (Keating, 2004, 6).

VIA COMMUNITY ENGAGEMENT

In the 1970s members of the New Left argued that bureaucratic structures had become too large and unwieldy and that the bureaucrats in them had become divorced from the public they were meant to be helping. Far from transforming people's lives, welfare expenditure had simply led to the 'regulation of the poor' (Squires, 1990; Smart, 1991). But whereas a similar neo-liberal critique of hierarchy led to a preference for governing through markets, the New Left argued for a radical democratisation of politics through the devolution of decision-making powers to local citizens and communities. In the 1990s community engagement became a favoured strategy of local and, eventually, central governments seeking to enhance their democratic credentials and legitimacy. Governments are

now awash with citizens' juries, consensus-building conferences, deliberative polling surveys, public hearings and focus groups. As a working
example of such an approach consider the system of Participatory Budgeting developed in Porto Alegre, Brazil, in the late 1980s and now practised
in around 300 cities across the world. Following a series of preliminary
open meetings to discuss past budget performance and future budget priorities, citizens elect a Budget Council, which negotiates final investment
priorities and a budget for the city (Fung & Wright, 2003; Stoker, 2006,
187–9).

VIA ASSOCIATIONS

In associative or network governance arrangements, the state works with
firms, private associations and interest-groups to develop and implement
policy. Through both corporatist and private-interest government arrangements (Streeck & Schmitter, 1985), states offer business associations and
other groups influence over the contents of public policy in exchange for
public support, access to information, and direct assistance in implementing policy. The involvement of non-state actors in the policy process is, in
itself, nothing new. What is said to have changed is the scale of interest-
group involvement and the legitimacy accorded to it (Sorensen & Torfing,
2008a, 4). Within a number of European countries, for example, peak
organisations representing the interests of labour or industry have on occa-
sion assumed the role of formal co-legislators who are able to negotiate
the contents of European Union directives (Treib, Bahr & Falkner, 2007,
10). Indeed, Rod Rhodes, whose work on governance we have already
mentioned, argues that the shift from what he describes as government
to governance is synonymous with the proliferation of networks in which
public and private sector actors exchange resources.

CONCLUSION

This chapter has outlined our critique of existing 'society-centred' accounts
of governance and introduced our 'state-centric relational' alternative to
them. Our basic aim here has been to emphasise two points: the continuing centrality of governments to the process of governance; and the degree
to which governments' capacity to govern requires the development of
effective working relationships with a range of non-state actors. In the following two chapters we develop these themes: first by critically examining

arguments that the state has been undermined by neo-liberal ideology, regulatory failure and globalisation; and then by looking in more detail at the notion of metagovernance. The remaining chapters then explore the role that governments continue to play in designing and managing governance through hierarchy, persuasion, markets, community engagement and association.

2 | The resilient state

ARGUMENTS ABOUT GOVERNANCE are closely connected to those about the fate of the nation-state. In many commentaries, the state is depicted as ineffective, fiscally constrained, weakened by globalisation and increasingly unable to respond to the demands placed upon it. In response, so the argument goes, states have off-loaded substantial responsibility onto alternative modes of governance. This chapter restores some balance to the governance debate by highlighting the ongoing importance of the state. Far from being hollowed out, governments and state agencies remain the central architects of governance strategies. Rather than receding, states are changing and adapting in the face of new challenges and experimenting with more elaborate forms of both hierarchical and relational governance.

It was during the 1970s that social scientists seriously began to question the existing capacity and future relevance of nation-states. At a time when the world economy was faltering and terrorist groups like the Baader–Meinhof Gang in Germany and the Red Brigades in Italy were threatening the stability of mature liberal democracies, it became common to talk of government 'overload' and an impending 'legitimacy crisis'. In the 1980s and 1990s the economic and political environment changed and, in most countries, improved. Yet many academics, buoyed by concerns about globalisation and regulatory failure, proclaimed the retreat (Strange, 1996), decline (Mann, 1990) or even death (Hobsbawm, 1990) of the nation-state.

Arguments about the state underlie discussions of governance and, in particular, the society-centred account of governance reviewed in the previous chapter. The so-called hollowing out of the state features as both a cause and an effect of the alleged shift from government to governance. It is a cause in the sense that it is thought to have required governments to reach out to non-state actors in the private sector, in policy networks and in communities, to help with – or even assume responsibility for – the process of governing. At the same time, it is an effect in the sense that the decision of governments to govern in different ways has undermined state policy capacity. Having had to learn to work with others, the state is now unable to work alone.

Yet academic arguments about the decline of the state, although viewed uncritically in many works on governance, remain controversial. In some cases, specific variants of the hollowing-out argument have been overtaken by events. The concern of many UK political scientists in the 1970s about government overload soon gave way to equally strident critiques of the 'authoritarian populism' (Hall, 1985) and 'executive dictatorship' (King, 1988) of Margaret Thatcher's Conservative governments in the 1980s. At other times, eye-catching academic theories about the infirmity of the state have encouraged government reform, as with arguments about policy implementation or policy coordination; or they have given way to more nuanced academic debates that recognise the strengths and weaknesses of the state, as with arguments about globalisation.

This chapter evaluates arguments about the weakening of the state as they relate to the public choice theory of 'state failure', the 'fiscal crisis' of the state, the implementation 'gap', the 'decentring' of national governments, the loss of state legitimacy, and globalisation. Chapter 1 argued that the extent of the shift from governance through hierarchy to governance through markets, associations and community engagement is often exaggerated *and* that the choice between society-centred and state-centric approaches to governance is a false one because governments, in establishing and operating governance strategies, must develop and maintain close relationships with a range of non-state actors. Building on this, we argue that the pressures that are supposed to have led to a weakening of the state have been exaggerated *and* that governments are changing and adapting in the face of new challenges and experimenting with more elaborate forms of relations with society.

PUBLIC CHOICE THEORY AND STATE FAILURE

Public choice (or, as it is often called, rational choice) theory involves the application of the methods of economics – principally the assumptions of methodological individualism, rationality and egoism – to the study of politics (Mueller, 2003, 1; Hindmoor, 2006a, b). Public choice theory, which was initially developed within American universities in the 1960s and early 1970s, had by the 1980s acquired a measure of both academic hegemony (Green & Shapiro, 1994, 3; Lalman et al., 1993, 79) and practical policy influence (Self, 1993; Sretton & Orchard, 1994).

Perhaps the easiest way to understand public choice theory is to see it as a reaction to the theory of market failure. One of the achievements of post-war economic theory was the demonstration that, in conditions of perfect information and perfect competition, markets will clear, allowing for the achievement of a welfare-maximising equilibrium (Arrow & Debreu, 1954). Yet, as many economists soon recognised, one obvious implication of this fundamental theorem of welfare economics is that imperfect markets characterised by, for example, monopolies, externalities, public goods and uncertainty will generate imperfect results, so providing a *prima facie* justification for state intervention. In concluding that the existence of market failure justified state intervention, public choice theorists argued that economists had simply assumed that politicians and state officials would be able and willing to act in the public interest. In their view, economists had made an entirely misleading comparison between imperfect markets and a perfect state and so had, unsurprisingly, found in favour of the latter. In fact, public choice theorists argued, the state would often fail, either because self-interested bureaucrats would inflate their budgets (Niskanen, 1971) or because self-interested politicians bent on securing re-election would manipulate the economy for political purposes (Nordhaus, 1975; Hibbs, 1977), use their monopoly control of economic policy to effectively 'sell' policy favours to firms and pressure groups (Rowley et al., 1988), or use the taxation system to redistribute income to marginal constituencies or key groups of swing voters (Tullock, 2005).

In denouncing a 'romantic' view of politics in which politicians and public officials can simply be trusted to act in the public interest (Buchanan, 1999), public choice theorists have come to view any and every instance of state intervention as both harmful and motivated by considerations of electoral or bureaucratic self-interest. For this reason they have argued for a balanced budget amendment (Buchanan, 1997); more local referendums to approve proposed expenditure increases (Tullock, 1993, 78–85); and more restrictive budget rules to prevent the kind of porkbarrel politics that led, most famously, to the proposal to build a $400 million 'bridge to nowhere' in Alaska as a part of the 2005 Transportation Equity Act (*New York Times*, 21 October 2005).

During the 1970s and 1980s, public choice arguments were popularised by think-tanks like the Cato Institute in the United States and the Institute for Economic Affairs in the United Kingdom. They provided intellectual ammunition and a burgeoning policy agenda for neo-liberal politicians determined to 'roll back the frontiers of the state' and make more use of markets as a governance mechanism. Yet in political science departments there has been a growing backlash against the assumptions made and conclusions reached by public choice theorists (see Green & Shapiro, 1994; Friedman, 1996; Bell, 2002; Marglin, 2008). One recurring argument is that they have exaggerated the propensity for the state to fail. In economic markets competition generates efficiency. Donald Wittman (1995) argues that competition from opposition parties and between interest-groups and the press to draw the public's attention to government malfeasance similarly ensures the efficiency of political markets. Globalised financial markets are also likely to punish politicians seeking short-term electoral advantage. The former governor of the Reserve Bank of Australia, Bernie Fraser, invokes markets as one reason for the disappearance of opportunities for loose or politically manipulated monetary policy.

> These days ... such manipulation will be caught out ... the financial markets in particular will see through the ruse and punish the perpetrators. Today's politicians appreciate that extended front page reportage of a plunging exchange rate, for example, could easily outweigh any positive effects of a politically inspired cut in interest rates [quoted Bell, 2004a, 120].

The irony is that reforms inspired by public choice theory in the 1980s and 1990s have enhanced state capacity. The encouragement to devolve responsibility for monetary policy to independent central banks (Buchanan & Wagner, 1977) has helped states control inflationary pressures during the last few decades (Alesina & Summers, 1993). The support offered by public choice theorists like William Niskanen (1971) to introducing competition *within* the public service has arguably enhanced the capacity of the state bureaucracies to deliver services efficiently. Finally, public choice arguments about the dangers of regulatory 'capture' (Stigler, 1971) have led governments to rethink the ways in which they interact with private firms and associations. Far from reining in the state, public choice assaults have in some ways helped to strengthen it.

GOVERNMENT OVERLOAD AND THE FISCAL CRISIS OF THE STATE

At the same time as those on the political right were using public choice theory to expose the alleged failings of the post-war state, left-wing academics influenced by various strands of Marxist thought were predicting an inevitable 'fiscal crisis' for the capitalist state (O'Connor, 1973; Offe, 1984). The basic argument was that governments were caught between the increasing need to invest additional money in support of private capital, and their inability to finance that expenditure through taxation. These arguments found an echo during the 1970s in other and more general writings about government 'overload' (Brittan, 1975; King, 1975; Crozier et al., 1975). The post-war years, it was argued, had seen a rapid and unsustainable growth in public expectations about what governments could manage, which, once challenged, had led to a growing loss of confidence not only in particular political parties but in the democratic process (Birch, 1984). Summarising this development, Anthony King (1975, 166) suggested that 'once upon a time man looked to God to order the world. Then he looked to the market. Now he looks to government. And when things go wrong people blame not "Him" or "it" but "them"'.

Concerns about government overload and the apparently inexorable rise in post-war public expenditure provided part of the intellectual justification for neo-liberal efforts to cut public expenditure in the 1980s and 1990s. Even today, fears about excessive government spending continue to drive political debates in the United States and Europe about the cost of public health care and pensions. As Gerry Stoker (1998, 18) wryly observed, the demand to reduce public expenditure means that 'governance' is often regarded within government as a code for spending cuts. Equally, Jon Pierre and Guy Peters (2000, 52) suggest that the 'emergence of the new governance', has been propelled by an 'astounding' decline in the financial resources of the state. Yet when we look at the data we find that, measured as a share of gross domestic product, overall state expenditure in nearly all the countries within the Organisation for Economic Co-operation and Development (OECD) has either remained constant or slightly increased over the last 20 years (OECD, 2005a, 212–15). Between 1980 and 2001 overall public expenditure across the OECD increased by almost four per cent of GDP (Castles, 2007, 22–3). The limited impact of neo-liberalism upon the state is even more apparent when figures on state expenditure are placed in historical perspective. In 1870 state expenditure accounted for around 10 per cent of US gross domestic product; by 1980 this figure had risen to 31 per cent. In Germany over the same period state expenditure rose from around 12 per cent to 48 per cent of gross domestic product (Tanzi & Schuknecht, 2000). Judged against this baseline, little has changed in recent years. There is no evidence that state expenditure is likely to fall to the levels experienced in the 1960s, let alone the 1870s. Moreover,

Table 2.1. Total social expenditure as a percentage of gross domestic product, selected OECD countries, 1980 and 2001

Country	Total social expenditure		% change, 1980–2001
	1980	2001	
Australia	11.3	18.0	+ 6.7
France	22.6	28.5	+ 5.9
Germany	23	27.4	+ 4.4
Italy	18.4	25.8	+ 7.4
Japan	10.6	16.9	+ 6.7
Netherlands	26.9	21.8	− 5.1
United Kingdom	17.9	21.8	+ 3.9
United States	13.3	14.8	+ 1.5

Source: Castles, 2007, 22.

welfare expenditure, one of the key targets of neo-liberal governments, grew sometimes dramatically in the 1980s and 1990s (Table 2.1).

Why has social welfare expenditure increased over the last few decades? In most countries it has done so in response to labour market insecurity, ageing populations and rising health care costs. Neo-liberals may see such expenditures as evidence of government overload, but governments regard societal acceptance of the market system and economic openness as contingent upon the continued existence of social protection and redistribution (Rodrik, 1997, 1998; Alesina & Perotti, 1996). The once conventional wisdom about globalisation was that it would generate irresistible pressures to reduce social expenditure as states competed to reduce taxes in order to attract and retain investment capital. Yet empirical studies show that indicators of globalisation, such as relative openness to trade or capital movements, are in many cases *positively* related to various levels of government expenditure (Rieger & Leibfried, 2003; Brady, Beckfield & Seeleib-Kaiser, 2005; Castles, 2007). As Dani Rodrik (1997, 53) argues:

> this puzzle is solved by considering the importance of social insurance and the role of government in providing cover against external risk. Societies that expose themselves to greater amounts of external risk, demand (and receive) a larger government role as a shelter from the vicissitudes of global markets. In the context of the advanced industrial economies specifically, this translates into more generous social programs. Hence the conclusion that the social welfare state is the flip side of the open economy.

Table 2.2. Total taxation as a percentage of gross domestic product, selected OECD countries, 1975–2007

	Total taxation			
Country	1975	1995	2007	% change, 1975–2007
Australia	25.8	28.8	30.6 (2006)	+ 4.8
Belgium	39.5	43.6	44.4	+ 4.9
Canada	32.0	35.6	33.3	+ 1.3
Denmark	38.4	48.8	48.9	+ 10.5
France	35.5	41.9	43.4	+ 7.9
Germany	34.3	37.2	36.2	+ 2.5
Italy	25.4	40.1	43.3	+ 17.9
Japan	20.9	26.8	27.9 (2006)	+ 7.9
Netherlands	40.7	41.5	38.0	− 2.7
United Kingdom	35.2	34.5	36.6	+ 1.4
United States	25.6	27.9	28.3	+ 2.7
OECD average	29.4	34.8	35.9 (2006)	+ 6.5

Source: OECD Tax Revenue Trends, 1965–2006 (2008 edition).

Have states managed to raise the taxation needed to pay for this increased expenditure, so averting a fiscal crisis of the state? Broadly, the answer is yes. As Table 2.2 shows, between 1975 and 2007 overall levels of taxation measured as a proportion of gross domestic product *increased* in a range of European countries and remained constant in the United Kingdom and the United States. Across the OECD as a whole (including a range of countries not included in the table shown here) average taxation increased from 30.3 to 36.3 per cent of GDP. Because most OECD economies have doubled in size over this period, absolute tax income has grown dramatically; indeed, as economies have grown, the 'tax state' has grown even faster. In Australia, for example, for more than a decade to 2007, corporate tax receipts grew at over three times the rate of GDP growth (Braithwaite, 2008, 7).

Although tax revenues within OECD countries have remained buoyant, there is a general trend to finance public expenditure through long-term public debt. As long as the world economy continued to grow these public debt levels were manageable. Between 1980 and 2001 net debt interest payments as a proportion of GDP only rose from 1.8 to 2.3 per cent in the United States and from 1.5 to 2.0 per cent across a broader sample of 18 OECD countries (Wagschal, 2007, 26). Whether the combination of a global recession and additional public borrowing to rescue private banks brings into question governments' ability to service their debt is, at the time of writing, an open question. In January 2009 the European Commission predicted that the UK budget deficit would rise to nearly 10 per cent of GDP and that, overall, public debt would be equivalent of 72 per cent of GDP. At this time, financial markets were awash with speculation that the credit rating of the UK government was to be downgraded and that this would limit its borrowing capacity.

THE IMPLEMENTATION GAP?

In 1964 US President Lyndon Johnson pledged to build a great society through the elimination of poverty and racial injustice. Over the next few years a series of new government programs were introduced, including Medicare and Medicaid, funds to assist children from low-income families, and a new housing act to provide rent supplements for the poor. Despite the huge sums of money involved, the results of these programs were generally considered to be disappointing. In trying to account for their failure, policy analysts stumbled upon the idea that programs had failed not because the programs themselves were inherently flawed but because they had been poorly implemented (Pressman & Wildavsky, 1973). According to one public official:

> we became increasingly bothered in the late 1960s by those aspects of the exercise of government authority bound up with implementation. Results achieved by the programs of that decade were widely recognised as inadequate. One clear source of failure emerged: political and bureaucratic aspects of the implementation process were, in great measure, left outside both the considerations of participants in government and the calculations of formal policy analysts who assisted them [quoted Brewer & DeLeon, 1983, 249].

Over the next few years academics came to recognise the difficulties – sometimes impossibilities – of successful policy implementation in policy environments characterised by multiple centres of decision-making, ambiguous policy objectives, high levels of uncertainty and uncooperative 'street-level' bureaucrats (Lipsky, 1980; Maynard-Moody & Musheno, 2003). A tidal wave of case-studies showed how frequently great policy expectations are dashed during implementation (for reviews see Sabatier, 1986; DeLeon, 1999). Consider, as one example, the fate of the Kyoto Protocol. Attention focused on the refusal of the United States and, to a lesser extent, Australia to sign the treaty (Australia eventually signed in December 2007, following the election of a Labor government). Less media attention has been devoted to the implementation of the protocol itself. As of January 2008, Sweden and the United Kingdom were the only countries likely to meet their Kyoto emissions commitments, calling into doubt the value of the further promise made by leaders of the G8 countries in June 2007 to at least halve carbon dioxide emissions by 2050.

In the 1990s research on the difficulties faced by governments in successfully implementing public policy was tied to the discussion of policy networks. In most policy arenas in most countries, public policy is formulated and implemented through networks of government officials and non-government actors who represent functional interests such as peak business associations, professional associations, farmers groups and welfare associations. Dave Marsh and Rod Rhodes (1992c) argued that these policy networks had become so entrenched in the United Kingdom that government efforts to bypass networks and unilaterally impose policy nearly always ended in failure. It is certainly true that governments can enhance their governing capacity by developing closer relations with non-state actors. Non-state actors provide legitimacy, expertise, and sometimes direct assistance in implementing policies. But the extent to which governments are constrained by the existence of policy networks can be exaggerated. Governments are not only leading players within networks, they retain the hierarchical authority to change governance rules if they can bear the short-term political costs of doing so. The discussion below on the alleged decentring of the state, for example, shows how the French government simply bypassed the two main farming unions when it came under pressure to reduce agricultural subsidies as part of trade talks in the early 1990s.

Three further points are worth making about the literature on implementation. The first is that the academic study of implementation failures has prompted governments at both national and local level to more closely invest in, monitor and control the implementation process. For example, in a study of implementing work requirements as part of social welfare policy in Wisconsin, Lawrence Mead (2001) 'confirms [the] success of a top-down model of implementation' by showing how the authorities effectively 'built up an employment bureaucracy' in efforts to further improve policy implementation. In similar centrist moves, the UK government created a 'delivery unit' in 2001 (Richards & Smith, 2004) and the Australian government a Cabinet Implementation Unit in 2003 (Wanna, 2006). The second is that the academic search for further cases of implementation failure and 'policy disasters' (Bovens & Hart, 1996) in the 1970s and 1980s risks creating a highly distorted picture of government performance which ignores instances of successful policy implementation. This is not to suggest that policy implementation is always perfectly managed: clearly it is not. But the third point to make here is that the perfect implementation of policy may itself be a sub-optimal result: the marginal benefits of investing additional money and staff in the implementation of a policy ought to be balanced against the marginal costs involved. Overall, implementation is a challenging task, but we argue that governments now have a better grasp of implementation issues and are addressing them more effectively than in the past.

A CRISIS IN LEGITIMACY?

Governance arrangements can be described as legitimate to the extent that they are popularly accepted. Fritz Scharpf (1997; 1999) suggests that legitimacy is a two-dimensional concept, relating to the inputs *and* outputs of the political system. On the input side, legitimacy requires that political choices are derived, directly or indirectly, from the preferences of citizens and that governments are accountable for the actions. On the output side, legitimacy requires a high degree of effectiveness in achieving goals.

Governance arrangements that are democratic and accountable but result in ineffective policies will not be considered legitimate. In the United Kingdom, the Child Support Agency, an executive agency of the Department of Work and Pensions, catastrophically lost public support when the Independent Case Examiner's Office revealed that it took an average of 300 days to process a claim (BBC, 14 November 2004). Eventually, the agency was abolished and replaced by the Child Maintenance and Enforcement Commission. By streamlining the process of determining and collecting child support payments from absent parents, the commission eventually acquired some measure of output legitimacy.

Equally, governance arrangements that result in effective policies but are undemocratic and unaccountable are unlikely to be considered legitimate. After the World Trade Organisation had been the focus of many anti-globalisation protests, its director, Michael Moore, sought to defend its record in liberalising trade arrangements and alleviating poverty in developing countries (Address to the European Parliament, 21 February 2000). This is unlikely to persuade critics who view the organisation as undemocratic and unaccountable. The political scientist Susan George suggests that the World Trade Organisation gives 'transnational corporations... the ideal tool to complete their globalisation and impose new rules', and complains that the way panels are appointed to settle trade disputes is 'obscure... the names of the "experts" who sit on them and who meet behind closed doors and hear no outside witnesses are not made public' (*Le Monde Diplomatique*, November 1999). This argument is not about policy outputs but about democracy and accountability.

What evidence is there that states are losing their legitimacy? First, we might point to declining levels of voting. In competitive elections in all countries between 1945 and 1990 turnout rose steadily to reach an average of 68 per cent. In the 1990s turnout began to fall back towards an average of 60 per cent (Stoker, 2006, 32). Falling turnout might show evidence of voter satisfaction with the status quo. But polls have also shown a rising cynicism about politicians and political systems. European Social Survey data shows that around 25 per cent of Europeans believe that 'hardly any politicians care' about what they think (Stoker, 2006, 120). In the United States Joseph Nye and colleagues (1997) showed that whereas three-quarters of people expressed confidence in the federal government in 1964, only one-quarter were prepared to do so by the late 1990s. Second, we might point to the resurgence in some countries of anti-system parties with non-democratic ideals whose members engage in unconventional, illegal or violent behaviour (Capoccia, 2002; Keren, 2000). More prosaically, the decision of Dutch, French and Irish voters to reject the European Union's constitution in referendums held in 2005 and 2008 was also interpreted as showing a profound dissatisfaction with existing political processes. Finally, widespread political protests and marches – whether against the Iraq War, rising fuel prices, job losses or globalisation – might be taken as expressions of a loss of legitimacy in either national governments or international bodies.

We might account for declining legitimacy in terms of a growing belief that politicians are venal or incompetent; a lack of social cohesion; a rise in post-material values that has eroded any sense of deference to politicians; a professionalisation of politics that has made it harder for ordinary citizens to participate; the corrosive effects of a cynical media eager to assume political wrongdoing; or even the effects of public choice theory (see Stoker, 2006, 47–67 for an overview). Yet we should not see a continuing decline in overall levels of legitimacy as being somehow inevitable. Governments have adopted alternative governance arrangements precisely in order to enhance their legitimacy. This is most obviously true of community engagement strategies intended to give ordinary citizens the opportunity to directly

Table 2.3. Public confidence in parliament, selected OECD countries, 1981 and 1999/2000

Question: *I am going to name a number of organisations. For each one, could you tell me how much confidence you have in them: is it a great deal of confidence, quite a lot of confidence, not very much confidence or none at all? Figures show proportion of respondents expressing 'a great deal' or 'quite a lot' of confidence in their parliament.*

Country	1981	1999/2000
Belgium	38.4	35.6
Canada	43.7	41.1
Denmark	36.6	48.4
Japan	26.8	21.7
United Kingdom	41	35.4
United States	52.5	38.1

Source: World Values Survey <http://www.worldvaluessurvey.org/>.

influence decisions. According to *A Manager's Guide to Citizen Engagement*: 'Public engagement strategies provide decision-makers with opportunities to improve the substance of public input, cultivate trust through the process, raise the legitimacy of decisions in the public eye, and lay the groundwork for lasting implementation' (Lukensmeyer & Torres, 2000, 16).

The shift toward governance through persuasion and association, discussed in Chapters 5 and 8, can also be understood as an attempt by the state to bolster its legitimacy. Governance through persuasion is attractive to states because it provides an alternative to coercive policy instruments that may attract public opposition. Governance through community engagement or association is meant to ensure that policies are viewed as legitimate by stakeholders.

The loss of state legitimacy in recent years should not, however, be exaggerated. As we have said, voters continue to demand that states act to mitigate the effects of natural disasters, bank failures, environmental catastrophes, social disorder and threats to public health. Indeed, the pressures being placed upon governments often reflect growing and sometimes unrealistic expectations about what governments can achieve. The public is not turning its back on government; witness the historic voter turnout in the 2008 US presidential election. The World Values Survey allows us to track the amount of 'confidence' citizens have in various public institutions. Table 2.3 shows the proportion of voters who had 'a great deal' or 'quite a lot' of confidence in their parliament in the early 1980s and in the late 1990s. With the notable exception of Denmark, confidence has generally fallen over this period. But it has not fallen dramatically. Only in the United States did overall confidence fall by more than 10 per cent.

In the 1930s the legitimacy of democratically elected governments was brought into question by the Great Depression and then challenged by both communism and fascism. In 1968 student-led protests in France, the United States, Belgium, Mexico and Brazil heralded a brief moment of acute political turmoil. In the 1970s stagflation and government overload precipitated the collapse of the Keynesian post-war consensus. As Gerry Stoker (2006, 32) observes, however, the paradox of growing public disillusionment with politics today is not so much that it has occurred but that it occurred during the long economic expansion of the 1990s and 2000s when confidence in democratic decision-making remains high.

THE DECENTRING OF GOVERNMENT

A further argument about the alleged hollowing out of the state is that states and governments have become increasingly less central to governance or have been 'decentred' (Bevir, 2002). The argument has two strands. The first is that governments have devolved much of their authority to market contractors or policy networks. The second is that governments have lost power or authority and can no longer effectively coordinate or steer the activities of the multitude of actors now involved in governance processes. Hence, it is argued, the authority of central government has been compromised. Matthew Flinders (2006, 223), for example, points to the inherent difficulties of managing complex governance processes: 'The state consists of a highly heterogeneous network of organisations and controlling, steering and scrutinising this increasingly diverse flotilla of organisations and partnerships, many of which enjoy significant levels of autonomy from elected politicians and legislatures, remains the primary challenge of modern governance.'

The Dutch academic Walter Kickert (1993, 275) similarly argues that 'deregulation, government withdrawal and steering at a distance . . . are all notions of less direct government regulation and control, which lead to more autonomy and self-governance for social institutions'. Donald Kettl (2002, 161) writes: 'Hyperpluralism, policy networks, devolution, and globalisation have all greatly diffused power. Government might retain its legal position, but exercising political sovereignty amidst such diffused power represents a major challenge.' It is the existence of such self-organising networks that animates the society-centred account of governance described in the previous chapter. Indeed, Rhodes goes so far as to equate the alleged transition from government to governance with the proliferation of self-organising networks. In our view these arguments, which find an obvious extension in the claim that states have been decentred or hollowed out, have been overplayed.

True, the relational aspects of governance might in certain circumstances see outside groups achieve considerable influence within governance arrangements. This is certainly the case in associative governance arrangements such as corporatism, as we argue in Chapter 8. In another instance, the American Medical Association and the health insurance industry were widely credited with derailing Hillary Clinton's health reform proposals in the 1990s (Burns & Sorenson, 1999, 120–32). Kettl (2002, 143) adds that dealing with an array of partners obliges governments to recognise and deal with the fact that the partners may have their own missions, operating procedures and other projects that do not necessarily align with central governance purposes. But these dynamics do not mean that governments across the board have lost power or that networks are autonomous or self-organising. There is a significant difference between arguing that networks or devolution complicate governments' efforts to steer policy, and arguing that governance networks operate independently of the state. The problem is that self-organisation and self-responsibility are demanding criteria against which to judge the existence of such networks.

Nor do the standard discussions of policy networks support the idea that non-state actors or interest groups dominate networks or operate autonomously. Central is the work of Marsh and Rhodes (1992a), who initially distinguished between two kinds of policy networks: issue networks and policy communities. Where groups lack resources, where contacts between interest-groups and government fluctuate in frequency and intensity and the basic relationship is one of *consultation* rather than negotiation, an issue network is said to exist. It seems clear, from this analytical account, that issue networks cannot reasonably be described as self-organising (for case-studies see Damgaard, 2006; Parker, 2007). Therefore networks *per se* do not lead to governance without government. Policy communities, on the other hand, are characterised by a limited membership; frequent, high-quality interaction on all matters related to policy issues; stability of membership and outcomes; shared basic values; the acceptance of the legitimacy of outcomes; and the possession, by each of the members, of some valuable resources. In the case of policy communities, however, interest-groups are assumed to be in a stronger position; indeed, policy communities are defined in these studies partly in terms of a balance of power between government and non-state actors. Yet, even here, it is clear that interest-groups are not viewed as working autonomously from government. Policy communities are defined precisely in terms of the exchange of resources and the development of a close relationship *between* government and interest-groups. Indeed, in most cases actors join policy communities precisely because they wish to influence government.

A critical issue is that networks almost always contain authoritative actors from the state. There may be varying degrees of interdependency within networks or within contractual arrangements, but such arrangements are typically established by the state for wider public purposes. In many cases governments can choose which firms and interest-groups to work with. Interest-groups and firms, on the other hand, often have no choice but to work with government if they wish to acquire policy influence. Also, because non-state actors participate in networks mainly in order to influence the state, the notion that they end up operating with significant autonomy from the state is doubtful. Indeed, interest-groups have an incentive to lobby governments because the latter retain hierarchical authority. ExxonMobil was prepared to invest resources in the effort to persuade the US federal government to relax restrictions on oil exploration in Alaska precisely because the government retains the authority to determine where and when exploration can take place.

Governments occupy a privileged position in networks and can change existing governance rules to bypass or even dissolve networks. In recent years governments have abandoned policy communities centred on health in Canada (Kay, 2006, 104–15), agriculture in Australia (Botterill, 2005), and industrial relations in the United Kingdom (Marsh, 1992). The relationship between governments and other network actors is usually asymmetrical.

The self-styled 'structural' approach to the study of policy networks developed by David Knoke (1990; 2001) can help us to understand how governments can 'dominate the exchange' (Chhotray & Stoker, 2009, 22). Knoke makes two claims. First, that we can identify the participants in a network and formally measure the strength of the relationships between them in terms of, for example, the frequency of their meetings or membership of shared committees. The second – and, for our purposes, more interesting – claim is that we can explain actors' success in achieving their goals in terms of their structural position within a network.

(i)   (ii)

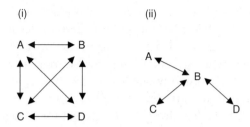

Figure 2.1. Network and structures

Figure 2.1 shows two possible network arrangements between four actors, A–D. In the first network every actor is connected to every other actor. In the second, A, C and D are connected only to B.

It seems obvious that B will be at a relative advantage in the second network. But why is this? One possibility is that network position determines the flow of information: a key bargaining resource within networks (Dowding, 1995, 158). In the second network A, C and D have to depend upon B for any information about the behaviour of other actors, while B can withhold or distort information to its advantage. A second possibility is that network position determines the opportunities actors have to form coalitions. In the second network A, C and D are at a disadvantage because they have no alternative but to work with B, who is therefore in a strong bargaining position.

In our view governments occupy a central location within associational networks equivalent to that enjoyed by actor B in the second network. As we have said, groups want to develop close working relationships with government officials because government possesses hierarchical authority – the authority to make binding policy decisions. This is not to say that non-state actors will operate in splendid isolation. Even when they are in direct competition for members and influence, groups want to exchange some information and, on occasions, develop joint negotiating positions. But the strongest network relationships are likely to be those between government and groups. A government's central position in a network gives it a number of advantages in steering the groups: the opportunity to control flows of information; to play interest-groups off against each other; and to demand that groups accept its preferences as the starting-point for negotiation. Of course the government cannot simply require groups to accept its policies. But the structural position of government within associational networks frequently imposes an asymmetrical form on this exchange.

In their influential book *Reinventing Government*, David Osborne and Ted Gaebler (1992, 30) called on governments to devolve responsibility for 'rowing' – the actual delivery of services to citizens – to non-state actors while retaining responsibility for 'steering' – raising resources and setting priorities. Crucially, however, they argued that by doing less rowing governments would *enhance* their capacity to steer – by creating more opportunities for strategic management (or metagovernance; see Chapter 3).

A critical issue is the government's capacity to exert control and to steer; it seems that in a wide range of instances governments continue to exercise considerable coercive power and regularly govern using hierarchical means. Indeed, Chapter 4 documents ways in which governments have *extended* their hierarchical control to meet the challenges posed by restructuring the state to boost governance capacities or those posed by new technologies, market failures and security and environmental threats. Here are some examples in which governments across the world have relied upon the threat or the actual use of coercive force to achieve particular goals:

- In 2005 the United States passed a 'Real ID Act' requiring states to redesign their drivers' licences in ways that would allow them to serve as a de facto compulsory identity card.
- In 2002 the United Kingdom introduced tough money-laundering legislation which requires banks and other financial institutions to report any suspicious financial activity to the Serious Organised Crime Agency.
- In the same year the Israeli government started to construct an 8-metre-high security barrier physically dividing the West Bank from Israel.
- In 2001 the Australian government courted international unpopularity in denying access to asylum-seekers seeking to enter Australian territorial waters, or by locking those that did in harsh detention centres.
- In 1998 the European Union effectively suspended the production or importation of genetically modified organisms, a decision which led to a near trade war with the United States.

It is also the case that government can restructure or overturn networks. A case in point is French agricultural policy, which was traditionally made within a closed policy community composed of the two main farming unions, the FNSEA and CNJA. These groups worked closely with the Ministry of Agriculture to defend the subsidy arrangements contained within the Common Agricultural Policy (Keeler, 1987). In the early 1990s the French government came under intense pressure to reduce overall protection levels as a part of the Uruguay round of trade talks taking place as part of the General Agreement on Tariffs and Trade (GATT). The French business community, represented through a different policy network centred on the Ministry of Finance, made it clear that a successful conclusion to the GATT talks was vital to its interests. The agricultural network predictably resisted making any concessions. At this point the president and prime minister, together with the minister for finance, decided that limited agricultural reform was nevertheless in the national interest and authorised senior officials to essentially bypass the agricultural policy community and conclude a trade deal. As Paul Epstein (1997, 357) concludes:

> when it became clear that a solution on agriculture was the key to progress in other sectors more important to the country's economic welfare . . . the influence of the traditional policy community was undermined, as interest-group leaders and high-ranking officials . . . found themselves playing second fiddle to those closer to the power centre of the French Government, specifically to the offices of the President and the Prime Minister.

The exercise of this kind of coercive power requires governments to possess legitimacy as well as a monopoly on the use of violence. This search for legitimacy has sometimes led governments to govern in conjunction with a variety of non-state actors. Yet, even here, governments can continue to exercise coercive power in metagoverning these arrangements, by choosing and revising governance rules, selecting participants, mobilising resources, monitoring effectiveness, establishing chains of accountability, and ensuring legitimacy. In the case of Australia's Job Network, for example, a complex contractual mode of governance delivering employment services, the federal government went to extraordinary lengths to control the market by setting service standards, imposing codes of conduct and determining prices (see Chapter 3).

As Flinders (2004, 895) observes, 'contemporary projects concerning "joined up" or "holistic" government represent an attempt to devise new mechanisms or tools to steer dense organisational webs'. Referring to the United Kingdom, he cites new regulatory bodies created for such purposes – including the Food Standards Agency and the Office of the Communications Regulator – as examples of state adaptation.

The claim by Flinders that a range of governance organisations possess significant levels of autonomy from governments also needs to be treated cautiously. Within the state itself, it is true that independent regulatory agencies may be granted parcels of authority, but these mandates are always on loan from governments. Indeed, governments have extended their efforts to monitor and render such organisations accountable. The mechanisms of steering and accountability may not always work well (Flinders, 2006, 237), but this simply underlines the metagovernance challenges, as well as ongoing efforts by governments to improve performance. This is especially the case when metagovernance failures reach the political arena, quickly shattering any illusions that devolved governance arrangements are somehow at one remove from government or 'depoliticised'.

In the United Kingdom, where the most empirical research on the governance capacities of the state has been undertaken, the argument that governments have lost control of governing processes has been widely challenged. For example Andrew Taylor (2000) finds that the use of taskforces and other mechanisms to coordinate policy across government has, far from hollowing out, helped 'fill in' government. Oliver James (2004) argues that the central coordination capacity of the 'core executive' has been strengthened using various instruments, particularly through Public Service Agreements (PSAs). Similarly, Ian Holliday (2000, 173) argues that an increasing emphasis on central government capacity, coordination and 'joined-up government' has meant that the 'enhancement of core executive capacity has been considerable' (see also Flinders, 2002). Francesca Gains (2003, 66) initially suggests that the creation of quasi-autonomous executive agencies within the public service has created power-dependent networks, but nevertheless concludes that '*political resources* legitimising the operation and the *authority to act* are still ultimately held by ministers' (emphasis in the original). Josie Kelly (2006) argues that devolution of authority to local councils has been accompanied by more stringent central auditing controls which have strengthened central authority and steering. Two studies by Ian Bache (2000; 2003), one on regional policy and one on education policy, also found that the devolution of parcels of authority has been accompanied by increased central control and steering. In fact, study after study of central control over local governing strategies has reached similar conclusions (Benyon & Edwards, 1999; Morgan et al., 1999; Davies, 2000). Central government continues to set the goals and rules of governance arrangements.

In reviewing these and other studies, Mike Marinetto (2003a, 592) concludes that 'central government is still highly resourced and has at its disposal a range of powers . . . it is difficult to see how recent developments have transformed the capacities of the core executive'. Adam Crawford (2006) argues that heightened social surveillance and an 'elaborate and complex mosaic of micro-management by government' show that 'ambitious interventionist government is alive and well' (2006, 455). Michael

Moran (2003, 6) argues that new audit and regulatory rules have 'widened the range of social and economic life subject to public power' (see also Power, 1997). According to Michael Saward (1997), hollowing-out processes such as privatisation and decentralisation are best seen as efforts to rationalise the state in order to promote central coordinating authority. In the case of privatisation, he contends that there is no 'strong evidence in favour of the hollowing out hypothesis. Indeed, we can see it as core actors flexing their political muscles' (p. 22). Similarly, Giandomenico Majone (1994, 79) argues that privatisation tends to strengthen rather than weaken the regulatory capacity of the state (see also Muller & Wright, 1994).

Carolyn Hill and Laurence Lynn (2005) note that 'the growing acceptance of governance as an organizing concept... reflects a widespread, though not universal belief that the focus of administrative practice is shifting from hierarchical government toward greater reliance on horizontal, hybridized, and associational forms of governance'. Yet in a review of over 800 individual studies of governance arrangements they find that 'hierarchical investigations of the nature and consequences of government action predominate in the literature'. They conclude that experiments in more horizontal forms of governance reflect 'a gradual addition of new administrative forms that facilitate governance in a system of constitutional authority that is necessarily hierarchical' (p. 173). Such arguments and conclusions have led Rhodes (2007, 1253), the originator of the hollowing-out thesis, to state that 'the weight of criticism meant that I had to reconsider my discussion of the changing role of the state'.

GLOBALISATION

The argument that states are being hollowed out is frequently associated with the claim that globalisation – the widening, deepening and speeding up of worldwide interconnectedness (Held et al., 1999, 2) – has heralded 'the end of geography' (O'Brien, 1992) and so 'undercut the policy capacity of the nation state' (Cerny, 1995, 612).

There are several parts to this argument:

- Globalisation has left states with little alternative but to engage in a race to the bottom by cutting taxes and regulatory standards in an effort to attract inward capital investment from transnational firms.
- Global financial markets act as a form of 'golden straitjacket' (Friedman, 1999), requiring states to adopt business-friendly policies.

- Globalisation has empowered regional authorities and city states to bypass national governments and work with each other to secure their economic development.
- Globalisation has transferred policy-making authority to international and, occasionally, supra-national organisations (Rosenau & Czempiel, 1992), multinational banks, accountancy firms and ratings agencies, which provide the infrastructure of global economic trade and to transnational NGOs.

These academic arguments have been challenged by evidence that there are no clear relationships between:

- overall levels of globalisation and patterns of state expenditure (Keating, 2004, 6; Castles, 2004, 8 and references therein)
- the levels of business taxation and inward capital investment in countries (Wilensky, 2002)
- the degree of globalisation within a country and the level of business regulation (Kenworthy, 1997; Vogel & Kagan, 2004; Basinger & Haller-berg, 2004)
- the degree of globalisation within a country and its level of social welfare expenditure (Swank, 2002; for an overview see Hay, 2005, 241–2).

In discussing the relationship between government expenditure and globalisation, for example, Mike Keating (2004, 6), a former head of the Australian public service, concludes that:

> even a cursory examination shows that government intervention, as mea-sured by the ratio of expenditure and taxes relative to GDP, has not fallen, and that the amount of government regulatory activity continues to increase . . . it is simply misleading to assert that governments have lost power and are withdrawing from their responsibilities.

Why has globalisation failed to result in the expected 'policy race to the neo-liberal bottom' (Garrett, 1998, 823)? One answer is that, with the exception of capital markets, the extent of globalisation has been exagger-ated. Most economic activity continues to take place within the boundaries of the nation-state, and those parts of it that span borders are largely con-tained within European, North American and Asia–Pacific regional trading blocs (Hirst & Thompson, 1996).

A second answer is that globalisation has actually increased the salience of the state's role – not only in protecting its citizens via social expenditure but in attracting inward investment and supporting businesses (Evans, 1997; Weiss, 1998). Rather than taxes, it is the quality of a country's education and skills training and other publicly provided business infrastructure that can best account for levels of inward investment (Hay, 2005, 252–3). Those governments that have worked most closely with non-state actors such as business associations and invested the most in vocational training and university education have benefited the most from globalisation.

A third answer is that the policy demands made by global markets, especially financial markets, are actually quite narrow. Layna Mosley (2000; 2003), for example, demonstrates that financial market decision-makers do not factor a wide range of government policy variables into their calculations but instead focus on two main issues: inflation levels and ratios between government deficits and GDP. These are regarded by traders as the key measures of a government's willingness to protect monetary values and ensure debt repayment. As she argues: 'Market actors forcefully demand particular values on key variables, but the number of key variables is small, so that many national economic policy choices . . . reflect domestic political and institutional constraints rather than external financial market pressures' (2000, 745). Even in arenas such as monetary policy, which is widely assumed to be highly constrained by market pressures, there is still evidence that national policy preferences and institutional dynamics matter in shaping the details of policy (Bell, 2005).

A final answer, contrary to race-to-the-bottom arguments, is that globalisation has, in some instances, been associated with a 'California effect', whereby manufacturers have standardised production values to align with those demanded in the toughest regulatory regimes. Originally, this referred to the practice of car manufacturers who set vehicle emissions standards to the high Californian levels rather than incur the costs of having different production processes for different states or of producing cars to a lower standard that could not then be sold in America's largest domestic market (Vogel, 1995; Fredriksson & Millimet, 2002). In principle, the California effect could also ratchet up product standards in international trade in so far as countries with large domestic markets set higher regulatory standards (Vogel, 1995, 259). For example, Canadian businesses are prepared to support some form of emissions-trading because 'big trading partners, including the United States, have either put a price on carbon or are about to do so [and] exporters worry that their products could be penalised if Canada does not follow suit' (*Economist*, 3 July 2008).

In another area of debate, the argument that globalisation has resulted in the transfer of policy-making authority to international organisations is, in some senses, irresistible. Organisations such as the European Union, the World Trade Organization, the Financial Stability Forum (which promotes international cooperation in financial supervision and surveillance) and the Internet Governance Forum either have been created or have acquired considerable new powers over the last few decades. States choose to join such groupings or regimes voluntarily because they expect to further their own strategic interests. States remain beyond such regimes, and although they may involve some constraints on policy autonomy, these constraints are accepted by states in order to further their wider strategic interests.

The European Union is the most extensive example of a supra-national body to which national states have surrendered significant elements of decision-making authority. It is also represents the most obvious exception to our earlier argument that states remain the 'final and absolute authority in the political community' (Hinsley, 1986, 26). In a range of policy areas – trade, competition, agriculture, energy, fisheries, immigration, regional policy – the European Union has acquired formal regulatory authority. Its 27 member states have undertaken a process of economic and monetary union requiring the adoption of a single currency and the transfer of monetary policy authority to the European Central Bank. Furthermore, an ongoing process of 'Europeanisation' means that there are now few, if any, areas of policy-making unaffected by a European dimension (Borzel, 1999; Featherstone & Radaelli, 2003). Following the near-collapse of the Northern Rock bank in September 2007, for example, the UK government argued that it had been unable to lend public money to the bank in order to secure its position because doing so would have breached European Union rules on the provision of state aid (Hindmoor, 2008).

European integration results in a process of 'multi-level' governance, comprising local governments, national governments, bodies like the European Council composed of representatives of nation-states, and supra-national bodies like the European Commission (Marks et al., 1996; Kohler-Koch & Rittberger, 2006, 34–5). In some policy areas, most notably foreign policy and justice and home affairs, the European Council – composed of the representatives of the governments of all the member states – remains the 'pre-eminent political authority' (Cini, 2003, 150). For this reason Andrew Moravcsik (1993; 2005) argues that the European Union ought to be viewed as an 'intergovernmental regime' rather than a nascent supra-national European state. It is clear, however, that a growing number of policy debates within the European Council are subject to qualified majority voting, and that supra-national bodies like the European Commission, European Parliament and European Court of Justice have acquired significant policy-making powers.

It is routinely argued that globalisation necessitates further European integration. The claim is that in order to tackle transnational problems like migration and climate change nation-states must sacrifice their sovereignty. In an address to the American Chamber of Commerce, the president of the European Commission, Jose Barroso (2008), claims, for example, that 'it is only through the European Union that the Member States can acquire sufficient collective weight to influence the worldwide debate on climate change, energy security and sustainable development'. Similarly, Tony Blair (2006) says that 'the nature of globalisation' requires nations to 'build strong alliances' and that for this reason 'an ever closer [European] union' is 'the only way of advancing our national interest effectively'.

Within 'realist' conceptions of international relations, sovereignty has traditionally been defined in terms of an internal supremacy over all other decision-making authorities and external independence over all outside authorities (Bull, 1977, 8). As Stanley Hoffmann (1987, 172) describes it, sovereignty is the doctrine that the state is 'subject to no other state and has full and exclusive powers within its jurisdiction without prejudice to the limits set by applicable law'. Membership of the European Union requires countries to surrender their external sovereignty. In a landmark ruling in 1964 the European Court of Justice confirmed that:

> by creating a Community of unlimited duration, having its own institutions, its own personality, its own legal capacity and capacity of representation, on the international plane and more particularly, real powers stemming from a limitation of sovereignty or a transfer of powers from the States to the Community, the member states have limited their sovereign rights [quoted Wallace, 1999, 510].

By limiting their external sovereignty, states have enhanced their capacity to deal with policy problems. On this reading, sovereignty has been pooled and enhanced rather than surrendered and diminished (Keohane, 2002, 744). States have chosen to comply with European regulation in order to enhance their influence (G. Sorensen, 2006, 200–1; Marsh, Richards & Smith, 2003, 328–31).

In terms of wider international regulatory issues, a major study by Daniel Drezner (2007) finds that the 'great power' governments of the United States and the European Union are the major players in creating and shaping transnational governance arrangements. Drezner (2007, 63–88) distinguishes between situations in which there is a high and low divergence of interest among the great powers and a high and low divergence

Table 2.4. A typology of regulatory coordination

Divergence of interests among great powers	Divergence of interests between great powers and other international actors	
	High conflict	Low conflict
High conflict	Sham standards	Rival standards
Low conflict	Club standards	Harmonised standards

Source: Drezner, 2007, 72.

of interests between the great powers and other international actors (see Table 2.4).

When the great powers agree on the need for regulatory action with other international actors, the result, Drezner argues, is harmonised standards formulated and monitored by international governmental and non-governmental organisations like the International Organisation for Standards and the International Accounting Standards Committee. Within these organisations, the great powers steer 'policy interventions behind the scenes' by making appointments and setting agendas (2007, 73). Where the great powers agree among themselves on the need for regulatory action but disagree with significant parts of the rest of the international community, 'club' standards result. Here, the great powers create new regulatory bodies and standards, and invite other countries to adhere to them. In the case of international finance, for example, the great powers effectively sponsored the Basle Accord requiring banks in signature countries to keep an agreed amount of reserve capital available. They did so in the knowledge that, over time, other banks, usually in developing countries, would be forced to meet these standards in order to engage in international commerce. Where the great powers disagree with each other about regulatory standards, as has been the case with genetically modified foods, the result is either rival standards or, if the disagreement is broad, sham global standards such as the labour standards promulgated but not enforced by the International Labour Organization. The overall import of Drezner's argument is that states remain the major players in international affairs.

CONCLUSION

This chapter has argued against the theory that the state is being hollowed out. Our approach to governance rests on the continued centrality of governments and state agencies because it is these entities that are the architects and key players in governance arrangements. This view does not overlook the fact that such arrangements involve various types of relations with society or major actors within society. Rather, governments and state agencies are attempting to increase their governing capacity by experimenting with an array of governance arrangements involving strategic relations with society.

Chapter 3 further explores the role of the state in governance arrangements by looking in more detail at the role of governments and state agencies in establishing and managing governance arrangements. We refer to this government of governance role as metagovernance. As we shall see it involves important design and strategic considerations and important normative elements as well, because governments remain responsible for ensuring that governance arrangements are effective, accountable, legitimate and democratic.

3 | Metagovernance and state capacity

GOVERNMENTS AND STATE agencies are participants in particular governance arrangements, but they also play a key role in metagovernance, or the 'government of governance'. As Mark Whitehead (2003, 8) argues, 'metagovernance... focuses explicitly on practices and procedures that secure governmental influence, command and control within governance regimes'. Yet, as Eva Sorensen (2006, 101) complains, 'governance theorists do not define the concept of metagovernance precisely'. An example of this can be found in a paper by Josie Kelly (2006) on the devolution of regulatory authority over local government in England to an independent regulatory agency (the Audit Commission, AC). She argues that 'the shift from direct to indirect regulation has resulted in the AC becoming a vehicle of metagovernance, acting on the government's behalf'. In our view the devolution of authority to the AC is more accurately seen as a governance strategy itself; essentially a reallocation of parcels of authority from one part of the state to another. By contrast, the central *metagovernance* role in the case explored by Kelly is how such governance relationships (between the government and the AC and between the AC and local councils) are developed, managed, resourced, audited, assessed and ultimately controlled by the central government.

The first part of this chapter defines metagovernance in terms of the performance of six functions. We show why metagovernance functions are the prime responsibility of the state, a view also adopted by scholars such as Renate Mayntz (1993) and Fritz Scharpf (1994). We then explore some of the challenges of metagovernance and examine the concept of 'state capacity' in relation to metagovernance.

THE FUNCTIONS OF METAGOVERNANCE

There are six core elements of metagovernance: steering, effectiveness, resourcing, democracy, accountability and legitimacy, conveniently summarised as SERDAL. These are the functions that governments typically perform, or at least arguably should perform, in relation to any governance arrangement.

STEERING

Steering implies the need for overall strategic management, goal setting, coordination and control of specific governance arrangements. It also covers the choice of mode or modes of governance to deploy in different settings and the roles to be played by non-state actors. Within any given set of governance arrangements, steering requires that governments provide (and, if necessary, change) the ground rules for governance; ensure the compatibility or coherence of different governance mechanisms; provide information and organise dialogue with which to shape the expectations and even the identities of actors within governance arrangements; act as a court of appeal for disputes between the actors involved in governance arrangements; and rebalance power differentials by strengthening the position of weaker actors (Jessop, 1997a, 575; 2002).

A good example of such a steering and regulatory role in relation to governance is Australia's Job Network. In 1998 the federal government dissolved the Commonwealth Employment Service and in its place created the Job Network, in which profit-making firms and organisations such as the Salvation Army competed for contracts to provide job search, job training and 'work for the dole' programs (Considine & Lewis, 2003). The involvement of these non-state actors has not prevented the government from controlling the direction and performance of the Job Network. As Michael Keating (2004, 91–5) demonstrates, governments have, over time, woven ever-tighter controls in order to minimise the discretion of contractors. This has included: controlling the number of eligible referrals to specific service providers; setting tight service standards; establishing codes of conduct; setting prices in what is, in effect, a managed market; establishing appeals processes; rating providers; and monitoring and policing service quality. These mechanisms 'have left the government very much in control of the market' (Keating, 2004, 95).

EFFECTIVENESS

Effectiveness is an obvious goal of metagovernance and closely related to the strategic management and steering of governance arrangements. Ultimately it is up to governments to establish, or at least approve, the goals, targets and evaluative criteria and methods used in overseeing governance arrangements. The government needs to monitor performance and take remedial action if the performance of specific governance arrangements is deemed inadequate.

As an example of the role governments can play in ensuring overall effectiveness, consider the complex governance arrangements for the provision of water in Guyana. Two publicly owned water utilities, the Georgetown Sewerage and Water Commission and the Guyana Water Authority, traditionally provided services. In 2001 the introduction of private sector management was made a condition of funding by the World Bank as a part of its country assistance strategy. At this time, less than 50 per cent of Guyanese houses had connections for water and less than 10 per cent had sanitation. In 2002 the Guyanese government created a new organisation, Guyana Water International, which subsequently awarded a contract to an English firm, Severn Trent Water International, to provide a range of services. The entire funding for this contract was met through a grant by the UK Department of International Development. Under these complex arrangements, responsibility for metagovernance was retained by the Guyanese government. In February 2007 a consultancy report showed that Severn Water had met only two of the seven key performance targets it had been set with regard to the provision of potable water and the collection of revenue. In the case of a target to supply 52 per cent of residents in the Amerindian settlements with potable water by 2005, the audit showed a 45 per cent shortfall. On this basis the Guyanese government announced that it was terminating its contract with Severn Water and that it would develop alternative strategies for developing effective water supply.

RESOURCING

Properly resourcing governance arrangements is an important aspect of metagovernance. Of course not all the requisite resources need come from governments or the state. Partnership arrangements with non-state actors are often forged by the state precisely because it lacks critical resources. But the depth of the government's financial resources, its access to a large professional bureaucracy and its monopoly on the legitimate use of violence mean that governments are, and in most cases probably should be, major supplies of governance resources. The resources in question might include leadership and authority, fiscal or administrative resources, in-depth policy expertise, information, or the capacity to promulgate laws or shape rules or norms.

An example of metagovernance via resourcing is the provision of mental health care services in southern Arizona, a case extensively studied by H. Brinton Milward and Keith Provan (2000; 2003). In 1995 a new not-for-profit organisation, the Community Partnership of Southern Arizona, was given overall responsibility for providing a range of mental health services in two counties. Four provider networks, each headed by a non-profit mental health agency, were also created and randomly allocated around 1000 clients. The health agency in each network was required to set up its own network of collaborating agencies, with which they could sign contracts for the delivery of services. Each health agency was paid the same monthly capitation rate for each patient and encouraged to use this money as it saw fit in the best interests of its patients. As a result, the direct involvement of the county's Department of Health Services in the day-to-day delivery of services was effectively ended and significant competition injected into the system. In terms of the standard society-centred view of governance, this seems to be a prime example of a transition from 'government to governance'. Yet under these arrangements government retains responsibility for funding and oversight. Furthermore, although only employing around 100 people, the Community Partnership of Southern Arizona received $180 million public funding in 2006, which it used to purchase contracts.

DEMOCRACY

Ensuring compliance with democratic practices and norms is an important metagovernance function. In Western systems of representative democracy elected politicians are generally regarded as the font of democratic authority, and the involvement and ultimate control of these politicians over decision-making processes is regarded as the guarantor of democratic legitimacy. The inclusion of unelected non-state actors in the governance process might therefore be thought to undermine democratic control. Consider, for example, the decentralisation of decision-making authority that has taken place within Denmark over the last 20 years (Greve & Jespersen,

1999; Greve, 2004). User boards have been established in schools, kinder-gartens and care homes to give recipients of these services some measure of control over the delivery of services. Legislation allows groups of clients to organise their own service delivery through self-owned institutions which can levy fees. Under these arrangements it looks as though decision-making authority is being taken from elected politicians.

In our view governments can enhance the democratic credentials of governance arrangements involving non-state actors in two ways. First, insofar as they continue to assume responsibility for steering, effectiveness and resourcing, governments will, through these activities, continue to provide a measure of democratic legitimacy. In the case of the Danish reform process, a report by the Ministry of the Interior stated that the role of municipal politicians should no longer be to make all decisions but to 'decide the overall priorities and define overall goals for the economy and for the service delivery'. Discussing this report, E. Sorensen (2006, 107) suggests that 'this new role for politicians is problematic for democracy because it gives politicians a marginal role'. Yet so long as there is a way to ensure that the strategic decisions of elected politicians are translated into action, the opportunity to metagovern by setting overall goals and priorities is a far from marginal activity and an important source of democratic input and legitimacy.

The same argument might be applied to the governance of independent central banks and other 'non-majoritarian' public organisations which are deliberately shielded from the pressures of day-to-day politics (Coen & Thatcher, 2005; Vibert, 2007). The creation of an independent central bank may seem to entail a loss of democratic control. Indeed, the credibility of central banks is usually thought to depend upon their freedom from political interference. Yet, even here, democratic controls remain in place. Elected governments determine the objectives that central banks must pursue. In most cases governments appoint the bank's governing board. Governments also usually retain the legislative authority to suspend independence in the event of a national emergency or in the case of misconduct by the central bank (see Bell, 2004a, 149–55; Blinder, 1996).

Democratically elected politicians can enhance the democratic qualities of governance arrangements in a second way. We have suggested that the involvement of non-state actors poses a problem for representative democracy because it risks separating elected politicians from decision-making. Others argue that democracy ought to be understood as *requiring* the engagement and empowerment of citizens. The central idea is that the devolution of authority to civil society groups or associations can enhance democracy by encouraging participation, checking centralised power, and increasing the opportunities for deliberation and compromise (Elster, 1998; Fung & Wright, 2003).

It is easy to see how the decentralisation of decision-making authority to user boards in Denmark might, thereby, be argued to have *enhanced* democracy. This appears to render redundant our argument that governments must provide democratic legitimacy through metagovernance. Yet even on this account, an important role for government remains. One obvious danger of decentralised systems of decision-making is that the community and stakeholder activists who involve themselves in the management of user boards, self-governing institutions and other bodies become an unrepresentative and self-perpetuating elite. For this reason Grace Skogstad (2003) concludes that mechanisms of participatory democracy are a useful supplement for, rather than an alternative to, government and representative democracy. A second lesson here might be that government should play an important metagovernance role in designing and monitoring mechanisms of participatory democracy in order to ensure that those who make decisions are representative of the broader community and, when they are not, that decisions can be appealed and reversed (see Fung & Wright, 2003). We will pursue this argument further in Chapter 7.

ACCOUNTABILITY

The capacity to be called to account is an important criterion of metagovernance because it implies the need for clear lines of responsibility and transparency. Accountability is essentially about responsibility, or where the buck stops. But accountability also covers responsiveness and control. As Richard Mulgan (2000, 563) puts it, 'accountability and control are intimately linked because accountability is a vital mechanism of control'. Accountability in all its forms is especially important not only when governments or state agencies act, but also when non-state actors become involved in governance arrangements as contractors or partners.

The division of decision-making authority between the European Council (the body within the European Union comprising the heads of state) and the supra-national European Parliament and Commission is often argued to have resulted in a loss of accountability within the European Union (see Arnull & Wincott, 2003). Similarly, the creation of networks composed of state and non-state actors is routinely argued to undermine accountability (Barrados, Mayne & Wileman, 2000). Rod Rhodes (2000, 77) suggests that networks 'substitute private government for public accountability' which 'disappears in the interstices of the webs of institutions which make up governance'. In these circumstances governments ought to retain (and, in our view, frequently do retain) a metagovernance responsibility for safeguarding accountability arrangements.

One possibility is that governments accept responsibility for performance even in those cases where a large number of actors are involved. Mulgan (2006) suggests that the arm's-length contracting arrangements underpinning the Australian Job Network raise potential accountability issues. He nevertheless states that, 'having flirted with the temptation of off-loading blame on to contractors', governments have 'come to accept the public expect them to remain accountable' (p. 49). This, he goes on to argue, has given governments a powerful incentive to exercise close control over contractors.

Second, and even on those occasions when it has not assumed responsibility for steering, effectiveness and resourcing, the state can hold *other* actors to account for their behaviour. The most obvious manifestation of this accountability is legal. Under laws relating to, for example, corporate manslaughter, private firms and individuals within them can be held to account for their actions through the courts. Following the deaths of 21 tourists in a canyoning disaster in Switzerland in 1999, six managers of the adventure company responsible for organising their trip were charged with negligent manslaughter. In most countries politicians can also hold non-state actors to account through hearings conducted by legislative committees. In February 2009 senior bankers were hauled before committees in the United States and United Kingdom, questioned about their bonuses and invited to apologise for having caused the credit crisis.

We are not naïve: there is no doubt that government sometimes seeks to evade accountability within partnership arrangements. Indeed, the possibility of off-loading blame onto other actors can be a key attraction of such governance arrangements. Yet even in these cases governments can still be held to account by legislatures, the media and the electorate. Governments can still seek to deny responsibility for the operational behaviour of non-state actors within governance systems. But this is hardly a novel problem. Ministers are equally reluctant to accept responsibility for actions taken by public servants of which they were unaware (Mulgan, 2002). In the aftermath of the Abu Ghraib torture scandal in Iraq, numerous critics called for the resignation of the US Defense Secretary, Donald Rumsfeld. In testimony before the Senate Armed Services Committee, Rumsfeld claimed that his office had received no warnings about the abuse and that in these circumstances his responsibility was only to 'evaluate what happened, to make sure those who have committed wrongdoing are brought to justice, and to make changes as needed to see that it doesn't happen again' (*New York Times*, 8 May 2004).

A good example of a metagovernance failure, at least in the initial phase, occurred in relation to accountability arrangements within Australian detention centres. Since the early 1990s Australia has had a system of mandatory detention for those arriving in the country without a valid visa. In 1998, 3500 people – the majority of whom were claiming political asylum – were detained in various holding centres across Australia, mostly in remote areas. By 2001 this number had risen to nearly 8000. In 1997 a contract was awarded to a private company, Australasian Correctional Management (ACM, a subsidiary of an American firm, Wackenhut), to run the detention centres. ACM was later widely criticised for conditions in the centres and held responsible by opposition parties and parts of the media for a series of riots and breakouts, self-mutilations and hunger strikes.

When questioned, ACM consistently argued that it was accountable for its behaviour under the terms of its contract with the Department of Immigration and Multicultural Affairs (DIMA). Critics argued that the contracting-out of services had resulted in a loss of accountability as DIMA ministers routinely referred questions about conditions within the detention centres to ACM or declined to answer them on the grounds of commercial confidentiality. In 2002 a report by the Regional Advisor of the United Nations High Commissioner for Refugees, Justice Bhagwati, concluded that 'the situation in the detention centres seems to be bedevilled by a lack of transparency and accountability' (Melbourne *Age*, 31 July 2002). A subsequent report by the Australian National Audit Office (2003) warned that 'the administrative practices in place did not establish accountability' and recommended that DIMA be made to report to Parliament on the results of its monitoring programs and details of its funding outlays.

This loss of accountability is unlikely to have happened by accident. At a time when the basic principle of mandatory detention was popular with the electorate but the details of the actual conditions in which detainees were being held provoked considerable disquiet, ministers had a strong incentive to minimise their accountability. The Inspector of Custodial Services in Western Australia, Richard Harding, suggested that accountability had been compromised because 'the government wanted this to be out of sight and out of mind' (ABC, 20 June 2004). Similarly, a former Attorney-General and Minister for Corrections in Victoria, Jim Kennan, argued that, 'one of the driving political motives for [the contracting-out

of detention centre services] was to distance the government from problems . . . they can say it is a matter for the contractor' (Melbourne *Age*, 9
January 2003).

The government's initial refusal to accept responsibility for the management of the detention centres provides a good example of metagovernance
failure. However, to argue that states can sometimes fail is not to argue
that states must always fail. As we observed in Chapter 2 when discussing
the limitations of public choice theory, the media, opposition parties and
interest-groups have an incentive to monitor government performance and
draw public attention to any failings. Governments may sometimes have
an incentive to avoid their metagovernance responsibilities but they risk
paying a heavy political price for doing so. Precisely because the public
expects states to retain overall responsibility for the delivery of services,
governments remain politically vulnerable to claims that they have failed
to effectively metagovern. In the case in hand, the failure to ensure the
public accountability of governance arrangements within detention centres
became a popular cause with the media and Opposition, causing the government long-term political difficulties. When a new contract was signed
with Global Solutions to manage the detention centres in 2004, accountability procedures were, as a consequence, overhauled. In this sense, the
expectation that the government will metagovern itself creates an incentive
for the government to do so.

LEGITIMACY

Legitimacy is an important criterion of effective metagovernance. Governance arrangements that are seen as fair in terms of processes and outcomes, have popular support, and are regarded as legitimate are likely to
be more stable and effective than arrangements that are thought to be
upheld through force or arbitrary power (Kjaer, 2004, 12). The legitimacy
of governance arrangements can best be secured as a byproduct of the performance of other metagovernance functions. Chapter 2 discussed the view
of Fritz Scharpf (1997; 1999) that legitimacy is a two-dimensional concept
relating to the inputs and to the outputs of the political system. On the
input side, legitimacy requires that political choices are derived, directly or
indirectly, from the preferences of citizens. On the output side, legitimacy
requires that organisations perform effectively. If governments effectively
steer governance arrangements, ensure effectiveness and provide necessary resources, the legitimacy of the outputs is enhanced. If governments

provide democratic oversight and ensure accountability, the legitimacy of the inputs is enhanced.

Where, for whatever reason, governance arrangements lack legitimacy, governments come under pressure to take action. Following the international credit crisis which began in late 2007, banks, investment firms, credit agencies and accountancy firms lost a significant measure of public support. Immediately, governments in the United States and Europe were urged to revise light-touch regulatory systems in order to prevent banks from taking excessive risks in the knowledge that taxpayers would ultimately have to cover any losses that threatened the integrity of the financial system. As *The Economist* argued:

> For three decades, public policy has been dominated by the power of markets—flexible and resilient, harnessing self-interest for the public good, and better than any planner-in-chief... [but] new rules became inevitable the moment the Federal Reserve rescued Bear Stearns and pledged to lend to other Wall Street banks. If taxpayers are required to bail out investment banks, the governments need to impose tighter limits on the risks those banks can take [3 April 2008].

METAGOVERNANCE AS A PROBLEM OF PUBLIC GOOD PROVISION

Metagovernance is exercised not only by state actors but also by various networks of public and private actors and a whole range of supranational, regional, and local levels in the formal political system. In fact, metagovernance can potentially be exercised by any resourceful actor – public or private. All it takes is resources and a desire to influence activities performed by self-governing actors [E. Sorensen, 2006, 103].

So far we have been assuming that metagovernance functions must be discharged by the state. Eva Sorensen challenges this assumption by suggesting that 'any resourceful actor – public or private' can metagovern. This raises two issues: whether private (that is, non-state) actors have the resources and legitimacy needed to metagovern; and whether they have the incentives or desire to do so.

We will start with a discussion of resources. Chapter 1 said that states retain a monopoly on the legitimate use of violence. This is a key metagovernance resource. States can metagovern because they can impose decisions, change governance rules, extract resources through compulsory taxation, and require actors to appear in court or before parliamentary committees to account for their action (also see Mayntz, 1998). With regard to the first of these activities, imposing decisions, non-state actors could, in the event of a dispute, agree to accept decisions made by an independent arbitrator acting as a metagovernor. But it is difficult to see how non-state actors might force each other to abide by decisions that they do not accept. It is even harder to see how a non-state actor performing this metagovernance function might force the state to accept such decisions where it is involved as one of the participants in a governance arrangement. The same holds true of the second and third functions. Lacking any coercive power, non-state actors will only be able to change governance rules and extract resources if all the groups affected agree.

There is one further resource states possess which enhances their metagovernance capacities: legitimacy. Even if firms or sectional interest-groups have the required organisational and financial resources, they may lack the legitimacy needed to metagovern effectively. It is not hard to imagine how a non-state organisation like the American Automobile Manufacturers Association might position itself to metagovern a policy to reduce vehicle emissions. But such an arrangement would be unlikely to attract the support of environmental groups or concerned citizens. In some cases NGOs may acquire sufficient legitimacy to metagovern. Chapter 8 on associative governance shows how the World Wide Fund for Nature has played a metagovernance role in encouraging private forestry firms to sign a charter committing them to sustainable forestry practices. In other cases criminal groups have come to perform some metagovernance functions. Diego Gambetta (1993) argues that in the 19th century the Italian state was so weak and corrupt that the Mafia was, within limits, regarded as a trustworthy and legitimate body to enforce commercial exchanges. These are, however, exceptional cases. When either a new policy problem emerges or the failings of an existing policy become apparent, people continue to expect states to provide solutions; this expectation is itself a key metagovernance resource.

Let us now turn to the more complex issue of incentives. Sorensen suggests that actors must have a 'desire' to metagovern but does not consider whether this desire will be forthcoming. We argue that it is often absent. Economists classify goods in terms of their 'excludability', and their 'rivalness' (Hindmoor, 2006a, 103):

- A good is excludable if its owner can prevent its consumption benefiting anyone else; it is non-excludable if the benefits deriving from its consumption are available to all.

• A good is rivalrous when its consumption by one person reduces the amount available to others; it is non-rivalrous to the extent that consumption by one person does not reduce the amount available to others.

Public goods like defence, sanitation, clean air, street lighting and law enforcement are non-excludable and non-rivalrous. Street lighting on public roads provides a benefit to everyone who walks or drives down them and this benefit is non-rivalrous in the sense that the light 'consumed' by one person does not reduce the amount of light available to others. Economists generally regard the existence of public goods as a key source of market failure. Because everyone benefits from the provision of a public good whether or not they contributed to its supply, everyone has an incentive to free-ride and none of the good will be supplied. Economists then conclude that the state must intervene to directly secure the supply of public goods using its coercive powers to, for example, extract taxation.

In our view the supply of metagovernance raises equivalent issues. Effective metagovernance provides benefits both for the participants in any governance mechanism and for the broader public. Let us look first at the function of steering. Without a court of appeal to settle disputes, governance arrangements risk being paralysed by disagreements between participants. Without the timely provision of information, actors risk being committed to sub-optimal plans. Or consider effectiveness. Individual participants in a governance arrangement may resist the imposition of performance targets but nevertheless recognise that others will perform more effectively if they are in place. The same applies to accountability. When a policy has failed, the public wants to see those responsible held to account.

The benefits provided through effective metagovernance are, however, non-rivalrous and non-excludable public goods. That the benefits of metagovernance are non-rivalrous is obvious. If one actor in the network consumes information about the demand for services, this does not reduce the amount of information available to others in the network. Equally, the benefits a taxpayer derives from knowing that someone has taken responsibility in accounting for the actions of the participants in a network do not reduce the 'amount' of accountability available to others.

The sense in which the benefits of metagovernance are non-excludable is initially less obvious. By way of an introduction, think about the provision of human rights and, more specifically, the right to free speech. There is no doubt that this right could be framed to exclude specified groups of people: suspected terrorists, organised criminals, or employees of tabloid newspapers. In this practical sense free speech is excludable. But an advocate of human rights will argue that a right to free speech which excludes certain groups of people is no right at all: that the principle of free speech is intrinsically non-excludable.

In an analogous sense we suggest that metagovernance is non-excludable. Assume that two of the three members of a network agree to share the cost of collecting and distributing general information about the demand for different kinds of services. It is not hard to see how they could refuse to provide this information to the third member. In this sense, the information is a non-rivalrous but excludable toll good. But if, as a result of their decision, this third organisation sets incorrect plans, we could say that the right information had not been provided, that the function of steering had not been discharged effectively and that there had been a failure of metagovernance. For the functions of metagovernance to be discharged, they must be discharged inclusively. Steering requires the steering of *all* the actors in the network; resourcing requires the provision of adequate resources for *all* the actors in a network; accountability requires the calling to account of *all* the actors in a network, and so on. Hence metagovernance is non-excludable.

Because the benefits provided through effective metagovernance are public goods, interest-groups, private firms and other non-state actors operating in networks and other governance arrangements have an incentive to free-ride on their provision. Actors might recognise that there is a need to collect and distribute information, coordinate plans, provide a neutral court of appeal, monitor the overall effectiveness of the network, and account for actions; but each recognises that any investment it makes in metagovernance will benefit not only the actors in the network but the taxpayers and others outside it and, conversely, that they will benefit from free-riding on any investment made by others. The 'market' for metagovernance is thus likely to fail because none of the actors in that market has an incentive to invest in metagovernance. Just as the state must correct for the existence of market failures by providing public goods like defence, law enforcement and sanitation, so, too, it needs to provide metagovernance if the other actors who benefit from its supply are driven by consideration of their own interest. Organisations may sometimes have an incentive to undertake metagovernance responsibilities if they have a general commitment to the welfare of *all* the actors in a governance system. We point to such an example in Chapter 8. Yet it would be a mistake to assume that, simply because a range of actors benefit from the provision of metagovernance, any non-state actor will find it in its interest to supply that metagovernance.

STATE CAPACITY: A STATE-CENTRIC RELATIONAL ACCOUNT

The challenges of metagovernance raise important questions about whether states have the capacity to operate coherently and forge effective governance relationships. Here the widely discussed concept of state capacity or 'governing capacity' is relevant. This approach provides a broad institutional and relational blueprint for understanding governing capacity by drawing on a range of comparative studies. States' capacity to formulate and implement policies varies both within and between countries (Weiss & Hobson, 1995, 28). As an example of varying capacity between countries, consider taxation. Chapter 2 showed that the amount of money raised through taxation has risen steadily within the largest OECD economies over the last 30-odd years. There are, however, striking differences between the capacities of states in this regard. In Sweden it is estimated that the state collects over 95 per cent of the revenue owing to it each year; in Russia the equivalent figure is thought to be as low as 10 per cent (Rothstein, 2005, 1–2). As an example of varying capacity within the state consider how, in the United States, a federal government that had successfully mobilised more than a quarter of a million troops for the invasion of Iraq was paralysed by the flooding and subsequent breakdown of public order in New Orleans in 2005 following Hurricane Katrina.

How do we account for such startling differences in governing capacity? Political scientists have tended to define both *institutional* and *relational* components of state capacity. Institutional arrangements can be vital in this respect. As Stephen Krasner (1984, 228) says:

> The ability of a political leader to carry out a policy is critically determined by the authoritative institutional resources and arrangements existing within a given political system. Industrial policy can be orchestrated in Japan through the Ministry of International Trade and Industry. There is no American institutional structure that would allow a political leader, regardless of the resources commanded, to implement a similar set of policies.

We can define institutions as formal or informal rules, norms or sanctions designed to shape human behaviour (Thelen & Steinmo, 1992; Thelen, 1999; Hall & Taylor, 1996). For pioneering researchers, such as Douglas North (1990, 4), an institution is 'any form of constraint that human beings devise to shape action'. The core claim of institutional researchers is that institutions matter because they shape the behaviour of individuals and the possibilities for governance. All strands of institutionalism share a common focus on institutionally 'situated' actors or individuals, whose behaviour is shaped by their institutional location and role and by the authority relations and ideational orientations that institutions embody. Institutions also matter because governance typically occurs in and through them, whether they are specific organisations or clusters of rules, norms, or other institutional arrangements. Existing institutional configurations also shape governance strategies and outcomes. Hence, we might expect that relatively centralised and unitary political systems such as those in New Zealand and the United Kingdom might be more inclined to govern via hierarchy. By contrast, more decentralised institutional arrangements may lend themselves to more negotiated governance approaches, especially across the multiple levels of government in federal systems. In turn, governance strategies shape institutions. For example, market-oriented governance strategies have tended to strengthen those institutions engaged in various forms of market regulation, such as the organisations administering competition policy.

As a further illustration of the importance of institutional arrangements in shaping state capacity, consider the case of nuclear energy. In the 1950s and 1960s most Western governments decided to invest heavily in commercial nuclear energy programs in the mistaken belief that nuclear power would prove to be an exceptionally cheap source of energy. These nuclear programs met with varying fates. In France 67 nuclear reactors were built and nuclear power now generates more than 70 per cent of France's electricity. In the United States and the United Kingdom nuclear power continues to provide around 15 per cent of electricity, but it fell out of favour in the 1980s and 1990s and has only recently been resurrected as a potential solution to the problems of climate change and energy security. In Germany 20 reactors were built, but a decision was taken in 1998 to phase them out. Austria (1978), Denmark (1985), Greece (1975), Ireland (1999), Italy (1990), and Switzerland (1990) have gone so far as to ban the future use of nuclear power (OECD, 2001, 228).

In each of these countries the capacity of government to hierarchically impose its preferred nuclear solutions depended upon existing institutional rules. In France, 'although there was considerable resistance to nuclear energy', the political weakness of local government, enshrined within the constitution of the Fifth Republic, meant that 'there were few paths' for protestors (Kitschelt, 1986, 79). In the United States, by contrast, a federal political structure that devolved considerable decision-making power to states severely constrained the capacity of central government to develop nuclear power (Joppke, 1993). In New York, for example, the Shoreham nuclear power plant, built in the late 1970s, was never switched on because the governor of the State of New York, Mario Cuomo, refused to sign the Emergency Evacuation Plan, so the plant could not receive a full power licence from the Nuclear Regulatory Commission. In Germany, meanwhile, the federal government's attempts to develop a nuclear program were eventually frustrated by a proportional voting system that resulted in the Green Party entering government in coalition with the Social Democratic Party in 1998 on the condition that Germany's nuclear power program be abandoned (Feigenbaum, Samuels, & Weaver, 1993).

A range of scholars who have explored the major institutional attributes of 'capable' states have suggested the following key components:

- *Centralised decision-making:* Strong states (or perhaps strong sectors within states) have centralised political and administrative authority and a minimum number of 'veto points' (Tsebelis, 2002). Such centralisation implies the ability to act as a coherent, corporate actor. This capacity may stem from the structure of the state or from mechanisms that can effectively coordinate activity across a number of arenas. In weak states (or sectors), by contrast, decision-making authority is likely to be fragmented, perhaps because of federal structures or a lack of effective coordinating or steering mechanisms. For example, recent Australian experience shows that the problems of dealing with salination and water management have been exacerbated by the institutional structures and state and regional divisions of the federal political system (Connell, 2007). Hence, capable states (or state sectors) typically have centralised, or at least clearly defined and coordinated, decision-making hierarchies.

- *A strong administrative apparatus:* States must also have the requisite resources at their disposal to be able to act effectively. Bureaucratic and administrative resources, including high-quality information, forums of active policy debate, and expert, dedicated and experienced staff in key areas of policy formulation and implementation, are also a vital component of state capacity. Skocpol (1985, 16) writes that 'loyal and skilled officials' are the 'universal sinews of state power'. As Max Weber, the original theorist of bureaucracy, pointed out long ago, the key elements underpinning an effective bureaucracy include highly selective meritocratic recruitment and promotion procedures, combined with high status and rewards, long-term career prospects and a sense of service and professionalism. In the case of taxation, for example, the capacity to tax citizens does not depend on simply imposing coercive power by issuing credible threats to fine or imprison those who refuse to pay. It also requires a large bureaucracy capable of tracking people's employment and salary (for income tax); their overall wealth (for property or capital gains tax); their place of residence (for determining liability on income earned overseas); the movement of goods in and out of the country (for tariffs); and the cumulative addition of monetary value through the production process (for sales taxes).

- *Fiscal resources:* The taxation example relates directly to another element of state capacity: fiscal resources. The capacity to extract financial resources through taxation remains a key source of state capacity. Historically, a state's fiscal capacity has always been a major determinant of its capacity to wage war, but increasingly projects of public infrastructure, industrial competitiveness and social compensation and welfare have made heavy claims on the fiscal state. The capacity to raise revenue via taxes reflects the state's 'extractive capacity' (Weiss & Hobson, 1995, 7).

- *Policy instruments:* Policy instruments are the actual means or devices that governments have at their disposal for implementing policies (see Hood, 2007, for an overview). States must have the necessary tools, inducements and sanctions to shape the behaviour of societal or external actors in appropriate ways. Policy instruments may include anything from subsidies or tax incentives to moral suasion or regulation. John Zysman (1983) suggests, for example, that the capacity of the Japanese and French states to develop new industries crucially depends upon the existence of 'state-led' systems of capital allocation within which the bureaucracy is able to control the flow of investment to private firms. In the United Kingdom and the United States, by contrast, the easy access of firms to capital markets and external sources of finance has limited the capacity of the state to direct economic development.

- *Legitimacy:* We have repeatedly pointed out that the successful exercise of state power requires legitimacy (Seabrooke, 2006). Government leaders must ultimately be regarded as having a mandate to rule and delivering effective policies if legitimacy is to be established or maintained. Hence, governments require the consent of those being governed. In the United Kingdom in the late 1980s, for example, the government found it almost impossible to implement a new tax, the community charge or poll tax, which large parts of the population regarded as illegitimate (Butler et al., 2004).

Our account of state capacity also has important *relational* components involving the nature of the links between the state and society. It was once orthodox to say that the strongest states were those that were relatively insulated from the push and pull of political conflicts and possessed the authority to impose or push through their own policy agendas. Theda Skocpol (1985, 9), for example, defines state capacity in terms of autonomy, and autonomy in terms of the ability of government to 'implement official goals, especially over the actual or potential opposition of powerful social groups or in the face of recalcitrant socioeconomic circumstances'. State capacity is thus simply defined in terms of a triumph over opposing groups. The problem with this account, however, is that it is too 'state-centric'; states are assumed to gain policy capacity to the extent that they operate independently from the societies they govern. Yet, as Michael Mann (1988) points out, states have been able to enhance their policy capacity over the last few centuries by *strengthening* their ties to society. In the 14th and 15th centuries rulers exercised almost unlimited despotic power over their subjects. Yet in many respects, these 'absolute' states (Gill, 2003, 98–102) were surprisingly weak. They lacked the capacity to promote economic development or control people's lives, and their expenditure probably accounted for no more than two or three per cent of gross domestic product. States have a greater capacity to govern today because they exercise 'infrastructural' as well as 'despotic' powers. Infrastructural power refers to the way in which states can 'actually penetrate civil society, and . . . implement logistically political decisions throughout the land' (Mann, 1988, 5).

Developing Mann's arguments about infrastructural power, writers such as Peter Evans (1997), Linda Weiss (1998) and John Hobson (2000) have argued that state capacity requires states not only to 'penetrate' society but to work closely with non-state actors. This argument obviously bears upon our state-centric relational account of governance. The notion that the state's capacity and authority may in part be derived from sophisticated links with key social actors is not new. Talcott Parsons (1963) made a distinction between active notions of state capacity and simpler but cruder forms of coercive state power several decades ago. But by documenting the ways in which, in particular, Asian governments have been able to construct successful economic relationships with non-state actors, political economists have identified an economic alternative to the Washington Consensus of free markets and shrinking government. Hobson (2000, 234) suggests that states are more likely to be able to achieve their goals if the interests of the state and society are advanced 'collaboratively rather than competitively'. Similarly, Evans (1992, 162) argues that the most capable states are now more likely to be those in which 'concrete sets of social ties . . . bind the state to society', allowing for the 'continual negotiation and renegotiation of goals and policies' (see also Onis, 1991; Martin, 1989).

Governments can often extend their capacity to govern by developing closer relations with non-state actors, and thus the relationship between government and interest-groups ought to be viewed as positive-sum rather than zero-sum. In order to successfully formulate and implement policy, governments often need to acquire the expertise, support or assistance of interest-groups and NGOs. In return, governments must offer these groups a measure of policy influence. The existence of these exchange relationships means that governments are often not in a position to unilaterally impose their policy preferences. Thus, our critique of the society-centric approach does not require us to regard the state as a behemoth capable of trampling over any opposition. Instead, our state-centric relational approach leads us to emphasise the ways in which the relationships government builds can *enhance* its policy capacity.

An interesting example of the significance of such relational capacity is offered by Heather McKeen-Edwards and colleagues (2004) in a paper on financial integration within North America and the European Union. Despite greater rhetorical commitment to the free market, the United States and Canadian financial markets are less integrated than those within the European Union, both in terms of regulatory control and cross-national ownership. This apparent paradox is explained in terms of the 'relationship between private and public actors in the policy process' (p. 336). The European Union has developed centralised corporatist structures of policy negotiation that mobilise major financial interests through peak organisations; this has made it easier for the state to negotiate market liberalisation. The United States and Canada have a 'more pluralist pattern of policy making'; thus government–business relations tend to be riven by conflict as firms lobby for narrow concessions rather than negotiate collectively on market structure (p. 342).

In a book dealing with 'policy networks', or the interaction of state and non-state actors in specific policy arenas, Michael Atkinson and William Coleman (1989) look at industrial policy and offer an account that helps explain these relational dynamics. They are interested in the ways in which different kinds of policy networks are structured by institutional factors, including the authority and institutional capacities of the state and the associative capacities of key non-state actors or groups. In turn, such structured policy networks can facilitate or constrain industrial policy, especially in relation to what they call 'reactive' and 'anticipatory' policy styles. The former is a short-term, incremental policy style responding to events or particular lobbying demands; anticipatory policy is more plan-oriented and implemented around long-term strategic goals. It might appear that governments are more likely to be able to develop anticipatory policies where the state is relatively 'strong' *and* business interests are relatively weak and fragmented and so unable to challenge the government's edict. Yet Atkinson and Coleman argue that successful anticipatory policy requires the presence of *strong* business interests mobilised through powerful peak associations interacting with an authoritative and centralised state. In such 'concentation' networks 'state officials seek an accommodation with business that not only meets the latter's need for freedom of action and economic support, but is also in step with a set of broader political objectives', most of which are 'negotiated over a period of time with business' (p. 59).

Post-war Japanese industrial policy offers a paradigm of this kind of relational policy capacity. In the aftermath of World War II Japanese leaders decided on a strategy of accelerated economic development in order to raise living standards, enhance national security (Weiss & Hobson, 1995, 187) and recover lost national prestige. How did Japan achieve its 'economic miracle'? The conventional answer is that it was achieved in a hierarchical fashion through a 'developmental state' (Johnson, 1995) which diverted resources to high-growth, high-technology industries. On this reading, the Japanese state was successful because organisations like the Ministry of International Trade and Industry (MITI) were able to create a 'governed market' (Wade, 1990) by issuing hierarchical 'administrative guidance' to private firms, imposing restrictions upon foreign ownership and imports, licensing the use of particular technologies, and subsidising research and development.

Yet as Daniel Okimoto (1989) observes, the Japanese state is far from being a leviathan. Unlike the United Kingdom, France, Italy and a number of other European countries, Japan did not own the industries it set about promoting. Furthermore, when the economic miracle was unfolding in the 1960s, state expenditure remained relatively low. The state was able to guide development only because it was able to operate through a web of formal and informal contacts with individual firms, industrial clusters (Keiretsu) and industry associations with whom it was able to negotiate long-term policy. 'Instead of labelling Japan a "strong" state therefore, perhaps it would be more accurate to call it a "societal" or "relational", or "network" state, one whose strength is derived from the convergence of public and private interests and the extensive network ties binding the two together' (Okimoto, 1989, 145).

In his analysis of Japanese industrial policy, Richard Samuels (1987) talks of 'reciprocal consent'. Linda Weiss (1998, 48), who uses the term 'governed interdependence' to describe similar relationships, suggests that the Japanese model was effective because policies were 'the result of regular and extensive consultation, negotiation and coordination with the private sector'. The Japanese state was not robbed of its policy capacity through the development of policy networks in which there were frequent, high-quality exchange relationships. Instead, as Atkinson and Coleman suggest, the state gained through the opportunity to work with a capable and well-organised business sector. The lesson is that state capacity is a function both of state structure and of associational capacities in society. Governments are more inclined to engage with groups not only when those groups possess valued resources but when they are effectively organised, a theme we return to in Chapter 8 on associative governance.

THE CHALLENGES OF METAGOVERNANCE

The metagovernance of complex governance arrangements presents major challenges to governments. For example, our argument that state capacity can be enhanced through the development of closer state–society relations has one important qualification. On the one hand, a state that is too insulated from society will struggle to implement its goals. On the other hand, there is a danger that governments end up being captured by the non-state actors with whom they are seeking to develop closer relations (Stigler, 1971; Laffont & Tirole, 1991). In public choice theory, where the notion of capture unsurprisingly originates, the concern is that governments do the bidding of interest-groups, firms and business associations. Such rent-seeking activity is thought to explain, for example, the US government's continued commitment to farm subsidies that harm not only exporters in developing countries but also American consumers (Tullock, 1989; 1993; 2005). In another example, a critical aspect of economic governance in capitalist economies necessarily relies on the activities of private wealth holders, investors and entrepreneurs. A capable state needs to be able to achieve *its* goals by working with and encouraging such private actors while retaining the necessary authority to avoid slipping into relations of clientism, capture, rent-seeking, corruption or other manifestations of government failure. In this sense, close ties between the public and private sectors, or between the state and the community, need to be managed or metagoverned in order to achieve *public* rather than private goals.

In what circumstances are state actors most likely to retain their authority and independence within governance networks? We may already have answered this question. States are most likely to do so when either individual ministries or the state as a whole possess authority and a clear sense of their own legitimacy and mission, and when there is a well-trained, well-equipped public service with a strong sense of its own identity. To this extent, then, we might conclude that state capacity requires both a relational state and a strong state. Furthermore, where state officials are captured, it is important that other state actors are in a position to intervene by challenging policy decisions made within the network and change its membership. Chapter 2, for example, showed how French authorities overturned an established agricultural network in order to achieve wider strategic goals. Another example is the Tariff Board, a statutory authority charged with tariff administration in Australia in the late 1960s, which eventually destroyed the post-war protectionist policy network. The Tariff Board worked to establish its authority, expertise and eventually enough key allies to challenge the dominant tariff policy network, led by the powerful Deputy Prime Minister John McEwen (Bell, 1989). Such an exercise can be thought of as a further form of metagovernance in the sense that it requires the state to steer governance arrangements in order to ensure effectiveness and accountability.

In the final analysis, then, governments are instrumental in the creation of governance networks and they can choose whether to revise such arrangements (Pierre & Peters, 2005, 68). A further example of such state capacity comes from Alan Greer (2002, 465) who examines the development of organic agricultural policy in Ireland and shows how the government set up 'an Organic Development Committee composed of representatives from state bodies, the organic farming sector, the food processing and retail sector, and consumers to oversee the formulation of a development strategy'. When structuring networks, governments may have to choose between the interests of competing groups. Policy decisions taken in one network can generate costly external effects for other actors. The adoption of lax food safety standards in agricultural policy, for example, might generate high political and financial costs for a health ministry that must deal with the resulting public health crisis. In such situations metagovernance and coordination by higher state authorities may be necessary.

Despite efforts to build central state capacity, the challenges of metagovernance are not always met. The analysis by Stephen Bell and Alex Park (2006) of water management through community engagement across a range of river catchments in New South Wales, Australia, provides an illustration of the problems involved. In the early 2000s the state government established 36 Catchment Management Committees comprising local and other stakeholders; they were tasked with formulating water-sharing plans to allocate water to users and the environment. However, the selection of participants in the governance arrangements, the resourcing and information flows provided to the committees, the specification of goals, and confusion over the rules relating to authority-sharing and decision-making arrangements, all caused consternation among participants. This was a classic case in which the authorities were relatively unskilled, under-resourced and over-stretched in attempting to metagovern a governance system.

Other problems associated with metagovernance are illustrated by Mark Whitehead (2003) in a study of decentralised urban regeneration schemes in the West Midlands in England. Contrary to the difficulties of control emphasised by Flinders (2006), Whitehead emphasises the continued presence of central government hierarchy in shaping such governance relationships and the powerful role played by government oversight bodies that insist on adherence to central strategies and perform ongoing monitoring and assessment procedures while employing a strategy of 'fear and discipline' to intimidate local units (p. 12). The intensity of these metagovernance arrangements has certainly increased steering and accountability. But it has done so, according to Whitehead, at the cost of 'choking and constraining the flexibilities' ascribed to such decentralised networks. The 'bureaucratic burden' stemming from metagovernance is 'deflecting important time and resources from the actual projects' the local units were attempting to pursue. Whitehead concludes that the 'practices of metagovernance are currently facilitating hierarchical rule, not local self-determination in policy decision making processes' (p. 13). A similar conclusion is reached by Tabatha Wallington and colleagues (2005, 13) in their study of regional governance arrangements in Australia; they point to the potentially contradictory tendencies of metagovernance in both fostering and inhibiting local decision-making capacity: 'The more that accountability is demanded by higher levels of government, the more likely that the regional bodies – created to be flexible, community-oriented vehicles for change – will become rigid bureaucratic structures, thereby nullifying their original purpose' (see also Flinders, 2002, 70). Similarly Donald Kettl (2002, 146) points to the concerns of academics in New Zealand who have studied the development of a contract-based state and concluded that such governance arrangements have compromised social capital and reduced opportunities for wider engagement and debate. As he argues, government strategies to increase control run the risk of 'weakening government's ability to manage the networks on which effective implementation of public programs depends'.

Despite such problems, the challenges of governance and metagovernance may require a degree of restructuring of the state and perhaps further strengthening of central state authority. Kettl (2002) argues that such challenges are being faced in American public administration without a theoretical compass and with 'theory and practice sagging under the strain'. The traditions of American public administration, he argues, have been built on centralised institutions and hierarchy that are struggling to adapt to new governance arrangements and networks. On the other hand, he also points out that, 'to a surprising degree, governmental institutions have shown remarkable resilience in adapting' (2002, 123). These adaptations have required government leaders and administrators to develop better relational skills, especially in networking, negotiating and contracting. Nevertheless, he argues that there is a continuing need to join up government and develop new systems of budgeting, accountability and personnel management better adapted to relational modes of governance (p. 120). This requires negotiation and compromise, but it also requires strong hierarchical arrangements and a strong central state to exert controls and mobilise resources. As Glyn Davis and Rod Rhodes (2000, 94) argue, the experience of the outsourcing 'contract state' may help strengthen the 'hierarchical state'; one featuring a 'permanent, autonomous, career-based and policy-focused core public service, with a commitment to neutral professional advice'.

CONCLUSION

The state-centric relational approach to governance places both the state and the nature of state–society relations at centre stage in analysing and understanding governance arrangements. The state may be a direct player in specific governance arrangements, but it also has a metagovernance role that transcends such arrangements.

The study of metagovernance is still embryonic. Relatively few scholars have explicitly explored it (see Scharpf, 1994; Jessop, 1997a; 2002; Bell & Park, 2006; Kelly, 2006; Whitehead, 2003; E. Sorensen, 2006; Sorensen & Torfing, 2008b), although some have implicitly done so by emphasising an overall 'state-centric' management role in overseeing governance arrangements (Skogstad, 2003; Mayntz, 1993; Fung & Wright, 2003). We need to know much more about metagovernance functions. First, governments and state managers must move beyond notions that governance arrangements can somehow be self-managing. For Gerry Stoker (1998, 17), 'governance can be defined as a concern with governing and achieving collective action in the realm of public affairs, in conditions where it is not possible to rest on recourse to the authority of the state'. From our perspective, this society-centric view of governance is problematic because it rules out the use of state authority and hence the possibility of metagovernance. In our view, the exercise of metagovernance results in a continuing role for hierarchical government in *any* governance regime. Even when governments choose to govern through markets, networks and community engagement rather than through hierarchy, they retain a key role in the governance process.

In a much-cited article Fritz Scharpf (1994, 41) suggests that governance always take place under the 'shadow of hierarchy'.

> In most western democracies . . . the unilateral exercises of state authority has largely been replaced by formal or informal negotiations, in policy formulation as well as in policy implementation, between governmental actors and the affected individuals and organisations . . . but these are typically negotiations under the shadow of hierarchical authority.

Hence, even when actors appear to be operating under governance arrangements apparently designed to secure a degree of autonomy from government, metagovernance casts the shadow of hierarchy over them. This is a necessary function of the state in pursuit of the SERDAL functions outlined early in this chapter. Metagovernance, however, is always vulnerable to under- or over-regulation. In the case of the New South Wales catchments (Bell & Park, 2006), weak or poorly thought through metagovernance was the main problem. In the case of urban regeneration in the West Midlands (Whitehead, 2003) it appears that onerous levels of metagovernance inhibited local creativity and flexibility. The challenge, then, is to develop effective metagovernance without inhibiting local capacity. Given the hierarchical nature of the state, this is indeed a challenge.

4 | Hierarchy and top-down governance

GOVERNANCE REFERS TO THE TOOLS, strategies and relationships used by governments to help govern. Hierarchical governance is distinguished by the direct application of state authority to target populations. It arises when states impose rules or standards of behaviour on other actors, backed by sanctions and rewards, in order to achieve collective goals. The claim that there has been a 'fundamental transformation' in the 'basic forms' of governance (Salamon, 2002, 1–2) can be understood as saying that governance through hierarchy is being gradually superseded by governance through markets, associations and community engagement. We believe that this society-centric argument is misleading; that the state is far from being passé and that we still need to recognise the 'distinctiveness or uniqueness of state action within contemporary governance' (Crawford, 2006, 458). The actors who control the modern state have at their disposal a set of powers and resources – from formal constitutional and legal authority to vast fiscal, administrative, informational resources and access to expertise – that are qualitatively and quantitatively unlike those available to other actors in society. These resources are frequently employed to govern hierarchically.

In later chapters we pursue our argument that states can enhance their capacity by developing close relations with a wide variety of non-state actors. This chapter argues that the extent to which governance through markets, associations or communities has replaced hierarchical governance has been exaggerated. Hierarchy is not simply holding its own against other governance mechanisms: in some cases it is resurgent. We recognise that reliance on governance through hierarchy varies across states and among policy sectors. Constitutional democracies are characterised by institutionalised safeguards against the exercise of certain forms of hierarchical control not present within authoritarian regimes (Bellamy & Castiglione, 1997). As Kenneth Dyson (1980) observes, there are also differing state traditions within constitutional democracies. A French statist political culture that invests substantial legitimacy in the exercise of centralised state authority can be contrasted with a more liberal American tradition. Comparing policy sectors rather than countries, we might note that defence and monetary policy are almost always developed exclusively by senior politicians and public officials. By contrast, in areas where successful implementation requires the cooperation of semi-autonomous professionals – health and education policy being the sterling examples – extensive networks of consultation often develop.

While recognising that such variations are relevant, we concur with those who point to the growth of the 'regulatory state' (Moran, 2002; Jordana & Levi-Faur, 2004; Braithwaite, 2008). The first part of the chapter acknowledges a partial retreat in the use of hierarchical governance in some areas of economic management and in some areas of public policy. However, hierarchical governance has expanded significantly to address perceived risks posed by new technologies, market failures and threats to civil security. We do not claim that nothing has changed or that governance today is little different from governance yesterday. Indeed, we go on to show how states have institutionally re-engineered themselves to exert more effective control, often as a direct response to weaknesses identified by academics and practitioners.

ROLLING BACK THE STATE?

Chapter 2 demonstrated that state expenditure measured as a share of gross domestic product, far from being rolled back, has increased in most countries over the last 20-odd years. However, this headline figure masks a significant retrenchment of hierarchical governance in relation to some areas of economic management. Governments have progressively withdrawn economic subsidies, exchange and credit controls and tariffs; loosened regulatory controls on capital creation; privatised state enterprises; and deregulated a range of markets. Two important measures of this change are worth highlighting. Table 4.1 shows that overall state expenditure on economic subsidies as a share of GDP fell on average by just over one per cent of GDP in a sample of 20 OECD countries between 1980 and 2004. Interestingly, this withdrawal of state support was not limited to countries like the United Kingdom and the United States, which first elected neo-liberal governments. The largest falls in state support were in those

Table 4.1. Total economic subsidies as a percentage of gross domestic product, selected OECD countries, 1980 and 2004

Country	Total economic subsidies		% change, 1980–2004
	1980	2004	
Australia	1.44	1.32	−0.13
Canada	2.74	1.17	−1.57
France	2.13	1.29	−0.84
Germany	2.08	1.27	−0.81
Italy	2.70	1.07	−1.63
Japan	1.50	0.86	−0.64
Norway	5.15	2.25	−2.90
Portugal	4.60	1.64	−2.96
United Kingdom	1.96	0.53	−1.43
United States	0.35	0.34	−0.01
Total (20-country OECD average)	2.37	1.24	−1.02

Source: Obinger & Zohlnhofer, 2007, 184.

countries, Norway, Sweden and Portugal, with the strongest traditions of state intervention. Second, Figure 4.1 shows that the telecommunication, airline and electricity industries have experienced a marked decline in market regulation in most OECD countries. Remarkably, in not one of these policy sectors did the level of market regulation increase in any country between 1975 and 2002.

These figures must be regarded with caution. In the first place, they focus exclusively on developments in Western countries. Reaction to the explosion in world commodity prices in 2007 shows that hierarchical governance remains a reflex response within many developing economies. Faced with rising domestic food prices and the prospect of political unrest, the governments of Argentina, Cambodia, Indonesia, Russia, the Ukraine and Thailand responded to rising prices either by raising taxes on exports of basic foodstuffs or by simply banning the export of rice, beef or wheat (*Economist*, 2 April 2008). In Egypt, the army was redeployed to bake more bread.

In the case of the so-called 'developmental state' economies of East Asia – Japan, South Korea and Taiwan – it is sometimes argued that these states have, over the last decade or more, abandoned their efforts to

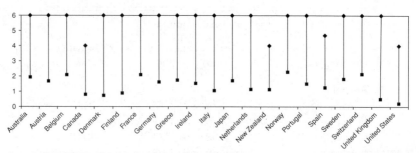

(i) Telecommunications

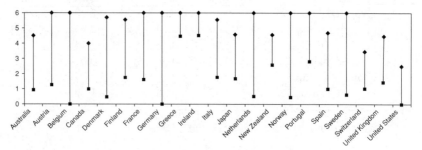

(ii) Aviation

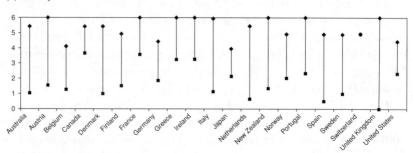

(iii) Electricity

Figure 4.1. Labour market deregulation in three industries, selected OECD countries, 1975–2003.
Note: Regulation is measured in each case on a 0–6 scale with 0 being the least regulated and 6 the most.
Source: Conway & Nicoletti, 2006, 52.

intervene strategically in their economics and have become more neo-liberal in orientation (Jayasuriya, 2001). It is certainly true that market instruments have been used more fully in such countries, but it is less true that they have abandoned state activism in the economy or their tradition of working closely with key firms (Weiss & Thurbon, 2006). In South Korea, for example, state elites led an aggressive campaign to restructure and reorient the activities of the giant conglomerates that dominate the economy – the *chaebol* – in the wake of the Asian financial crisis (Cherry, 2005). Similarly, using as his case-study the creation of a new bio-technology industry, Joseph Wong (2006, 653) demonstrates that, although the Taiwanese state's ability to direct 'industrial transformation from the top-down has weakened', it continues to provide important support for the development of key sectors. Thus, the Ministry of Economic Affairs provides tax deductions for corporate investments in research and development in bio-technology, and offers 'improvement loans' for small and medium-sized industries contemplating work in this area. In addition, the ministry confers generous tax exemptions on profits acquired through patented intellectual property and has overseen the allocation of nearly $1 billion of private funding in bio-technology. The Taiwanese state does not own any bio-technology firms: it does not need to. The state has achieved its development goals by developing closer relations with private actors.

Even within Western liberal democracies, hierarchical economic control, although in partial retreat, frequently remains significant. The economic logic of privatisation may have been accepted in most countries in the world, but the OECD (2005b, 29) estimates that the asset value of state-owned enterprises in France, Greece and South Korea still exceeds $1000 billion. Furthermore, where governments have privatised industries they have often found ways of retaining a measure of control. In the Netherlands and Norway governments have retained majority shareholdings in the firms they have privatised. In France governments have retained a 'golden share', which allows them to appoint two non-voting members to the board of directors and block the sale of any privatised firm to a foreign company. In Italy governments have restricted the sale of state assets to a small group of trusted shareholders – usually banks and industrial conglomerations – that they have worked with closely in the past and trust to protect their interests. These companies are prohibited from selling their shares for a certain period and, after this, can only sell their shares to a firm approved by the government. Furthermore, privatisation, where it has occurred, has led to significant extensions in regulatory powers as governments have sought to protect consumers from monopoly abuses by privatised companies (Vogel, 1995).

In the case of trade policy, it is certainly true that the Kennedy, Tokyo and Uruguay rounds of trade talks under the GATT system prompted significant liberalisation in the era following World War II. But, more recently, the Doha round of talks ended in an impasse when the United States and the European Union refused to dismantle agricultural subsidies and trade protection in return for greater access to markets in developing countries. A study by Kym Anderson and Alan Winters (2008) estimates that state-created trade barriers continue to cost the global economy up to $3 trillion each year. The bottom line is that states still subsidise production in order to pursue domestic policy agendas, such as protecting the livelihoods of farmers and rural populations. The United States prohibits overseas firms with assets in the US from trading with Cuba and has blocked foreign take-overs of oil companies and ports.

Even where governments have come to rely on alternative governance strategies, states continue to exert strong oversight and metagovernance controls. An example comes from Giandomenico Majone's discussion of the use of devolved authority or government by proxy using third parties to regulate or help deliver services. As Majone (1996, 146) says, 'indirect government involves . . . new forms of control and accountability' – in our language, more metagovernance. 'If policy makers wish to control or influence agencies and other organisations operating at arm's length, they must do so by contractual arrangements, and by means of rules and regulations.' Further evidence of hierarchical control in the midst of apparent devolution of governance control can be seen in what Michael Power (1994; 1997) has described as an audit 'explosion' as governments seek to monitor and sanction the behaviour of charities, businesses, sports associations, housing associations, and other bodies that receive public funding. Several factors drive this change: intensified competition in markets, increased individualism, the decline of earlier norms of trust and social cohesion, a greater appreciation of principal-agent problems, and increased recognition of risk factors in societal and governance processes (Beck, 1992). Hence, the perceived escalation of risk in modern societies has occasioned increased efforts in both the public and private sectors to impose more control and auditing in attempts at the 'remanagerialisation of risk' (Power, 1997, 138).

There are other, non-economic, issues on which it is possible to point to the erosion of hierarchical governance over a longer period of time. Legislation criminalising homosexuality was repealed as long ago as 1893 in Belgium and 1933 in Denmark, in the 1960s in the United Kingdom,

Canada and Germany and as recently as 1994 in South Africa. Laws relating to the possession of certain types of drugs, prostitution, pornography and blasphemy have also been loosened or repealed in many countries over the last few decades. Yet in these cases it may be a mistake to equate state-sanctioned tolerance with the decline of hierarchical governance. In the case of gay rights, repeal of discriminatory legislation has recently given way to legislation recognising same-sex marriages (Netherlands, 2001; Canada and Belgium, 2003; South Africa, 2006) or same-sex civil unions and state-recognised partnerships (Denmark, 1989; Sweden, 1995; Germany, 2001; United Kingdom, 2004). In these the state has directly intervened to give same-sex relationships legal status. Limited decriminalisation of recreational drugs has occurred at the same time as far stricter regulatory regimes have been introduced to monitor and sanction performance-enhancing drugs within sport. Finally, the repeal of blasphemy laws has been balanced by the promulgation of hate laws in more than 40 countries since the early 1990s.

NEW TECHNOLOGY

New technologies, new perceived sources of market failure and concerns about growing risk and social disorder have provided three specific stimulants to hierarchical governance. The rapid growth of the digital economy and information flows has prompted states to build or underwrite the construction of new communication networks (Zysman & Newman, 2006). It has also required states to legislate to define and protect intellectual property rights. States have played a major role in defining property rights in new global services markets such as aviation and telecommunications. In a study of such developments, Peter Cowhey and John Richards (2006, 301) conclude that the 'hand of governments has gripped the markets firmly'.

State responses to the development of genetically modified organisms (GMOs) have confirmed the durability of long-standing regulatory differences. Working with other food exporters including Argentina, Canada, Chile and Uruguay in the so-called Miami Group, the United States has lobbied for a permissive regulatory regime for genetically modified crops (Drezner, 2007, 161). Adopting the precautionary principle in responding to widespread public alarm about the use of so-called Frankenstein foods, the European Union has, by contrast, sustained an effective moratorium on GMOs. This is despite an adverse ruling by the World Trade Organisation that it had acted illegally in banning imports of genetically modified crops between 1999 and 2004 (BBC News, 29 September 2006). This pattern of hierarchical control has been largely reversed in the case of stem cell research. In 2001 President Bush announced that federal funds would not be used to support research on human embryonic stem cells. The following year the European Union identified stem cell research as a funding priority.

In the case of the internet, it was once regularly claimed that because 'cyberspace slips seamlessly and nearly unavoidably across national boundaries', governments have been 'pushed effectively to the sidelines' (Spar, 1999, 82). Such a claim now seems less sustainable. Nation-states have played a leading role in funding initial research into the internet, in subsidising the creation of broadband and wireless access, in setting internet technical protocols and in fixing rules on e-commerce and data privacy. Through firewalls, proxy servers, routers and software filters, as well as simple prohibitions on the possession of personal computers, states have been able to block the content of websites considered to be morally or politically undesirable.

The extent and varying methods of internet control have been documented by the Open Net Initiative (http://opennet.net/). Three examples will suffice, the first two taken from authoritarian governments. Saudi Arabia requires all web access to be routed through a proxy server, which blocks access to politically or religiously sensitive material. In China, the state employs an estimated 30 000 public servants to monitor the content of websites (*Guardian*, 14 June 2005), and companies like Yahoo, Google and Microsoft have been required to censor their own material in order to gain access to the Chinese market. This provoked a political storm in 2006 when Yahoo was widely criticised for releasing information to the Chinese authorities about the use of the internet by a political dissident. Yahoo executives argued that they had no choice but to abide by the 'laws, regulations and customs' of the countries in which they operate (*Time*, 3 October 2005). Finally, in South Korea, a law was passed in 2008 requiring the users of all major internet portal sites to verify their identity following the earlier removal of some sites that had expressed personal criticism of politicians.

MARKET FAILURES

Market failures occur when the individual pursuit of self-interest in a market setting leads to collectively sub-optimal outcomes. Externalities or non-priced impacts (such as damage from pollution) on third parties who are not part of direct market transactions are a case in point. We have already seen in Chapter 2 that public choice theory offers a riposte to the orthodox theory of market failure, arguing that state intervention can be a source of inefficiencies. Recognition of the costs of state intervention has certainly encouraged privatisation and deregulation. Yet over the same period, new forms of market failure have been identified and dealt with through hierarchical intervention.

In the environmental arena, scarce resources such as water have increasingly been managed through hierarchical forms of state intervention. In Australia, for example, the federal government imposed a quantitative cap on water extractions in the largest river system in the country, and uses markets and other means to price water to reflect its scarcity value (Connell, 2007). There are proposals in Australia to transfer difficult and contentious water allocation decisions to an independent authority, along the lines of the policy authority held by independent central banks. More broadly, the use of hierarchy in environmental management is widespread. As we noted in Chapter 1, a wide-ranging study by Andrew Jordan and colleagues (2005, 490) found that, despite the development of a range of new environmental policy instruments, the state remains a central player and that there has been 'no wholesale and spatially uniform shift from government to governance'.

In the case of climate change, much has been made of market-based emissions trading schemes. We examine the European Union's Emissions Trading Scheme in Chapter 6. The fourth report of the Intergovernmental Panel on Climate Change (2007) says clearly that states must continue to play the lead role in steering investment decisions, promoting the use of alternative energy sources, encouraging the development and transfer of technologies, and investing in public transport in order to reduce carbon emissions. States have also relied on hierarchical governance mechanisms to tackle other environmental market failures, such as traffic congestion. London, Milan, Stockholm and Singapore have exploited new technology to introduce congestion charges. In London charging has resulted in a 20 per cent fall in inner-city congestion since 2003. In Germany trucks are now charged for their use of roads according to the distance they travel and their emission levels. Finally, in the case of pollution caused by plastic bags, some states have moved beyond moral suasion of the sort examined in the following chapter to impose taxes, levied at the point of sale, upon consumers. The introduction of such a tax in Ireland resulted in a 90 per cent reduction in the production of bags (DELG, 2002).

Governments have also identified obesity (especially in children), pension provision and population decline as policy problems that competitive markets are unable to resolve. Hierarchical governmental action to address obesity includes requirements that manufacturers list ingredients clearly and bans on the sale of junk food in schools. In 2006 the New York City Board of Health attracted publicity when it prohibited the use of artificial trans fats in public restaurants. In the case of pension provision, deregulation in the 1980s and 1990s resulted in the misselling of pensions and a long-term shortfall in provision. To address this market failure, states are increasingly *requiring* individuals to contribute a certain proportion of their income to state-regulated pension schemes. Finally, worries about declining population levels in Italy, Sweden, Japan, France and South Korea have encouraged governments to try to boost birth rates through 'baby bonuses', tax incentives, and improved maternity and paternity payments (OECD, 2007). In France, all-day nurseries, income tax reductions and subsidised rail transport have all been employed. Such measures supplement the Medal of the French Family which, since the 1920s, has been awarded to any woman who gives birth to more than eight children.

Perhaps the most dramatic recent example of hierarchy being used to deal with market failure is the role of governments in dealing with the global credit market crisis since late 2007. In September 2008, for example, central banks, led by the US Federal Reserve, the European Central Bank and the Bank of England, injected over $620 billion of liquidity into the banking system by, effectively, lending taxpayers' money to banks that were refusing to lend money to each other. In order to reassure savers, the Irish government subsequently took the extraordinary step of guaranteeing all deposits held in high-street banks for a two-year period. This created a competitive pressure similar to the California effect documented in Chapter 2. Once Ireland had guaranteed savings in its banks, the governments of Greece, Germany, Austria, Denmark and Sweden succumbed to intense pressure to guarantee savings in their banks in order to prevent capital flight. When it became clear that these measures had not restored confidence and that stock markets were continuing to crumble, a number of governments then proscribed the short-selling of shares while the governments of Austria, Iceland, Russia, Romania and the Ukraine simply suspended share trading altogether.

When even these measures failed and the global financial system came close to meltdown, governments directly intervened to effectively part-nationalise the world's banking system. In the United States, the giant insurance company American International Group was the beneficiary of a $85 billion loan, which its former chief executive officer characterised as nationalisation. Before the political dust had settled, America's two giant mortgage corporations, Freddie Mac and Fannie Mae, were taken into the 'conservatorship' of their regulator, the Federal Housing Finance Agency, at an immediate cost to the US taxpayer of at least $200 billion. After protracted negotiations and much political grandstanding during an election year, Congress agreed to spend more than $700 billion to buy 'toxic' debts from failing banks. In the United Kingdom two banks, Northern Rock and Bradford & Bingley, the latter specialising in 'self-certifying' mortgage applications, were taken into public ownership *before* a further £500 billion of taxpayers' money was found to take equity stakes in a number of banks. In return, the UK government extracted guarantees that these banks would limit executive pay and resume lending to businesses, mortgage applicants, and other banks. Following its lead, the French, German, Austrian and Spanish governments pledged upwards of €800 billion of taxpayers' money to rescue crippled banks and inject further liquidity into European capital markets.

Beyond the immediate crisis, policy debate began to focus on the need for long-lasting reform in the management and organisation of the world's financial markets. The important point to make here is that all the proposals for reform required the extension of hierarchical authority. At the time of writing in November 2008, in no particular order of either significance or feasibility, proposals included:

- restrict the use of derivatives and securitisation; one specific option was to require those who securitise debt to retain a part of the risk of the securities they create
- proscribe the creation of hedge funds that seek to minimise client risk by engaging in short selling
- tighten capital adequacy requirements in order to prevent banks from exposing themselves to too much debt
- create new insurance schemes to guarantee savings, the schemes being funded out of bank profits during periods of economic boom, rather than by taxpayers at a moment of bust
- require financial institutions to reveal their debt liabilities to each other
- establish new rules requiring central banks to target not only underlying inflation but the 'asset bubbles' that frequently precede financial crises
- restrict executive pay and tax, or simply prohibit incentive schemes that encourage risk-taking to meet short-term performance targets
- empower international bodies, whether the International Monetary Fund, the G7 or the G20, to standardise international financial regulations.

It might be objected that the financial crisis was caused by financial deregulation and sustained by an apparently limitless neo-liberal faith in markets and that it is therefore ironic to cite the crisis as evidence of a resurgent state. The global credit crisis certainly exposed the limitations of an ideology which maintained that the pursuit of individual self-interest in competitive markets would always and everywhere secure the collective good. Its inadequacy is now recognised even by neo-liberals such as the former chairman of the Federal Reserve and chief cheerleader for financial deregulation, Alan Greenspan (in testimony to Congress in October 2008). Although a supporting role was played by Congress – which, for its own political reasons, pressed Freddie Mac and Fannie Mae to underwrite the 'sub-prime' mortgages being offered to poor American families – it is difficult to avoid casting financial deregulation as the villain of the financial debacle. Yet the coordinated and extraordinary response to the credit crisis showed that the state remains capable of intervening decisively in deregulated and globalised financial markets. The failure of governments across the world to anticipate and prevent the crisis from occurring reflected a failure of political will rather than of governing ability.

Partly in response to the regulatory challenges of globalisation and partly due to a desire to integrate markets, states have worked together to enhance their national policy capacity in a wide range of areas. This will certainly be a central issue in dealing with the global financial crisis. In another arena the development of the European Union has seen the rise of a Europe-wide 'regulatory state' dominated by Brussels and using a wide array of relatively independent regulatory agencies, such as the European Central Bank (Majone, 1996). The continuing relevance of hierarchical regulatory rule-making within the European Union can be seen in the 'almost exponential growth, during the last three decades, of member directives and regulations produced by the Brussels authorities each year' (Majone, 1997, 144). Moreover, the 'Europeanisation' of regulation continues to empower national regulators linked to complex European regulatory regimes.

On a similar transnational regulatory note, and as we saw in Chapter 2, a major study by Drezner (2007) argues that state authority, especially that of the major states, is the driving force behind new extensions of state regulation in fields from the internet to international finance and the international pharmaceutical industry. Because of the growth of regulation and legal standards as extensions of state authority to regulate or police the international arena, scholars have also observed the growth in the 'juridification' of international relations and regulatory policy (Jayasuriya, 2001). Even in international arenas once considered the domain of private transnational corporations, such as the oil industry, it is now increasingly the case that national oil corporations, in many cases backed by state authority, have been out-manoeuvring oil giants such as Shell and Exxon Mobil in securing oil reserves around the world. Moreover, critical studies of global governance find plenty of evidence that international organisations from the United Nations to the World Trade Organization possess only limited autonomy from their most powerful member states (Murphy, 2000), and that the leading nations, such as the United States, still exert considerable hegemony in shaping the rules of the international policy and regulatory arena (Gowan, 1999; Wade, 2003; Beeson & Bell, 2009).

POLICING SOCIETY

In developed countries the last few decades have witnessed a significant extension of policing and surveillance. This has occurred amidst a general set of fears, articulated by both the right and the left, about a breakdown of social responsibility following the erosion of traditional forms of social conditioning and restraint such as religion, community and family.

In the welfare field, new forms of 'welfare contractualism' now exemplify new or additional layers in the state's regulation of behaviour. Prompted by concerns about the growth of a dependency culture and fraud, welfare payments have been made conditional upon a recipient's willingness to look for work or retrain or undertake voluntary work. Following the development of a number of state-based programs, in 1996 President Clinton signed into law a new federal welfare system, Temporary Assistance for Needy Families. This requires welfare recipients to retrain and imposes a lifetime limit of 60 months upon the payment of support (Lurie, 1997). A number of countries – including the United States, the United Kingdom, Australia and France – have adopted conditional welfare payments for the unemployed, lone parents, and the disabled (Clegg & Clasen, 2007). In Australia, contracts are being used to codify, monitor and regulate the behaviour of welfare recipients through arrangements developed under the Howard government's system of 'mutual obligation'.

States have used tax incentives, subsidised nursery places and job-sharing schemes to encourage mothers to return to work. In Mexico, Brazil and other South American countries, conditional cash transfers provide financial incentives for mothers to take nutritional supplements, keep their children in school, and ensure they attend regular health check-ups. Parents are paid only if they effectively police their own activities. This kind of disciplinary power has also been employed in New York, where private charities, funded through the mayor's office, have offered cash payments to students in poor neighbourhoods who excel in exams.

In parallel with such developments, and possibly overshadowing them, there has been an increase in policing and the micro-management of society. The case of speeding fines is a classic example of governments ratcheting up legal sanctions and technologically sophisticated methods of surveillance in order to extend (increasingly successful) controls over drivers' behaviour. The spread of random breath testing to detect alcohol and other drugs among drivers is a related example of the state further encroaching on societal behaviour. Writing about trends in the United Kingdom, Adam Crawford (2006, 455) argues that 'ambitious, interventionist government is alive and well'. He documents the rise of a 'complex mosaic of micro-management' in previously semi-autonomous schools, universities and other public bodies. More generally, he points to enhanced efforts to regulate a wide range of behaviour through such hierarchical instruments as anti-social behaviour and parenting orders (see also Burney, 2005). The 1000 new criminal offences encoded in law in the United Kingdom between 1997 and 2005 included measures allowing the state to prosecute and jail the parents of persistent truants. There have also been increasing incursions designed to curb 'anti-social' behaviour in public places, including police crack-downs, curfews, dispersal orders and court orders to restrict freedom of movement. Over the same period, the development of a network of linked closed-circuit television cameras has allowed the police to track the movements of individuals and cars in city centres. It is estimated that the average UK citizen is now caught on a surveillance camera more than 300 times a day (BBC News, 2 November 2006). The authorities are even deploying technologies such as miniature remote-controlled drone aircraft fitted with surveillance cameras, and 'talking' surveillance cameras that can shout public rebukes to offenders dropping litter or engaging in other anti-social behaviour (*Economist*, 27 September 2007). The former abode of George Orwell, the author of the authoritarian dystopia *1984*, now has surveillance cameras outside it. Recently, in response to continuing concerns about binge drinking, the government proposed measures to ban pubs and restaurants from running promotions offering women free drinks.

The rhetoric of 'crisis' is increasingly an excuse for sidestepping routine policy processes and strengthening the hand of centralised government. A classic example occurred in Australia where the federal government (in the run-up to a tough election) declared a national emergency in 2007, following the publication of a report that alleged that child sexual abuse was occurring in 'almost every' Aboriginal community in the remote Northern Territory (Toohey, 2008, 45). The decision to intervene was made hastily by a small inner circle without wide consultation with the Northern Territory government (whose chief minister subsequently resigned). The relevant legislation was rushed through the federal parliament. With the assistance of the army and police and the notable absence of any community engagement or stakeholder consultation, the federal government forcibly acquired five-year leases over township land, quarantined welfare payments, introduced new restrictions on the sale of alcohol and pornography, and announced compulsory health checks for all children.

Finally, fears of terrorist attacks and rogue states have been used to justify a wide range of military interventions, security and surveillance measures, new powers of detention, curbs on civil liberties, extended detention without charge, 'offshore' detention centres such as Guantanamo Bay, as well as the use of torture and practices such as 'extraordinary rendition'. The US government has invested an estimated $3 trillion and the lives of over 4000 of its soldiers fighting the war in Iraq (Stiglitz & Bilmes, 2008). The former US Secretary of State, Condoleezza Rice, argued for a system of 'preventative detention', claiming that 'you can't allow somebody to commit the crime before you detain them'. A wide range of such security incursions has been deployed in the United Kingdom, the United States and Australia. In the United States, legislation introduced shortly after September 11 enabled the federal government to monitor and freeze bank accounts suspected of being used to support terrorism (Woodward, 2002, 45). Subsequently, the Patriot Act has relaxed controls over phone-tapping and other forms of surveillance. In the United Kingdom the government opted out of parts of the European Convention on Human Rights in order to pass legislation allowing it to hold indefinitely and without charge any foreigner who is deemed a national security risk. Following legal challenges to this measure the government introduced indefinitely renewable control orders, including electronic tagging, a ban on phone and internet use, and strict curfews on any suspected terrorist, British or foreign (*Economist*, 4 October 2007).

HIERARCHICAL GOVERNANCE: CHALLENGES AND ADAPTATIONS

Despite such continuing incursions, a body of work points to various problems of hierarchical control and the dangers of regulatory overreach (Sunstein, 1990). Echoing a widespread view in the governance literature,

Jon Pierre and Guy Peters (2000, 3) argue that 'states can no longer control society in a conventional command and control mode'. Arguments first developed in the 1970s about the difficulties of policy implementation (Jordan, 1999; Lampinen & Uusikyla, 1998; Goggin et al., 1990) and state failure (Winston, 2006; Orcalli, 2007) continue to be applied to new subject matter. Such arguments should be taken seriously. There are problems with implementation failure; vested interests can exert powerful pressures on regulation; and there can be complex disputes over legal interpretation and enactment.

On the other hand, the difficulties involved in hierarchical governance ought not to be exaggerated. The claim that governments always fail has no more veracity than the claim that governments never fail. It is clear that, sometimes against all expectations, hierarchical governance remains an effective means of addressing some policy problems. For example, in a review of clean air regulation in the United States, Daniel Cole and Peter Grossman (1999) challenge accounts of regulatory failure and argue that top-down regulation has proved reasonably effective in many instances. They invite critics to be more sensitive to the historical, technological, institutional and political environment of regulation; and they review a range of studies to demonstrate that these contextual factors shape the efficacy of command and control strategies compared to alternative strategies, such as market-based instruments. Despite the difficulties countries have experienced in meeting their obligations under the Kyoto Treaty, internationally coordinated hierarchical intervention to deal with environmental problems can be effective. In the 1980s and early 1990s countries negotiated a series of deep cuts to the production of chlorofluorocarbons (CFCs) used in refrigerators and many industrial processes at an estimated long-term cost of $20–40 billion (Sandler, 2004, 215). These gases were implicated in the creation of a growing ozone hole above the Antarctic. As a result of these agreements, overall global consumption of CFCs has more than halved, while the atmospheric concentration of most ozone-depleting gases started to drop in the late 1990s.

States have also adapted and reconfigured themselves in ways that have increased centralised control and hierarchical authority. First, government leaders in a number of countries have increasingly centralised executive power and authority, a trend commentators have referred to as the presidentialisation of politics (Poguntke & Webb, 2005), the strengthening of a culture of command (Walter & Strangio, 2007; Walter, 2008), or the rise of post-democratic leadership (Hocking, 2005). The powers exercised by Prime Ministers Tony Blair and John Howard and President Bush exemplify this dynamic, which emphasises 'strong leadership' in the face of real or constructed 'crises'. The centralisation of executive power is reflected in the strengthening and growing insulation of inner circles of policy formulation and advice, often featuring the rise of political advisers and spin doctors, the bypassing of party structures and parliamentary arenas of decision-making, and the sidelining of departmental advice or input and even, at times, of cabinet government itself. Wide consultation and community engagement are obvious casualties of this approach.

Second, states continue to rely upon – and indeed strengthen – hierarchical governance options partly because their own reform efforts have made such options more attractive. As Michael Moran (2002, 410) observes, some of the 'biggest upheavals that have taken place are actually within state structures themselves'. Attacks on state intervention in the name of public choice have actually encouraged politicians to undertake reforms that strengthen state capacity. States are combating principal-agent problems by tightening authority structures and escalating the use of audits and other internal disciplinary measures such as competition and the use of tightly specified contracts.

Governments have also sought to institutionally redesign their own state systems to make them more responsive and authoritative. Across most Western governments, for example, there have been extensive reforms of the public sector in recent decades, often under the banner of 'new public management'. This has resulted in a shift in the focus of management systems from inputs and processes to outputs and outcomes; towards greater measurement of results; and a preference for leaner, flatter and more autonomous organisations (Hood, 1991). In the United States, the United Kingdom, New Zealand, Australia, Canada and Sweden and, to a lesser extent, in France, Germany and the European Commission, the application of such ideas over the last 20 years has entailed greater use of targets and performance indicators, tighter budgetary controls, the creation of semi-autonomous executive agencies, and performance contracts between finance and delivery agencies (see Pollitt & Bouckaert, 2000, 192–298, for country-by-country reviews). Performance contracts have exerted greater ministerial control over the bureaucracy. Such management reforms have aimed to abolish the security of tenure of senior bureaucrats, placing them on short-term contracts where performance is judged against specified targets. As we said in Chapter 2, such reform measures, as well as the use of taskforces and other mechanisms to coordinate policy, rather than hollowing out government have helped to fill it in and strengthen central coordination and the authority of central state institutions.

As a part of this reform process, there has been an explosion not only in the degree to which state agencies regulate non-state agencies but in the regulation of state agencies by other parts of the state (Hood et al., 1999). Over the last few decades watchdog bodies have acquired additional staff, budgets and regulatory powers. For example, in the United States the Office of Management and Budget monitors the performance of federal agencies; in the United Kingdom the Office for Standards in Education monitors and reports upon the performance of state schools; the European Court of Auditors must declare whether the European Union's budget has been implemented correctly; and in Australia assorted Crime and Misconduct Commissions investigate allegations of public sector corruption.

In an important survey of governments that have increased central steering and control in the face of external risks and the imperatives of internal control, Moran (2002) documents the growth of the 'regulatory state'. Similarly, writers such as Martin Loughlin and Colin Scott (1997), Francis McGowan and Helen Wallace (1996) and Kanishka Jayasuriya (2001) argue that the institutional architecture of the state is changing, with an increasing emphasis on institutional self-regulation, technocratic rule, and patterns of intervention designed to support and police markets and other arenas of social life. According to these authors, central state powers have been consolidated and insulated, and core policy-making has been distanced from disruptive politics and partisan intervention. This has been associated with moves towards independent and partly self-regulating policy institutions whose rules and behaviour take on an increasingly juridical character at one remove from the government (see also Majone, 1996).

A range of factors have been adduced to explain the increasing delegation of powers to independent agencies within government. In particular, the establishment of quasi-autonomous agencies offers politicians the prospect of boosting the expertise and authority of regulators, enhancing the credibility of a policy in the eyes of third parties, and perhaps shielding politicians from the political heat of making tough regulatory decisions (Gilardi, 2002; Elgie, 2006). The recourse to specialised regulatory remits and the honing of specialised expertise are important developments that have helped build or rebuild the authority of states in complex environments.

Although his work concentrates on the United Kingdom, Moran (2003; 2006) offers us one way to summarise the general effect of such changes in the way states order their activities. He charts a shift away from an earlier form of closed and genteel control by cloistered elites, which he refers to as 'club government', in favour of the development of a new form of 'high modernism' and a new and more hierarchical 'regulatory state'. The latter is characterised by stronger central controls, and extensive auditing and quantitative measurement of performance (see also Porter, 1995; Baldwin, 2004). In response to claims by Rhodes (1997) about weakening central controls and the hollowing out of the state, Moran (2006, 35) suggests: 'to maintain this paradigm in the face of the evidence of the state's transformed role – notably its invasion precisely of those self-regulating networks that were once central to British regulation – involves serious intellectual contortion'. Similar observations regarding the strengthening of the UK state in the context of the drive for neo-liberal reforms, particularly under Prime Minister Thatcher, have been made by Andrew Gamble (1998), who talks about the combination of a 'free market and the strong state'. More broadly, Stephen Vogel (1996) shows that the creation of 'freer markets' has resulted in the imposition of more rules. Echoing earlier classical themes in political economy, especially as developed by Karl Polanyi (1957), Moran (2006, 42) argues that the 'road to a more market liberal society was cleared and sustained by a massive state intervention and a sharp rise in state control of regulatory systems'. He traces this process in various developments, from the tightening of controls over financial markets and the City of London to the imposition of new top-down governance agendas in arenas as diverse as school performance and the administration of sports. This is a discussion to which we will return in Chapter 6.

SELF-REGULATION IN THE SHADOW OF HIERARCHY

Criticisms were first made in the 1970s and 1980s about the difficulties of successfully regulating the activities of non-state actors through hierarchical control. In response there has been an important movement toward various systems of self-regulation, or light-touch, smart or responsive regulation, particularly in business and the professions (Cunningham & Rees, 1997; Ayres & Braithwaite, 1992). We will consider this reform process in detail because it offers a good example of state-centric relational policy capacity.

The growth of self-regulation in business sectors, financial markets and the professions reminds us that states must frequently forge governing coalitions with societal interests in order to achieve their policy goals. In other words, state capacity is achieved *through* coalition with other powerful non-state interests to achieve joint aims. As this book argues, state capacity ought to be understood not only as a product of the state institutional capacities but also as a network or *relational* concept. The relationship between state and non-state actors in such systems of self-regulation is not, however, one of equality; it should not be interpreted simply as an abandonment of hierarchical governance. As Ian Bartle and Peter Vass (2007, 902) point out, under self-regulation we may have moved beyond 'conventional hierarchy', but 'the state still retains a special place ... in a self-regulatory world, that place, at the very least, is *primus inter pares*'.

If states are always central players in shaping patterns of self-regulation, it is also useful to point to the impact of state traditions and institutional structures in shaping cross-national variations in regulatory practice. David Vogel (1986) looked at differing 'national styles of regulation' some time ago, suggesting that a formal and legalistic pattern of regulation in the United States could be contrasted with informal and cooperative modes in the United Kingdom. Abraham Newman and David Back (2004) pointed to a similar distinction in patterns of self-regulation, arguing that in the United States there is stronger recourse to direct threats by the state to impose punitive action if industry does not meet self-regulatory standards.

These relations of cooperation and hierarchy in self-regulatory practice have been analysed by Ian Ayres and John Braithwaite (1992) in their influential model of 'responsive regulation'. They emphasise that effective self-regulation can be fostered by continuing persuasion and dialogue between regulators and those being regulated. In the place of a confrontational relationship they show how expectations, agreements, and codes and norms of compliance can over time be agreed cooperatively (see also Cunningham & Grabosky, 1998). As Chapter 5 emphasises, persuasion is increasingly recognised as an important aspect of governance. But responsive regulation requires more than persuasion. Ayres and Braithwaite are clear that the compliance of non-state actors with understandings and expectations agreed through dialogue is best fostered in a pyramidal set of relations. The base of this pyramid represents the ongoing arena of persuasion, norm-building, codification and voluntary compliance within the regulated sector. Yet such activity occurs in the shadow of hierarchy, with recourse, if needed, to the top of the pyramid, through the imposition of coercive power if there are failures or breaches in self-regulation or compliance. Self-regulation works if, as well as speaking softly, the state carries a big stick.

In surveying the role played by the Occupational Health and Safety Administration in the United States, Charles Caldart and Nicholas Ashford (1999) found that cooperation between state and non-state actors to ensure more responsive regulation required strong systems of deterrence and authority. Similarly, in a study of competition policy and corporate regulation in Australia, Christine Parker (2002) describes a process whereby the role of the state has changed from direct command and control to a system of state-guided 'metaregulation', entailing the constituting of markets and overseeing systems of self-regulation. Parker compares the performance of two regulatory agencies, the Australian Competition and Consumer Commission and the Australian Securities and Investments Commission. She argues that both agencies adopted a strategy broadly in line with Ayres and Braithwaite's pyramidal, responsive regulation model. In her view the former has been a more successful metaregulator because it has more effectively connected the use of moral suasion and cooperation to state coercion.

To what extent have such responsive partnerships weakened the state and drained its power? Lester Salamon (2002, 15, 12) reflects a common view when he argues that collaborative forms of governance entail mutual dependencies between state and non-state actors, in which 'no entity is in a position to enforce its will on others' and 'negotiation and persuasion replace command and control' (see also Pierre & Peters, 2000, 99). In these conditions states are forced to 'surrender significant shares of authority' in order to make such collaborations effective (Salamon, 2002, 12). We disagree. Governance through partnerships, whether by means of self-regulation in associative networks or through community engagement, has allowed states to strengthen their capacity by reducing much of the burden of previously cumbersome regulatory controls. Yet in systems of self-regulation the state, operating under the shadow of hierarchy, remains the weighty actor. Indeed Chris Berg (2008) argues that responsive regulation has allowed governments to *increase* their regulatory reach in the economy because firms have been pressured into accepting 'voluntary' agreements that they must abide by.

We have concentrated here on responsive regulation, but in other cases the state's commitment to power-sharing can be even more limited. States do sometimes grant parcels of decision-making authority to non-state actors, but such grants are likely to be limited, highly conditional and potentially reversible. This is partly because states do not like to share power and usually consent to do so under only special or restrictive conditions. It is also because, even in a brave new public management world, politicians know that voters expect government to be ultimately accountable for outcomes. Thus governments set the parameters of acceptable agreements, and they may even overturn negotiated outcomes or plans submitted by devolved negotiating forums. In recent years, following a series of public scandals over the misbehaviour of doctors, the UK government withdrew from the British Medical Council the authority to determine a doctor's fitness to practise. At the same time, in order to meet an ambitious target to build 3 million new homes between 2008 and 2020, the government created a new Homes and Community Agency with the legal authority to issue binding directives to housing associations which, although publicly subsidised, have previously operated as independent not-for-profit NGOs.

A further example of states enhancing their capacity by developing close relations with non-state actors is offered by Geert Teisman and Erik-Hans Klijn (2002), who examine various partnership arrangements in the redevelopment of Rotterdam Harbour. Their main finding is that government actors wanted to 'retain their primacy' in the processes and were largely unwilling to share power (p. 204). Similarly, in a study of ecological modernisation policy in Sweden, Lennart Lundqvist (2001, 332) sets out to test Rhodes' arguments about 'governance without government' and finds that, 'contrary to Rhodes' assertions, central government has been found to hold the initiative in the process of implanting Sweden's new strategy of ecological modernisation'. The central government went out of its way to build new processes and institutions that increased its power in relation to interlocutors such as independent expert agencies and municipal governments.

THE GROWING VOLUME OF GOVERNANCE

This chapter argues that, contrary to the conventional wisdom, governance through hierarchy remains an essential part of the policy armory of governments. However, we do not argue that governing and governments have remained unchanged. The following chapters illustrate the development of governance through persuasion, markets, community engagement and associative governance. Is there a contradiction in arguing that governance through hierarchy is resurgent *and* that there has been growth in the use of other governance mechanisms? We think not. The use of governance mechanisms can be measured in relative and absolute terms. Relatively, there has been some shift towards governance through markets, community engagement and associations. Yet because the total volume of governance has grown, the absolute level of governance through hierarchy has also increased.

The total volume of governance has increased within many countries because the range of the collective goals that governments pursue has

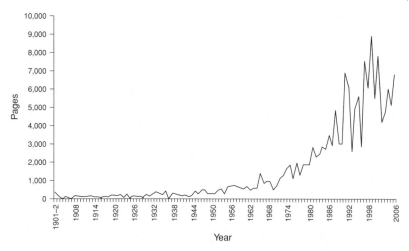

Figure 4.2. Number of pages of Commonwealth Acts of Parliament passed per year, 1901–2006.
Source: Berg, 2008, 12.

increased. As the first part of this book argued, we live in an age in which, despite the apparent political appeal of neo-liberal promises to 'roll back the frontiers of the state', people still expect governments to solve policy problems and steer society. It is true that governments once pursued policy goals that are long abandoned: for instance, most Western countries abandoned food rationing in the late 1940s. By and large, governments no longer attempt to control the movement of currencies across national boundaries, and in many European Union countries internal border controls have been dismantled. Yet as new policy problems have been identified and new technologies developed, the range of activities that governments seek to encourage, discourage, regulate, monitor, prohibit or offer advice on has grown. Obesity, species extinction, water conservation, smoking, carbon emissions, anti-social behaviour, the use of mobile phones while driving, busking, hate speech, cloning, the numbers of senior female business executives, the transfer of personal data between organisations, doping in sport, road pricing, the transmission of major sporting events on terrestrial rather than satellite television, stalking, binge drinking, the number of gold medals won at an Olympics – all have become the subject of political debate and government action.

As a measure of the absolute growth in governance through hierarchy, consider the graphs shown here. Figure 4.2 shows the total number of pages of legislation contained in new acts of the Australian Parliament

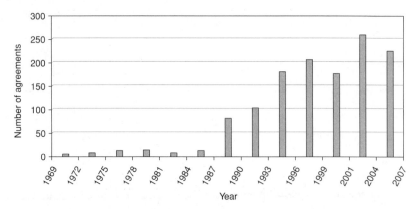

Figure 4.3. Total number of agreements signed by the European Community/Union with third countries and international organisations, 1969–2007
Source: <http://eur-lex.europa.eu/en/accords/accords.htm>.

between 1901 and 2006. It shows a spectacular increase in the late 1960s which, far from reversing itself with the election of a succession of increasingly neo-liberal governments in the 1980s and 1990s, has accelerated. Figure 4.3 shows the total number of formal agreements signed by the European Union with other countries and international organisations over three-year periods between 1969 and 2005. The subject matter of these agreements is incredibly varied. In 2007 the European Union signed, among other things, a fisheries partnership agreement with Mozambique; a partnership agreement with the Republic of Tajikistan; a scientific and technological cooperation agreement with India; a protocol with Thailand relating to manioc production, marketing and trade; a convention on jurisdiction and the recognition and enforcement of judgments in civil and commercial matters with Switzerland; and an agreement with Serbia on the issuing of visas. The important point to note is a dramatic increase in the overall number of agreements. In the 1970s when the then European Economic Community was first formulating many of its policies dealing with trade and agriculture, fewer than 20 agreements were being signed every three years. Between 2002 and 2005 alone, 260 such agreements were signed. Finally, Figure 4.4 shows the total number of regulatory agencies contained within 16 policy sectors across 49 countries between 1960 and 2002. It also shows that a dramatic expansion in regulation started at precisely the moment in the early 1980s when resurgent neo-liberal parties were promising to 'roll back the frontiers of the state'.

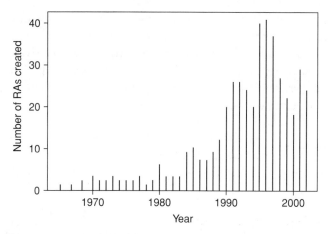

Figure 4.4. Expansion of the number of regulatory agencies across 16 sectors and 49 nations, 1960–2002
Source: Braithwaite, 2008, viii.

CONCLUSION

This chapter has provided evidence that hierarchical governance, far from retreating, continues to expand in response to new policy challenges. States are clearly building in new governance instruments and expanding their reach. We agree with Moran (2003, 6) and Crawford (2006, 471), who argue that there has been 'an extraordinary growth of the "regulatory state"' and that 'recourse to command and control continues to occupy a prominent place in the contemporary social regulatory armoury'. States are the only policy actors that have the authority to kill, deport, tax, imprison, usurp property, or send people to war. As Christoph Knill and Derk Lehmkuhl (2002, 43) argue, states are often in a unique position to 'accommodate conflicting interests and define governance priorities'.

In deference to public sensitivities, neo-liberal ideology or even, perhaps, academic writing, governments have sometimes eschewed the rhetoric of hierarchical control and coercive power. Politicians and state officials have found the notion of an 'enabling' state particularly attractive. Yet as we explain in our discussion of governance through community engagement in Chapter 7, there is danger in confusing rhetoric with reality. We have described governance in terms of an exchange of authority and resources between states and societies. This is the essence of our state-centric relational approach to governance. This chapter has documented an extraordinary growth in a wide range of forms of top-down authority. Some extensions of authority have been criticised as excessive and may be amended or repealed, while others have been accepted by society as legitimate exercises of power. Either way, the political exchange between state and society is ongoing.

5 | Governance through persuasion

MUCH OF THE LITERATURE ON GOVERNANCE focuses on the means of hierarchy, markets and associational networks (Thompson et al., 1991; Borzel & Panke, 2008). We have argued for a broader conception of governance that allows for the possibility of community engagement, which we discuss in the following chapter, as well as governance through persuasion, the focus of this chapter. This can be contrasted with governance through markets or hierarchies in terms of the motives of those governed. Markets and hierarchies rest upon the application of rewards and sanctions, whether in the form of profits and losses or prohibitions and subsidies. When governing through hierarchy and markets, governments achieve their goals by making it in the interests of other actors to behave in particular ways. Governance through persuasion takes a different form, in which governments or other actors seek to convince people that they ought to behave in a particular way. Governance through persuasion leads not simply to a change in behaviour but to a change in people's ideas about how they ought to behave.

The capacity to exercise power by changing someone's beliefs and values constitutes an important source of power analysed in Michel Foucault's work on 'governmentality': a term coined to refer to the styles of reasoning characteristic of governing practices (1991). One of Foucault's most important books, *Discipline and Punish* (1979), opens with a lengthy and horrifying account of the torture and public execution of a murderer in Paris in 1757. This is contrasted with the austere and soulless order of a young offenders' institute in France in 1838. For Foucault, the difference between these two regimes symbolises a more general transition during this period from 'repressive' to 'disciplinary' power; a transition that vividly illustrates the differences between governance through hierarchy and governance through persuasion.

Repressive power, as characterised by Foucault, is exercised in the name of the sovereign and is, in its nature, episodic, violent and destructive. The purpose of repressive power – exemplified through military occupations and the suppression of insurrections as well as executions – is not simply to punish those who break established laws but to destroy them. Repressive power is exercised *on* individuals. By contrast, disciplinary power is pervasive, bureaucratic and productive. Disciplinary power is exercised with the intention of changing people's behaviour. Where repressive power is destructive, disciplinary power is productive, in the sense that it operates *through* individuals not to break them down but to reconstitute them in ways that render them fit to be governed.

Although disciplinary power was initially confined within what Goffman (1968) called 'total' institutions such as prisons, hospitals, psychiatric institutions and military barracks, Foucault suggests that it has become a pervasive – indeed, defining – feature of modern society. Factories, schools and hospitals have come to resemble prisons (Foucault, 1979, 225). Supervisors, teachers, administrators, probation officers, career advisers, doctors, social workers, psychiatrists and, yes, lecturers, have all come to share with prison officers a responsibility for setting and monitoring standards of 'acceptable behaviour'. Constant regulation within the disciplinary or 'carcereal' society has the cumulative effect of shaping not only people's preferences but their very identities. Foucault challenges the notion that there is an autonomous individual whose preferences the government and other actors can shape. In Foucault's work there are no autonomous individuals who lie behind and remain unaffected by the exercise of power. Power 'constitutes' people.

There is an apparent paradox here. The rise of the disciplinary society has coincided with the triumph of a liberal governmentality that prescribes strict limitations upon government intervention. The Foucaultian answer to this paradox is that, if people are to be left to their own economic devices, they must first possess the required liberal virtues of self-discipline, frugality, entrepreneurship, morality and sexual restraint. So the state must intervene in order to create the conditions for its subsequent non-intervention. Yet in Foucault's view it is not only representatives of the state such as social workers and probation officers who exercise this disciplinary power. Power also 'circulates', to use one of Foucault's favourite phrases, within churches, universities, workplaces, community groups and the media.

Foucault's arguments about the exercise of disciplinary power raise an important issue about the relative significance of state and non-state actors as agents of persuasion. In Chapter 1 we showed that states retain an effective monopoly over the exercise of coercive power and that this underpins the continuing relevance of governance through hierarchy. Governance through persuasion, however, requires the exercise of a different kind of power, and it is not immediately obvious why the state must always play the same leading role in its application. This chapter provides examples of non-state actors engaging in governance through persuasion and demonstrates that, on occasions, non-state actors may have a greater capacity to change people's behaviour. This is important because governance through persuasion might therefore constitute an important example of 'governance without government'.

Yet as the chapter unfolds we point to a number of reasons why governance through persuasion depends crucially on the continued involvement of governments:

- The resources that states possess – their financial muscle, expertise and legitimacy – usually provide a significant capacity to shape people's preferences.
- Even where non-state actors are engaged in efforts to change people's behaviour, governments retain responsibility for the metagovernance of governance arrangements.
- Because the state has a monopoly on the exercise of coercive power, it is often the target of others' persuasive efforts.
- States have a key advantage over non-state actors in that they can combine attempts to change people's behaviour through persuasion with the application of rewards and sanctions. Hierarchical governance is not simply an alternative to governance through persuasion; in many cases it enhances the efficacy of governance through persuasion.
- States play a major role in the development of social capital: one of the key institutional prerequisites for effective persuasion.

LEGITIMACY, PERSUASION AND GOVERNANCE WITHOUT GOVERNMENT

Non-state actors routinely attempt to persuade each other to change their behaviour. Advertising and marketing conducted by and for privately owned firms constitute a massive exercise in persuasion. In 2007 Procter & Gamble spent $4.6 billion on advertising in the American market; General

Motors spent $4.3 billion; Time Warner spent $3.4 billion; and AT&T, $2.4 billion. Although precise estimates are difficult to obtain, the US federal government spent around $5 billion on advertising in 2001 (Weiss, 2002, 222).

Many of these efforts at persuasion may be considered to have little direct political consequence. Yet efforts to persuade people to buy particular brands of cigarettes, drive sports utility vehicles, or buy fast food obviously have the potential to undermine government efforts to persuade people to smoke less, reduce their carbon emissions and eat more healthily. But non-state actors also contribute *positively* to the achievement of collectively valued goals through persuasion. Consider the following examples.

- Over the last 30 years governments have sought to reduce rates of HIV/AIDS infection. The most effective work in promoting safe sex has often been undertaken by not-for-profit charities. In the United Kingdom the Terrence Higgins Trust, named after one of the first Britons to die of AIDS, has sought to promote sexual health through information campaigns and HIV testing programs; it has acquired a reputation for being able to communicate effectively with gay men and change their behaviour. In Brazil (Levi & Vetoria, 2002), Australia (Mameli, 2001) and Hungary (Danziger, 1997), programs to reduce the incidence of HIV/AIDS have also largely relied upon the involvement of NGOs.

- Chapter 4 pointed to efforts by governments, governing through hierarchy, to tackle obesity by, for example, banning the sale of junk food in schools. Non-state actors have also contributed to the achievement of the same goal. McDonald's, which was subject to a barrage of bad press following the 2004 release of the film *Super Size Me*, has promoted a range of healthier menu options and committed itself to providing clear and accessible information about the nutritional content of its food. At the same time, it has sought to promote children's exercise through, for example, a national exercise program run in conjunction with primary schools in Canada, sponsorship of a junior-league soccer competition in South Korea, and the construction of gym clubs in France.

- Non-state actors are also routinely involved in attempts to persuade people to contribute to the provision of collectively valued goods. A variety of airlines and companies like Climate Care, the Carbon Neutral Company and Offset My Life have sought to persuade people to offset their carbon emissions by paying to have trees planted (Smith, 2007, 14). The fair trade movement, created in the early 1960s, has collaborated with charities like Oxfam to persuade supermarkets to stock products from manufacturers in developing countries who pay fair wages and employ environmentally sustainable methods of production. Today, the fair trade movement is regulated through the Fairtrade Labelling Organisations International, which sets common labelling standards (Moore, 2004).

These examples of governance through persuasion raise an important issue about individual rationality, which we will pause to discuss. Economists and public choice theorists assume, and arguments for the use of markets tend to presuppose, that people can be trusted to further their own interests through the choices they make. Yet the fact that we sometimes regret the choices we make suggests that people do not always act rationally. Jon Elster (1979; 1983; 1989) has shown how information asymmetries, weakness of will and wishful thinking frequently lead people to act in ways that are inconsistent with their own interests. In the absence of rewards or sanctions, people can therefore be persuaded to change their behaviour in order to serve their *own* interests by, for example, practising safe sex or eating more healthily. Governance through persuasion can, however, take a second form. Economists also tend to assume that people are exclusively self-interested and that acting rationally means acting egoistically. Yet the empirical evidence is that people's normative commitments frequently lead them to act in ways that are contrary to their narrowly defined self-interest (see Hindmoor, 2006a, 122–5; Ostrom, 1990; Funk, 2000; Caplan, 2007, 148–9 and references therein). This does not come as a surprise. We know that in certain situations people's normative commitments can lead them to make dramatic personal sacrifices. We live in a world where politicians sometimes go to jail for their beliefs; thousands of people have chosen to take their own lives (and those of others) in suicide attacks; and millions of people have volunteered to defend their country in times of war, or given blood, or donated time and money to charity. More prosaically, there is a wide body of evidence that public sector managers and workers are motivated by a commitment to public service (Brewer, Selden & Facer, 2000; Taylor-Gooby et al., 2000).

People's willingness to act upon their normative commitments creates an opportunity to seek to persuade people to contribute to the collective good by, for example, offsetting the carbon footprint of a flight. Foucault's arguments about 'disciplinary power' paint a bleak picture of a carceral society in which, collectively, people can be manipulated to act in ways that are contrary to their own best interests. An equally bleak picture is painted by Steven Lukes (1974), who shows how powerful elites can shape people's preferences in ways that undermine their real interests. Our account of governance through persuasion is more positive. Any power can be abused, but the power to shape people's preferences can be used to further people's long-term interests and those of the communities in which they live.

Having discussed the relationship between rationality and persuasion, we return to the central issue of this chapter: the relative significance of state and non-state actors as agents of persuasion. The involvement of non-state actors in governance through persuasion can be linked to arguments about the declining legitimacy of the state. One obvious way in which a loss of legitimacy may manifest itself is in people's growing reluctance to be persuaded to behave in certain ways by politicians and government officials. In the United Kingdom, efforts to persuade parents of the safety of a newly introduced vaccine for measles, mumps and rubella were undermined by what is now known to have been rogue research suggesting a possible link between the vaccine and the onset of autism. The government declared that there was absolutely no additional risk in using the combined vaccine. But a widespread belief that the vaccine was only being introduced in order to save money combined with memories about a previous government that was thought to have deliberately misled people about the dangers of mad cow disease, so that, at one time, up to 30 per cent of parents refused to have their children immunised (Magennis, 1999, 136–8).

Where governments lack legitimacy and are not trusted, it is easy to see why non-state actors may be influential in persuading people to change their behaviour. In the case of the vaccination saga, the UK government eventually turned to the British Medical Council for support. In the case of HIV prevention, the Terrence Higgins Trust acquired a significant role when it became clear that a significant proportion of the gay community did not trust a government which, it believed, was ideologically opposed to gay rights (Street, 1988).

Chapter 2 explained that the extent to which national governments have lost legitimacy can be exaggerated. Voters still expect governments to solve policy problems and steer society. Indeed, the problems that governments face often reflect growing, and occasionally unreasonable, expectations about governments' capacity to resolve policy problems. There are specific cases in which governments are not trusted and non-state actors have a greater capacity to successfully engage in governance through persuasion: the management of HIV/AIDS offers a striking example. Yet Table 2.3 showed that, with the notable exception of the United States, levels of confidence in national parliaments have not fallen dramatically over the last few decades. Furthermore, in most countries the public's confidence in government exceeds its confidence in private firms whose efforts to persuade people to eat more healthily or take regular exercise are regarded as being tainted by self-interest.[1] One interesting, although dated, study into efforts to promote energy conservation in New York found that the behaviour of consumers was more likely to be affected by a message from the New York State Public Service Commission than by an identical message from their local utility company (Craig & McCann, 1978).

As described in Chapter 4, one way in which states have enhanced their governing capacity is through the creation of arm's-length and semi-independent agencies. In situations where the government lacks legitimacy, such agencies have a vital role. Take, for example, efforts to ensure an adequate supply of blood for medical purposes. Globally, it is estimated that about 18 per cent of all blood is donated on a voluntary basis; 15 per cent is donated specifically to help relatives; and about five per cent is donated in return for cash payments (WHO, 2007, 12). In South Africa, Canada and Singapore, voluntary donations are organised through not-for-profit charities. In most countries, however, blood donation is organised through quasi-autonomous governmental organisations like the National Blood Service in the United Kingdom, the Irish Blood Service or the New Zealand Blood Service. Even where trust in government has declined, it appears that these organisations have retained a reputation for political impartiality and expertise. It is striking that in the United Kingdom, Ireland and New Zealand, the overall number of voluntary blood donations each year has remained stable at a time when confidence in government has declined slightly. In China, voluntary blood donation increased from 45 to 91 per cent of all donations between 2000 and 2004 following a concerted government campaign (WHO, 2007, 29). In Bolivia, the establishment of a national blood program and concerted media campaign by the government resulted in the rate of voluntary donations rising from 10 per cent in 2002 to 50 per cent in 2006.

Governments can also seek to *enhance* their legitimacy by governing through persuasion. Consider instances in which states attempt to change the behaviour of a large but dispersed and unorganised group which broadly agrees about the desirability of achieving a goal. Persuasion will be an attractive governance mechanism in such instances because it is non-coercive (Vedung & Doeelen, 1998; Weiss, 2002). We have shown how the reach of the regulatory state has been extended. Yet except for a wartime emergency, most states would quail at the thought of trying to institute a system of compulsory blood donation. As well as the financial and logistical difficulties of constructing and policing such a system, the government would suffer political costs from loss of legitimacy if people believed this to be an inappropriate and excessive use of coercive force. Hence, governments can economise on their legitimacy by governing through persuasion.

Similarly, governance through persuasion is attractive to governments where it can create the appearance of decisive action. In cases where policy issues are regarded as important but intractable, states can seek to enhance their legitimacy – or at least avoid a loss of legitimacy – by being seen to tackle a problem. There is little evidence that large-scale government campaigns to persuade schoolchildren of the dangers of drugs, or citizens of the need to report suspicious activity in order to prevent terrorism, reduce levels of addiction or terrorist attack. They may, however, create a politically useful sense of urgency.

As governments have sought to persuade citizens to behave in particular ways, they have enhanced their communication strategies. Governing parties increasingly regard themselves as fighting a 'permanent campaign' for media and public attention. James Stanyer (2007, 42) writes:

> An obsession with promotion increasingly shapes all government communication efforts . . . many of the techniques pioneered in the public relations and public opinion industries, and practiced during election campaigns, have become the mainstay of government communication, the belief being that such promotional techniques are essential for administrations to get their message across.

Reflecting upon such developments, Sydney Blumenthal, formerly a senior adviser to President Clinton, suggests that campaigning has become the new ideology underpinning government (quoted in Lilleker, 2007, 144). In order to enhance their capacity to communicate with citizens, according to David Deacon and Peter Golding (1994, 4–6), modern states have turned themselves into 'public relations states' in which the 'marketing of government activity has become a central activity of modern statecraft'. The employment of media advisers, consultants and spin doctors is nothing new, but Deacon and Golding show how governments have *institutionalised* such activities (see also Ward, 2007).

Communication strategies have become professional, political and central. They have been professionalised through the appointment of marketing consultants in the place of public servants; the consultants have adopted – outside the usual campaign environments – focus groups, tracking polls, planning grids, rebuttal units and 'information subsidies' (the strategic deployment of information to trusted sources in order to maximise favourable coverage, Gandy, 1982). Innovative and increasingly sophisticated techniques have been employed to sell government messages. Stanyer (2007, 64) describes how the Clinton administration paid television networks producing popular shows like *ER* and *Beverly Hills 90210* to include in their scripts references to the government's anti-drugs campaign. In the United Kingdom the government paid Jeremy Kyle, the host of a controversial 'car crash' television show in which men take on-air paternity tests, to host a chat show discussing the ways in which the government can help people find work. At the same time, communication strategies have been politicised as the boundaries between informing the public and selling the government have blurred. During the lead-up to the 2003 Iraq War, the US and UK governments exploited their hierarchical control over the release of intelligence information to inflate the threat posed by Iraq (Kaufmann, 2004) and marginalise critics of the war. Finally, communication strategies have increasingly been centralised within and around the office of the president or prime minister as governments have sought to coordinate the activities of disparate departments and ministers (Stanyer, 2007, 48; Maltese, 2003). In 1997 the newly elected Tony Blair decreed that ministers would be required to agree the timing and content of any speeches, press releases, or media interviews with the Downing Street Press Office.

THE METAGOVERNANCE OF PERSUASION

Even where non-state actors engage in governance through persuasion, states usually retain the responsibility for the metagovernance of such arrangements. In the case of HIV/AIDS prevention, the decision to forge closer links with the Terrence Higgins Trust was taken within the Ministry of Health. Politicians and senior public servants decided which organisations they were prepared to work with and eschewed campaigning groups like Stonewall which, at the time, were thought to be promoting too radical an agenda. The Ministry of Health set the overall goals and targets for the HIV/AIDS campaign and provided most of the resources used to fund campaigns. Today, the Terrence Higgins Trust (2007), although apparently independent of government, continues to receive about three-quarters of its budget via statutory government grants or contracts.

In other cases, governments assume a metagovernance role in coordinating and steering governance efforts. In 2002 the UK government launched a high-profile campaign to encourage people to eat five portions of fruit and vegetables a day, amidst reports that up to 42 000 people were dying each year as a result of their failure to do so. Much of this campaign was delivered in conjunction with 500 partner organisations, including NGOs like the British Heart Foundation and profit-making companies like Weight Watchers, supermarket chains and food manufacturers (Collins et al., 2003). Yet responsibility for the content and management of the campaign was retained by the Ministry of Health; it intervened when, for example, a food manufacturer, Heinz, started to promote its range of tinned spaghetti with the slogan 'five-a-day the Heinz way'.

Our state-centric relational account of governance emphasises the ways in which governments have strengthened their governance capacity by developing close relations with non-state actors. Governance through persuasion offers another example of the potentially positive-sum relationships involved. Consider, once again, efforts to prevent the spread of HIV/AIDS. The UK government's initial efforts to inform people of the dangers foundered when it became clear that large parts of the gay community saw it as out of touch and politically hostile. The devolution of responsibility to organisations like the Terrence Higgins Trust helped the government to achieve its goals. Yet, as we have argued, the relationship between government and NGOs is unequal. Governments continue to set objectives, provide resources and monitor effectiveness.

PERSUADING STATES

When states are not the agents of persuasion, they are frequently its recipients. Because states retain a monopoly of coercive power and, with this, a monopoly on the authority to construct and revise governance rules, non-state actors routinely attempt to persuade states to change their behaviour. Chapter 6 shows how businesses routinely use the political process to try and achieve a competitive advantage. More generally, charities, interest-groups, trade unions, universities, local governments and community associations all lobby government in pursuit of their goals.

The notion that non-state actors attempt to change the behaviour of states is hardly novel. Chapter 2 mentioned many studies of policy networks that seek to explain how governments trade policy influence for support in formulating and implementing policy. Yet there is a conceptual problem in viewing these relationships as examples of governance through persuasion. The studies of policy networks view the relationship between governments and pressure groups in entirely instrumental terms. Networks are animated by, and constituted through, the efforts of actors to bargain with each other, exchange resources and achieve mutually beneficial outcomes (Rhodes,

1986, 16–23; Marsh & Rhodes, 1992a, 10–11; Rhodes, 1997, 36–7). There is no obvious room for persuasion here. Governments and pressure-groups know what they want and flex their muscles in order to achieve it. Preferences are, in the language used by economists, exogenously given and fixed.

Yet pressure-groups do not simply bargain with government. Just as it is open to governments to try to persuade individuals that they have misconstrued their interests and should change their behaviour, it is open to interest-groups and other actors to persuade the government that a particular policy promotes not only their own interest but the public interest. In 2001 during the crisis over foot-and-mouth disease, the UK government was widely criticised for its refusal to abandon its policy of selective slaughter of animals in favour of one of preventative vaccination.[2] Several inquiries later concluded that the costs of closing the countryside to tourists, an inevitable consequence of the slaughter policy, far outweighed the benefits of protecting British meat exports. So why did the government get its policy so wrong? At the time, newspaper commentators routinely argued that the government had wanted to vaccinate but that the National Farmers Union (NFU), which opposed vaccination, had been allowed to exercise a 'veto' over policy (Whittam Smith, *Independent*, 30 April 2001). In its report on the handling of foot-and-mouth disease, the European Parliament (2002, para. 34) denounced the way in which a 'relatively small special interest group', the NFU, had been given an 'undue influence over decisions affecting the wellbeing of whole regions'.

There is a major problem with this argument: there is no evidence that the UK government ever favoured widespread emergency vaccination as an alternative to slaughter, let alone that the NFU prevented it from implementing this policy (the following draws on Hindmoor, 2009). Of course, the NFU's opposition to the vaccination was relevant, but the access the NFU was given to policy-makers throughout the crisis enabled them to repeat to ministers and senior officials the arguments for selective slaughter and the potential costs and uncertainties of vaccination. The NFU was a large group which could, if it wanted to, make life politically uncomfortable for the government during an expected general election campaign. The government granted high-level access to NFU officials because it believed that it was in its interest to do so. Groups like the Soil Association, the National Consumer Council, the National Trust, the Royal Society for the Protection of Birds, Friends of the Earth and the Wildlife Trust favoured vaccination, but they were considered politically lightweight and were largely ignored. The important point here is that the relationship between the NFU and the government was not simply one of bargaining. In interviews, speeches, press releases, articles and, no doubt, private meetings with government officials, the NFU sought to persuade the government of the merits of its case. Rather than bargaining with the government, the NFU persuaded it; the government publicly endorsed many of the arguments the NFU had advanced against vaccination.

COMBINING MODES OF GOVERNANCE: PERSUASION AND HIERARCHY

We have so far examined governance through persuasion in isolation. Yet one source of the comparative advantage that states have over non-state actors in persuading people to change their behaviour is that they can combine persuasion with hierarchy. Public health campaigns to encourage people to eat more fruit and vegetables have been combined with bans on advertising junk food on children's television programs and the provision of free fruit in schools. Campaigns to persuade people to quit smoking have been combined with bans on smoking in public places and punitive taxes on cigarettes. Campaigns to persuade people to drive safely have been combined with increased penalties for those caught drink-driving or speeding.

There are two reasons why the application of hierarchical sanctions and rewards is likely to make efforts at governance through persuasion more effective. In the first place prohibitions, taxes and subsidies send a clear signal to people about the significance a government attaches to an issue and so are likely to attract their attention. Second, sanctions and rewards reassure people who are willing to contribute to the provision of a collective good but fear that free-riders may take advantage of them. In these circumstances, the provision of sanctions and rewards may persuade people that they will not be exploited.

As we saw in Chapter 4 in relation to 'responsive regulation', governments can combine efforts at horizontal coordination and moral suasion with (if needed) the application of hierarchical controls. It is worth re-examining this approach in a different context. Over the last decade a combination of government and consumer pressure has led many firms to create or join voluntary compliance regimes in which members promise to meet certain standards of ethical or environmental behaviour. Voluntary programs have proved a popular method of dealing with environmental problems in the United States (Potoski & Prakash, 2004), Japan (Welch & Hibiki, 2002), the European Union (Borkley & Leveque, 1998), and developing countries such as Costa Rica (Rivera, 2002). To take one example, the US Environmental Protection Agency's WasteWise program has attracted the support of nearly 1500 companies and public sector bodies (Delmas & Keller, 2005). There is no fee to join the program; participants agree to set waste reduction targets and report on their progress in meeting them. In return, the Environmental Agency provides information on how to reduce waste and sponsors case-studies and award ceremonies.

Sceptics might argue that voluntary agreements are of no more than symbolic value as they allow firms not only to set their own standards but also to break them routinely. In some cases firms only agree to join a voluntary scheme in return for a guarantee that they will not be prosecuted for any failure to meet the standards set out in an agreement (Steinzor, 1998). In the case of the WasteWise program it is notable that only about 20 per cent of member firms even submitted reports to the Environmental Protection Agency indicating whether they had met their performance targets (Delmas & Keller, 2005, 93; for other critical accounts see Darnall & Carmin, 2005).

The more effective schemes combine voluntary efforts at persuasion with the threat of hierarchical regulation (Mackendrick, 2005). There appear to be two models on offer here. In the first, voluntary agreements are signed as a supplement to, rather than replacement for, existing regulatory standards. In these cases firms may not meet the new standards contained in the voluntary agreement but there can be no erosion in overall standards. In the second model governments indicate that tougher hierarchical controls will be introduced unless voluntary standards are met (Reitbergen et al., 1999). In the late 1980s the Netherlands government introduced long-term agreements on energy efficiency in an effort to reduce carbon emissions by 3–5 per cent by 2000 (Welch & Hibiki, 2002, 410; Wallace, 1995). Over 90 per cent of Dutch firms signed these agreements, which were negotiated with peak-level industry associations. The agreements required firms to report upon their performance against agreed targets, and they allowed the Environment Ministry to revoke the operating licence of any firm that consistently failed to meet minimum standards.

SOCIAL CAPITAL AND GOVERNANCE THROUGH PERSUASION

Social capital can be defined as 'all those features of social organisation, such as networks, norms and social trust, that facilitate coordination and cooperation for mutual benefit' (Putnam, 1994, 67). A useful distinction is between 'bonding' and 'bridging' social capital. Bonding capital refers to the range and depth of relations between similar groups of people in a society; bridging capital refers to the range and depth of the relations among different groups of people. Over the last decade or so social capital has attracted huge interest from academics and policy-makers. This is because empirical studies of, in particular, bridging social capital – measured through such indicators as interpersonal trust, membership of voluntary organisations, community volunteering and engagement in social and political affairs – have shown that it seems to be closely linked to such valued policy goals as high economic growth (Knack & Keefer, 1997), rising education standards (Dika & Singh, 2002), good health, and low levels of crime (OECD, 2001). Social capital has come to be viewed as a panacea for all policy problems.

The existence of high levels of social capital may also underpin the efficiency of market mechanisms. Economic sociologists such as Mark Granovetter (1985) argue that markets work more efficiently when actors are embedded in interpersonal social networks, with 'dense' networks facilitating information exchange and the development and enforcement of norms. Empirical research by Wayne Baker (1984) found that, as the number of traders in particular markets increased (thus reducing the density of social networks), so too did price volatility. The point is that, contrary to mainstream economic analysis, market relationships are not impersonal transactions based on narrow, short-term calculations of utility; they are typically rooted in deeper sets of cultural and social understandings, expectations, norms and even obligations. Ash Amin and Jerzy Hausner (1997, 5) refer to this as the 'soft institutional parameters' of the market.

Correlation does not mean causation: the existence of a strong empirical relationship between social capital and valued policy outcomes is not conclusive. It may be that social capital is a consequence, and not the cause, of economic growth, low crime and so on (Scanlon, 2004). However, it is easy to see how high levels of social capital may make it easier to persuade actors to contribute their share to the provision of a collectively valued good. Indeed, there is a tendency in the literature to *define* or at least measure social capital precisely in terms of a person's willingness to contribute to collectively valued goods. Consider, for example, the World Bank's (1998) definition of social capital in terms of a 'common sense of civil responsibility'. High levels of social capital also facilitate efforts at governance through persuasion by encouraging people to believe that they ought to contribute their share to the provision of some goal and also that others are likely to do so as well. In this way high levels of social capital may provide an institutional catalyst to resolve collective action problems. Finally, high levels of social capital are likely to result in higher levels of trust not only in people but in government (Keele, 2007). Governments that are considered trustworthy are, of course, more likely to persuade people to change their behaviour. For all these reasons governance through persuasion, whether by state or non-state actors, benefits from the existence of high levels of social capital.

In his influential book *Bowling Alone,* Robert Putnam (2000) argues that social capital in general and bridging capital in particular are in rapid decline in the United States and that this is compromising the quality of millions of people's lives. Putnam says that Americans are leading increasingly isolated lives: commuting alone, working at a desk in a competitive office and, on returning home, collapsing in front of the television in their own room in a house. Academic studies, however, seem to indicate that the rapid loss in social capital that has occurred in the United States since the 1960s has not occurred elsewhere. In the United Kingdom (Hall, 1999), the Netherlands (De Hart & Dekker, 1999), Japan (Inoguchi, 2000) and France (Worms, 2000), people are less likely to engage in traditional activities such as attending church or joining political parties, but they are often *more* likely to socialise with friends and engage in voluntary community work.[3]

If there is a clear empirical lesson in the mass of data that has been collected on social capital, it is of the sheer variety in, rather than decline of, social capital. Table 5.1 tracks people's trust in other people between the first wave of the World Values Survey in the early 1980s and the third wave of surveys in the late 1990s. The survey shows that levels of generalised trust increased in almost as many countries as it declined in, and that there are huge disparities in trust between Argentina and France on the one hand and Australia, Canada and Denmark on the other.

Despite this mixed empirical record, many countries have expressed a determination to invest in the production of social capital. Joining the parts of our argument together, this will, all other things being equal, enhance the capacity of state *and* non-state actors to govern through persuasion. Yet it is clear that most of the methods of building social capital require not simply state action but hierarchical governance. In the conclusion to *Bowling Alone* Putnam (pp. 402–14) offers a manifesto for the restoration of social capital and American society. He calls for the development of community programs in schools; family-friendly policies in workplaces; less urban sprawl; the provision of more arts and entertainment facilities in communities; the reform of election finance laws to encourage citizens to contribute time as well as money to their political causes; and the

Table 5.1. Social trust, selected countries, 1980–4 and 1998–2000
Question: Generally speaking, would you say that most people can be trusted or that you need to be very careful in dealing with people?

	% saying that most people can be trusted	
Country	1980–4	1998–2000
Argentina	24.5	15
Australia	46.3	39.5
Belgium	25.1	29.4
Canada	42.1	38.4
Denmark	45.9	64.1
France	22.3	21.4
Ireland	40	46.8
Japan	37.4	39.6
Nigeria	21.7	25.3
South Korea	36	27.3
United States	39.2	35.5

Source: World Values Survey (http://www.worldvaluessurvey.org/).

decentralisation of government authority. Others have suggested that social capital might be enhanced through the sponsorship of community groups; better traffic management schemes to encourage people to walk to school or work; and the provision of more public festivals (Productivity Commission, 2003, 60). According to Rothstein (2005, 71–92), the provision of universal welfare services that benefit everyone regardless of their income is an important source of social capital and must be maintained in the face of demands for greater welfare selectivity. Similarly, Gittell and Vidal (1998) argue that the provision of high-quality public services is a key source of social capital. Where education and health services have been allowed to decline, they argue, the private sector has flourished and this has resulted in the segregation of services and the loss of bridging capital.

Yet most of these reforms require hierarchical government intervention to change planning regulations, subsidise public transport, reform electoral laws and welfare systems, decentralise decision-making authority, and so on. It is possible to imagine how non-state actors might be given contracts to develop community programs in schools, organise public festivals or build arts and entertainment centres. It is also possible that some profit-making firms will perceive it as being in their own long-term interests to develop more family-friendly employment policies. Yet the policy agenda for investing in social capital is largely an agenda for hierarchical state action. As Simon Szreter (2002, 613) concludes,

> far from being an alternative to the state and to government activity, [social capital] is symbiotically related to it . . . social capital is not a form of do-it-yourself civil elastoplast, for patching together polities with poor systems of central and local government and depleted public services . . . the first task in building social capital in poor communities is, paradoxically, to restore collective faith in the idea of the state as and in local government as a practically effective servant of the community.

Even where non-state actors are engaged in governance through persuasion, their efforts will be parasitic upon state action. States provide the environment within which governance through persuasion can be effective.

CONCLUSION

There are plenty of academic studies on governance as it relates to markets, hierarchies and networks, but little has been written about the possibilities of governance through persuasion (but see Bemelamans-Vedic et al., 1998; Weiss, 2002; Collins et al., 2003). Does this matter? If we were to follow the public choice approach – regarding individuals as not only exclusively self-interested but possessing fixed views about how best to achieve that interest – there would indeed be little scope for governance through persuasion. But as political scientists have recently come to emphasise, ideas matter (Campbell, 2004, 90–101; Blyth, 2002; Fischer, 2003; Menahem, 2008). They matter because people's normative commitments, their values, attitudes, and morals, can lead them to act in ways that are contrary to their self-interest. They matter because it is people's empirical notions about how the world works, about cause-and-effect relationships, programs and paradigms, which lead them to believe that certain courses of action *are* in their interest. As Colin Hay (2002, 209) puts it: 'if actors lack complete information, they have to interpret the world in which they find themselves in order to orientate themselves strategically toward it. Ideas provide the point of mediation between actors and their environment.' It is because ideas matter in politics that persuasion is possible. People can be persuaded to act out of a commitment to the collective good *or* to change their views about how best to pursue their own interests.

In Michel Foucault's view, the kind of preference-shaping activity we have examined in this chapter destroys individual autonomy. He equates what we have called governance through persuasion with the rise of the 'disciplinary society'. Our account is less bleak. We agree with Foucault that efforts to shape people's preferences, or perhaps even identities, are becoming more common. We also agree that the state, in partnership with a range of other organisations, plays a leading role in such activities. Yet governance through persuasion offers an effective and non-coercive means by which governments can achieve collectively valued outcomes. There are instances in which non-state actors are engaged in governance through persuasion, and even some cases of governance without government, but the state retains a crucial role. States have attempted to enhance their legitimacy by governing through persuasion. They have also attempted to enhance their governance capacity by working with non-state actors. Under such arrangements, however, governments retain responsibility for the areas identified in Chapter 3: steering, effectiveness, resourcing, democracy, accountability and legitimacy.

6 | Governance through markets and contracts

A MARKET CAN BE DEFINED AS A SOCIAL arrangement allow-
ing for the voluntary exchange of goods and services. Markets are characterised by the existence of private property rights, competition, and the use
of the price mechanism to allocate resources. The use of markets is usually
defended on efficiency grounds. Private property rights, when combined
with competition, are believed to give firms and entrepreneurs incentives
to develop new products and anticipate consumer demand. Prices provide participants in the market with a constant flow of information about
demand and supply (Hayek, 1945; Kirzner, 1973). In these ways, the invisible hand of the market is, according to liberal ideology, said to harness
individual self-interest for the collective good. As we have observed, the
idea that competitive markets represent the most efficient way of allocating
resources has become a paradigm of (neo-liberal) governance. In recent
decades in a range of countries an ongoing process of 'marketisation' has
resulted in waves of privatisation and deregulation, contracting-out and
the creation of new markets. Not only have the boundaries between the
public and private sectors been redrawn, but the public sector itself has
been partly recreated in the image of the market.

Economists continue to debate the economic consequences of marketisation. Critics suggest that, in many cases, market failures and high
transaction costs outweigh efficiency gains.[1] Our focus in this chapter,
however, is on the relationship between marketisation and state capacity.
There are two strands to the argument. The first is that marketisation has
resulted in significant powers being surrendered to private businesses operating independent of government control. If governance means steering,
marketisation, it is argued, has led to a reduction in the total amount of
governance. Indeed Susan Strange (1996, 14) suggests that 'the diffusion of

authority away from national governments' has resulted in 'ungovernance'. The second strand is that states have also lost control in those situations where markets have been used as an alternative means of pursuing policy goals. The contracting-out of public services to private firms is argued to have led to a hollowing-out of the state.

There are indeed cases where marketisation has led to a loss of state capacity and a failure of metagovernance. In one of the cases we examine, the outsourcing of defence contracts in Iraq, marketisation led to an eventually catastrophic loss of accountability, legitimacy and life. Emblematic of this failure are newspaper reports that one contractor, KBR, threatened to stop feeding the US army in Iraq unless it was immediately paid in full for a disputed contract (*New York Times*, 17 June 2008). Yet, as might be expected, we are sceptical about arguments that present the relationship between the state and hierarchy on the one hand and markets on the other in zero-sum terms. The extent to which markets, or indeed major players in them such as business interests, have replaced hierarchy as a mode of governance can easily be exaggerated. Furthermore, marketisation and the metagovernance of markets frequently require the exercise of massive hierarchical authority. In short, we concur with Michael Keating (2004, 6), who suggests that 'the shift to marketisation largely represents an attempt by government to enhance or restore their power to achieve their economic and social objectives'.

THE MARKETISATION OF GOVERNANCE

What we describe as the 'marketisation of governance' covers some related but distinct reforms. We will look at them in turn.

PRIVATISATION

Governments across the world have privatised state-owned enterprises either by selling shares in those companies on stock markets, by selling firms to private companies or by giving shares to citizens (OECD, 2005b). Pioneered in the United Kingdom, New Zealand and Australia, privatisation has had the greatest impact in those countries which had the largest number of state-owned enterprises. In Portugal, the Czech Republic and Hungary, the cumulative proceeds of privatisation sales have amounted to more than 20 per cent of current annual GDP (OECD, 2005c, 24). Even where privatisation has been rejected, the impact of the philosophy has been such that governments have committed themselves to rules requiring them to run state-owned enterprises on a commercial basis through independently appointed boards of directors, a process often referred to as 'commercialisation'.

DEREGULATION

This is the process by which states seek to eliminate, reduce or at least simplify restrictions on the activities of individuals or firms with a view to creating freer and more competitive markets. Chapter 4 noted that in OECD countries the telecommunications, aviation and electricity industries were, to varying degrees, deregulated in the 1980s and 1990s. Deregulation, along with technological change, has been a key driver of globalisation. Reductions in trade barriers, the elimination of restrictions upon the operation of foreign banks in domestic markets, and the removal of restrictions on the overseas transfer of capital have resulted in a massive expansion in international trade, overseas foreign investment and currency speculation.

EXTERNAL MARKETS

When governments privatise firms, a market for the products of those firms already exists. In the case of what we call external markets, the state actually creates markets by establishing new property rights and encouraging trade with a view to resolving specific policy problems. In response to a continuing drought exacerbated by intensive farming, the Australian government created a new market in water by limiting the amount of water farmers can extract from rivers while simultaneously creating water entitlements and allowing farmers to buy or sell their water allocations (Bell & Quiggin, 2008). The policy prescription is that, for any given limit upon the amount of water to be extracted, market trading ought to ensure the lowest loss in production as more efficient farms buy additional water from less efficient ones. External markets are still a relatively novel governance approach. In recent years, however, markets have been created to allow the exchange of a range of pollutants, including emissions of sulphur dioxide (associated with acid rain) and carbon dioxide (one cause of climate change).

CONTRACTING-OUT

In contracting-out (or competitive tendering), services once performed by state agencies are exposed to competition. Contractors are selected on a range of criteria including, most obviously, cost. As Chapter 1 pointed out, there is nothing new in the principle; but contracting-out has proliferated, spurred on by a neo-liberal ideology and the prevalence of outsourcing in the private sector. Defence provides an interesting example, given our earlier discussion about sovereignty and the state's monopoly on the legitimate use of violence. Having abolished military service, a previously reliable source of labour, armies across the world have come to depend on private firms to provide support functions such as training, base maintenance, health services and supply transport (Avant, 2005; Singer, 2001). In the United States more than 50 per cent of the navy's military research, development, testing and evaluation have been outsourced to private, profit-making firms, along with large parts of the work of nuclear laboratories and test centres at Los Alamos and Lawrence Livermore (Markusen, 2003).

In other cases, government services, particularly for health, education and personal well-being, have been contracted to not-for-profit organisations with commitment to the delivery of high-quality services in a particular area. The most recent comprehensive survey estimates that, globally, not-for-profit 'third sector' organisations account for around five per cent of world gross domestic product and employ around 40 million people (Salamon, Sokolowski & List, 2003). In the United States, the United Kingdom and Australia, the third sector employs an average eight per cent of the economically active population. Indeed, in the United Kingdom the crime-reduction charity NARCO, which has criticised the use of prison as a deterrence strategy and warned that Britain is in danger of becoming the 'prisons capital of Europe', has worked with a private security firm, Group 4, to tender to run two new vast 'superprisons' in Liverpool and London. According to NARCO's chief executive, 'if we're both [Group 4 and NARCO] involved in working together on the design, planning and regime of a new prison, it increases the chances that [the] regime will be one which helps to reduce re-offending by resettling prisoners effectively' (quoted, *Guardian*, 7 September 2008).

PUBLIC–PRIVATE PARTNERSHIPS

Public-private partnerships (PPPs) extend the role of private firms in the provision of public services to include the design, construction, maintenance and operation of infrastructure assets traditionally provided by the public sector (OECD, 2005a, 140). The arrangements vary but usually governments either pay rent for infrastructure designed, built and maintained by a private firm, or allow that firm to charge customers a fixed rate to use the facilities. Such PPPs were pioneered in the United Kingdom in the early 1990s to fund massive programs to build hospitals and schools. Elsewhere, PPPs have financed road construction in Portugal, a high-speed rail network in the Netherlands, and a new airport in Athens (OECD, 2005a, 140–3).

INTERNAL MARKETS

In the pursuit of public sector efficiency, governments across the world have pursued a program of 'new public management'. This has entailed the hierarchical imposition of benchmarking exercises, targets, performance-related pay and short-term contracts. Governments have also pursued reform through the creation of internal markets or quasi-markets in which public sector organisations are encouraged to compete against each other to provide cheaper or better services (Barlett & Le Grand, 1993; Le Grand, 2003). The most significant example of such a market was established within the National Health Service (NHS) in the United Kingdom. Tra-ditionally, the NHS has been hierarchically managed through top-down budgets. In the early 1990s general practitioners were given more con-trol over their budgets and encouraged to purchase treatment for their patients from local hospitals. The expectation was that doctors would send their patients to those hospitals with the shortest waiting times, the lowest costs and the best standards of care, and that the resulting competitive pressures would force every hospital to improve its performance. This did not amount to a privatisation of the NHS: medical treatment remained entirely free at the point of delivery. The money circulating within the internal market was, ultimately, all taxpayers' money.

COMMON FACTORS IN MARKETISATION

What do these market-based reforms have in common? Recall here our definition of markets in terms of competition, property rights and prices. First, contracting-out requires private firms and public sector agencies to compete to provide the best and cheapest service. Similarly, deregulation is meant to make it easier for new firms to enter existing markets. Second, these reforms have created new property rights. Australian farmers have always had the right to extract water from their land; the creation of a water market has given them an additional right to exchange this resource. Privatisation has created new property rights for shareholders, while dereg-ulation has extended the existing rights of property owners. Third, these reforms have resulted in a greater reliance on prices as a mechanism to allocate resources. Privatisation is meant to ensure that investment, pricing and employment decisions are sensitive to changes in price. By creating a price for water and pollutants, external markets are meant to ensure that use of resources reflects their environmental impact.

The marketisation of governance has not usually led to unfettered competition, unqualified property rights and absolute dependence upon prices. Governments have often chosen to privatise state-owned enterprises as monopolies in order to maximise revenue from their sale (Marsh, 1991). In the case of the internal health market in the United Kingdom, property rights are carefully controlled. Doctors are not given the option of selling their surgery and, until recently, could not choose to send their patients to a privately owned hospital at the taxpayer's expense. In otherwise deregulated markets, residual controls on prices also remain. The amount airlines must pay for landing slots at major international airports like Heathrow and Los Angeles and the fares they are allowed to charge on many international routes are still heavily regulated (Cowhey & Richards, 2006). Yet if we think of competition, property rights and price-based decision-making as a matter of degree rather than as binary alternatives, it is clear why the changes described here might be said to constitute a marketisation of governance.

STATE CAPACITY AND MARKETS

Alberta Sbragia (2000, 243) observes that 'market forces are widely viewed as threatening, diluting or eroding the powers of the state . . . the power of public authority to protect its citizens over the long-term is seen as diminished'. Susan Strange (1996, 4) argues that 'where states were once the masters of markets, now it is the markets which, on many critical issues, are the masters over the governments of states'. Christopher Pierson (1996, 124) suggests that the globalisation of markets has 'strengthened the bargaining position of capital [and] . . . undermined the authority and capacity of the interventionist state'. Similarly, Hans-Peter Martin and Harald Schumann (1996, 10) argue that 'the whole of politics' has become 'a spectacle of impotence' and that the 'democratic state has lost its legitimacy' as a consequence of the diffusion of market forces. Governments, in this view, have not simply disappeared but have been relegated to a 'market-supporting' rather than 'market-steering' role (Levy, 2006, 3–4). Governments have become the handmaidens of markets; they must enhance labour market participation, remove trade barriers and set minimal standards of regulation. Using alternative terminology, Jon Pierre and Guy Peters (2005, 104) suggest that the 'enabling' policy style adopted by many governments in the 1990s was one in which the state 'defines its role in society as one of removing obstacles to economic growth. More broadly, the enabling state is less intervening, less steering, and less proactive than a state pursuing a more traditional policy style.'

How, precisely, has marketisation challenged and undermined the role and capacity of the state? There are various theories. One is that privatisation has denied to governments an important policy tool by which they once directly influenced wages, employment practices and investment decisions within countries. Another is that deregulation in general, and the globalisation of markets in particular, have acted as a 'golden straitjacket' requiring states to adopt business-friendly policies (Friedman, 1999). The Asian financial crisis in 1998 and the global credit crisis beginning in 2008 showed that financial markets may have slipped beyond the control of regulators.

Turning to contracting-out, critics argue that a loss of in-house expertise and experience has made it impossible for states to manage or oversee the tangle of relationships they have voluntarily entered into (Milward, Provan & Else, 1993). Contracting-out is also said to have led to a loss of legitimacy and accountability. In Sydney there was a public outcry in 2006 when the state government refused to publish the full terms of a contract it had signed with a private sector consortium to build and operate a road tunnel. This was controversial because one clause in the contract was reported to require the government to close alternative traffic routes if business fell below projected levels (*Sydney Morning Herald*, 17 November 2006). Patricia Ranald (1997) argues that the lack of transparency entailed by 'commercial confidentiality' clauses in contracts constitutes a removal of citizens' democratic rights, since it denies public debate.

Finally, by encouraging competition, internal markets have been argued to undermine the public service ethos upon which government, in the long-term, must depend (see Le Grand, 2003, 41–4 and references therein).

THE RESILIENCE OF HIERARCHY

The use of markets to solve policy problems has attracted considerable academic attention. We have already argued in Chapter 4 that, even in

Western liberal democracies, hierarchical economic control remains significant, although it is diminished in some areas of the economy. In the case of deregulation, the elimination of rules in some industries has occurred at the same time as new regulations have been introduced relating to airport security, genetic research, data privacy, smoking, advertising and the use of mobile phones. In the United States, the spiritual home of the deregulation movement, a number of states have recently introduced regulations requiring people to pass a written examination and acquire a formal licence before advertising their services as an interior designer (*Economist*, 27 October 2007). Globally, important resources are still placed beyond the reach of price-based markets. Most countries prevent payments for surrogate-pregnancy arrangements. With the exception of Iran – which created a highly regulated market in the sale of kidneys for transplant purposes in 2006 – governments have sought to prevent decisions about organ donation being influenced by price.[2] Finally, we pointed in Chapter 2 to studies that emphasise the limits of globalisation and the continuing significance of national economies.

In regard to the contracting-out of services, the OECD (2005b, 134) observes that almost every developed economy has now outsourced routine support services such as cleaning, facilities management and security. At the same time, it notes that only a handful of countries have outsourced core state activities such as the provision of emergency services, policy advice, and audit and inspection. Even the contracting-out of basic services remains inconsistent. One study in the United States found that the majority of bus services and libraries continue to be provided directly by local government (Lundsgaard, 2002, 112). PPPs are flourishing in the United Kingdom but still fund only about one-tenth of capital investment projects (for a general discussion of the limits of such partnerships see Bloomfield, 2006). Outside the United Kingdom, internal markets and PPPs have been used sparingly (OECD, 2005a, 140). Finally, while carbon markets have been established in the European Union and California and are set to be introduced in Australia in 2010, a number of studies have confirmed that market-based solutions to environmental problems remain the exception rather than the rule (Wurzel et al., 2003; Rittberger & Richardson, 2003; Jordan et al., 2005). Also, after examining the case of water markets in Australia, Bell and Quiggin (2008) found a range of limitations in the use of market instruments, particularly related to difficulties in establishing property rights, high market transaction costs, and severe deficiencies in the capacity of market instruments to achieve environmental goals.

THE METAGOVERNANCE OF MARKETS: MARKETS THROUGH HIERARCHY

In both political and academic discourse it is conventional to draw a sharp distinction between public and private and between markets and hierarchy. This, however, takes for granted the elaborate institutional infrastructure that underpins the effective functioning of markets. Markets are based on systems of state-enforced property rights that define ownership rights and the appropriate use of resources. The exchange of goods and services requires the continuing presence of, for example, courts, police forces, competition and fair trading authorities and contract law, along with education, health and welfare policies to provide an adequate and trained workforce (North, 1990; Fligstein, 1996; 2001; Evans & Rauch, 1999). In other words, as Karl Polanyi (1957, 139) observed, there is 'nothing natural about laissez-faire'. Graham Wilson (1990, 4) makes the same point:

> It is the state which, by laws, establishes 'the market' whose existence is sometimes treated as if it were an act of nature. Markets require a vast institutional underpinning. Without courts to interpret and enforce agreements, for example, commercial life would become chaotic. Without laws to define, and police to enforce them, property rights would be non-existent. The modern corporation itself – the limited liability joint stock corporation – is, in historical terms, a comparatively modern creation of the state.

Market systems also rely on institutions to ensure fair and transparent market competition. The private sector and the wider society also play important roles in supporting markets. As Adam Smith and other founders of market theory have pointed out, markets rely on a moral underlay of trust which is crucial in ensuring the fulfilment of contracts (Hirsch, 1978).

Where these institutional conditions do not exist, attempts to introduce governance through markets often fail. In Russia, for example, the transition to a market-based economy through privatisation and the withdrawal of state subsidies has been compromised by the absence of stable property rights and an independent judiciary. According to Andrei Sharonov, a former adviser in the Economics Ministry, the absence of any legally enforced property rights shows that 'we have turned our back on healthy competition. The system rewards those who are closer to the centre of power, not those who work better. It is easier to get a competitor into a jail than to compete with him' (quoted in *Economist*, 28 February 2008). The NGO Transparency International has recently ranked Russia as one of the 30 most corrupt countries in the world.

In order to govern through markets, governments must first create those markets through the exercise of a hierarchical authority. The construction of global financial markets, for example, required governments to devise and enforce regulations relating to insider trading, standard accountancy practices, banking standards, and the disclosure of business information in order to ensure shareholder confidence. Hence the central paradox that 'the development of financial markets and the increasing prevalence and import of market relations, so often linked to the diminution of state power and authority, have been accompanied by a substantial and ongoing expansion of law and prescriptive regulation' (Cioffi, 2006, 186).

Governments thus retain responsibility for the metagovernance of the markets they create. This requires ongoing steering and resourcing, as well as the monitoring of effectiveness and the provision of accountability and legitimacy. Privatisation may have created freer markets, but it has also led to more regulations (Vogel, 1996). Where privatisations have occurred, 'hierarchical safeguarding' has been introduced to protect public values such as universal services and affordability (De Bruijn & Dicke, 2006; see also Heritier, 2002b). In Belgium, for example, the public value of social inclusion has been translated into an obligation on privatised electricity providers to maintain uniform price structures. Eiji Kawabata (2001) shows how the privatisation of the Nippon Telegraph Company (NTT) in the 1980s actually enhanced the authority of the Ministry of Posts and Telecommunications. In return for acquiescing in the sale of NTT, the ministry received exclusive jurisdiction and the coercive authority to require firms to make their infrastructure available to rivals, veto the entry of firms it believed would be unable to effectively compete with NTT, and approve proposed price changes. Where services are contracted out, governments, as well as providing the funds, decide which services to outsource, the criteria by which bids are judged, and the final terms of any contract. Governments also retain responsibility for monitoring performance and applying sanctions where performance is judged unsatisfactory. Trevor Brown and Matthew Potoski (2004) show that in the case of a simple contract to manage refuse collection in Ohio, public service managers continuously intervened to stimulate competition and sanction errant firms.

In the case of more complex contract arrangements, the metagovernance of governance arrangements is ongoing. Chapter 3 briefly examined the contracting of private firms and voluntary organisations to provide training and employment services for Australia's Job Network. The contractual authority of these organisations to assess a client's willingness to work and to withhold welfare payments seems to give significant discretion in decision-making to NGOs. Yet contractors, whether from the private or voluntary sectors, are expected to adhere to detailed regulations set by the Department of Employment and Workplace Relations. As Mark Considine (2003, 75) affirms:

> the quasi-market is controlled by a government department that is the monopoly purchaser of services. This gives senior bureaucrats enormous power to steer this market from behind the safe walls built upon the commercial-in-confidence tender process, and the contracts then written leave the agencies with little room to manoeuvre.

Considine raises an important point. Studies of contracting often express the fear that it renders governments vulnerable to 'hold-ups'. These occur when a firm that has obtained a contract acquires, over time, knowledge and 'transaction-specific investments' that prevent other firms from mounting a credible bid against it in the future. Hold-ups obviously make governments vulnerable to predatory pricing and poor performance (Williamson, 1985; Klein, 1996). Such fears are not without foundation. The UK tax collection agency, the Inland Revenue, spent £9 million *paying* suppliers to bid against its incumbent IT supplier, the American-owned Electronic Data Systems (Lonsdale, 2005, 225). Yet if governments must sometimes confront a monopoly seller, it is worth emphasising that private firms must always sell their services to a limited number of local and central government organisations and that they also make transaction-specific investments in these contracts. Martin Sellers (2003, 608) argues that this level of dependence has, over time, led to a process of 'publicisation':

> private companies become more like public agencies because competition for contracts is keen and they must be perceived by the contracting agent, government, as being agreeable with the government's demands in order to be contracted with again . . . government makes suggestions, sets requirements, and provides recommendations which, over time, cause the private companies to look more and more like government agencies.

Hierarchical metagovernance is also a salient feature of government-created external markets. The world's largest carbon market, the European Union's Emission Trading Scheme (ETS), was launched in January 2005. Under the rules of the agreement, large emitters of carbon dioxide – currently around 12 000 installations accounting for about 40 per cent of total emissions – must match their emissions to an annual allowance they are given each year. Firms that wish to emit more pollution must purchase other firms' allowances (Watanabe & Robinson, 2005; Soleille, 2006). At first glance, emissions trading represents a significant loss of regulatory control because governments cannot fix the amount of carbon to be emitted by any one country, let alone firm. Yet governments, acting collectively, play a crucial metagoverning role in steering this market by setting overall limits on carbon emissions and by facilitating and policing subsequent exchanges.

The capacity of national governments to manage the ETS is clear when the limitations of the policy itself are considered. Expectations that it would lead to a significant reduction in carbon emissions have, so far, been dashed. This is because national governments have awarded carbon allowances to firms which, cumulatively, often exceed existing emissions levels. In April 2006 pollution allowances were trading at around €30 per tonne of carbon dioxide. In 2007, after it became clear that national governments had issued so many allowances, the price fell to €0.05. Promising to play a leading role in combating global climate change, European leaders subsequently promised to issue fewer allowances in iterations of the market. Yet at a summit held in March 2008 national leaders agreed to offer special protection to energy-intensive industries exposed to international competition. On current evidence it is difficult to judge the ETS a success. This is not because of a lack of state capacity. The market has failed because governments have, for current political reasons, chosen to structure the market in such a way that total emissions are unlikely to fall.

POLICY LEARNING AND METAGOVERNANCE

We do not wish to appear too sanguine about the possible consequences of marketisation. Privatisation and contracting-out can, if managed ineffectively, lead to a haemorrhage of state capacity. Governments usually retain the resources and incentives necessary to metagovern markets effectively but, as Chapter 3 acknowledged, failures of metagovernance do occur. We will describe two examples of costly failures: the contracting-out of children's residential home care in the United Kingdom and the contracting-out of military support services to Blackwater USA in Iraq. These failures reflected, in the first case, poor strategic planning and, in the second, an absence of political will. However, they do not show that contracting-out *inevitably* leads to baleful consequences and a loss of state capacity. Indeed, the interesting point in these cases is the evidence that governments have learnt from their mistakes and reasserted control.

In the late 1980s local authorities in the United Kingdom started to pay privately owned firms to house vulnerable children in their care. In a careful review of this policy Ian Kirkpatrick, Martin Kitchener and Richard Whipp (2001) show that the creation of this market had some unfortunate results. Large numbers of children were moved into homes located outside the boundaries of their local authority, making it harder for social workers to monitor their progress and standards of care. Some children with specialist needs were 'warehoused' in unsuitable accommodation, and authorities awarded expensive contracts to private firms without soliciting alternative bids or linking payments to performance. One manager is quoted as saying that their local authority was 'getting stung, left, right and centre' because 'social workers who are not very good at negotiating on money' were left to write contracts (p. 60). Another suggests that the failure to seek out alternative sources of supply meant that 'most of the local authorities have behaved as if they are hostages to fortune and the providers have set their fee levels and said take it or leave it' (p. 57).

Although generally critical of the performance of the market in children's care, the authors show how, over time, some of the authorities involved learnt to metagovern. One local authority established a Children's Contract Unit to negotiate with and monitor the performance of private firms. Another offered formal training to social workers on negotiating and writing contracts. Working through the Association of the Directors of Social Services, others developed a register of approved suppliers. Others replaced short-term contracts with long-term 'relational' contracts with firms that had already established a reputation for providing a high-quality service.

We have already noted that nations – most prominently the United States – in recent years have contracted-out a range of military support functions (Avant, 2005). It has been estimated that during the occupation of Iraq private contractors working for the US military there outnumbered US Army personnel (*Los Angeles Times*, 16 October 2007). In 2004 one private firm, Aegis, was even awarded a contract to coordinate and oversee the activities of all the other private contractors working in Iraq (Scahill, 2007, 158–9). However, it was Blackwater USA (renamed Xe in February 2009) that captured the public's attention. In 1997 Blackwater was established by a former Special Forces soldier, Erik Prince, whose stated ambition was 'to do for the national security apparatus what FedEx did to the postal service' (Scahill, 2007, xix). In 2003 the State Department awarded a contract to Blackwater to guard diplomats and the US embassy in Baghdad. Blackwater obtained several other lucrative contracts and by 2005 had more than 1000 employees working in Iraq. In 2006 a Blackwater vehicle crashed into a US Army Humvee in Baghdad. Enraged by the incident, the Blackwater employees disarmed the soldiers and held them at gunpoint. In December 2006 an off-duty and apparently drunk Blackwater employee shot and killed a member of the Iraqi vice-president's security detail. In September 2007 Blackwater contractors escorting a supply convoy shot and killed 17 Iraqi civilians in what a large number of witnesses described as an entirely unprovoked attack. In total, data collected by the State Department shows that between 2005 and September 2007 Blackwater employees were involved in 163 incidents in which they shot at someone before they had been shot at.

These incidents raised important questions about the accountability of Blackwater's employees and the legitimacy of its operations in a war zone. Soldiers serving in Iraq are individually responsible for their actions and can, in theory if not always in practice, be tried through military courts. Those working for private firms appeared to operate outside the law. Not one contractor was investigated by the military or the police or other civil authorities between 2003 and 2007. Indeed Blackwater and other private security firms led 'a lobbying effort... to try to block congressional or Pentagon efforts to bring their companies and employees under the same justice code as active-duty soldiers' (*Minneapolis Star Tribune*, 23 May 2004).

In considering the relationship between marketisation and state capacity it should be emphasised that Blackwater employees were not called to account for their actions because the Pentagon and the State Department *chose* to allow them to remain unaccountable. Under an order signed by the head of the Coalition Provisional Authority, Paul Bremer, two days before the establishment of the new sovereign Iraqi government, US contractors working in Iraq were exempted from Iraqi laws. In Congressional hearings the Democratic chairman of the House Oversight and Government Reform Committee, Henry Waxman, suggested that US authorities went on to become Blackwater's 'enabler' in Iraq. The State Department had arranged an immediate flight home for the contractor accused of shooting the vice-president's bodyguard, thus preventing a thorough Iraqi investigation of the incident (*New York Times*, 3 October 2007). The failure to metagovern Blackwater and other private security firms was not an oversight: it was a deliberate political strategy.

Yet the Blackwater debacle shows that governments can, if they wish, reassert control over private firms. When news broke of the shooting of the 17 civilians, the Iraqi government announced that it would prosecute anyone who it believed had broken Iraqi law and threatened to revoke the operating licence not only of Blackwater but of all the other private security firms in Iraq. In response, the US government described the September shootings as a potential crime and dispatched the FBI to investigate them. A few days later the State Department official responsible for monitoring the activities of private contractors in Iraq was sacked. New rules were introduced requiring a representative of the State Department to accompany convoys operated or protected by Blackwater, and Blackwater itself to install video camera equipment in all its vehicles and keep a record of all communications. Finally, in October 2007, the Congress passed a bill, with the overwhelming support of both Democrats and Republicans, making all private contractors working in Iraq subject to prosecution by US courts.

RELATIONAL CAPACITY

Chapter 1 explained that governments, in establishing and operating governance strategies, develop strategic relationships or partnerships with a range of non-state actors. Governments choose to work with private firms and other actors in market-based governance arrangements because they believe that, by doing so, they can enhance their capacity to achieve certain policy goals. Up to now we have emphasised the extent to which states retain control over markets. Here we point out that, even in situations where governments have largely forsworn such hierarchical controls, the use of markets can enhance state capacity.

A good example is the role played in the global economy by a handful of credit rating agencies like Moody's and Standard & Poor's. These firms issue judgments on the creditworthiness of borrowers. Such is the significance attached to these that it is almost impossible for a firm or sovereign government entering the bond market to borrow money without first obtaining a credit rating. The rating agencies argue that they have acquired such a dominant position because they have established a record for reliable advice. Critics suggest that their dominance is due to government regulations *requiring* firms to possess a favourable credit rating from one of a list of credit agencies approved by the US Securities and Exchange Commission.

Several rules require firms to obtain a credit rating. First, regulations designed to protect the long-term interests of investors in pension funds prohibit pension fund managers from investing in a company unless it has the highest possible credit rating. Second, regulatory provisions relating to the disclosure of financial information have been tied to credit ratings: firms that have been judged as a low financial risk are not required to disclose as much information to the market. Third, finance ministers and central bankers operating through the G10 group of countries have, in part, founded global regulatory requirements for banking on credit ratings. Banks that are not in a position to undertake internal credit assessments of sufficient sophistication to comply with the Basle II Accords can instead calculate their capital reserve requirements using ratings issued by credit agencies. As Christopher Bruner and Rawi Abdelal (2005, 193) comment, the 'private authority of the rating agencies is not so private after all. Governments have both valorised and codified their authority.'

The authority delegated to credit rating agencies has led to a concern that a small number of exclusively US firms have been left 'wielding de facto government power . . . a market-based authority that is almost as centralised as the state itself' (Bruner & Abdelal, 2005, 207). Dieter Kerwer (2005, 464) suggests that credit rating agencies have been turned into 'quasi-public regulators' and that this raises important questions about their accountability and legitimacy. The argument about accountability is straightforward. Credit rating agencies can be hauled before Congressional committees to answer questions about how they operate. But under the terms of the first amendment to the US Constitution protecting free speech, they are not legally accountable for the judgments they issue so long as they are made in good faith. What legitimacy do these firms have in the absence of such an accountability mechanism? The agencies claim that they have the output legitimacy which comes from a generally successful record, but this record is controversial. Poor judgments made by the agencies have been implicated in the 1997 Asian financial crisis, the 2000 dot-com crash, the failure of Enron and Worldcom in 2001, and the global financial crisis that began in 2008. In the latter case, agencies have been widely castigated for issuing the highest possible credit ratings to banks trading in sub-prime debt which were subsequently shown to be insolvent. Sceptics point to a conflict of interest because the rating agencies have an incentive to compete for business by giving the firms who pay their bills a higher rating. Critics also argue that the agencies lack legitimacy because their judgments about creditworthiness overemphasise fiscal orthodoxy and the presence of weak labour unions (Kerwer, 2002).

Yet in assessing the relationship between the credit rating agencies and governments, it should be remembered that the US government has *chosen* to foster closer relations with the agencies. From the government's perspective there are good reasons to tie business regulations to credit-worthiness. Light-touch regulation for firms demonstrating a strong credit position allows regulators to focus on more risky firms. Preventing pension funds from making high-risk investments may save the state from meeting the costs of more people's retirements. Governments could, if they wanted, reach their *own* judgments about the creditworthiness of firms.

For the US government there are advantages in using the judgments reached by private firms. In the first place, they are less costly. Credit ratings are available free of charge to market participants: the firm seeking a rating must pay for that service. Governments would have to devote considerable resources to devising their own ratings. Second, it is less politically risky to rely upon private firms. A government which classified as creditworthy a firm that subsequently went bankrupt would be accused of incompetence and held liable by voters and taxpayers for the losses incurred. By relying on the judgments reached by private firms, the US government has a ready-made scapegoat. As Bruner and Abdelal (2005, 209) wryly observe:

> When Enron collapsed with no warning from the rating agencies, capping a series of perceived failures including several global financial crises in the 1990s, Congress and the SEC could call hearings, investigate, and berate the agencies, querying whether ratings-dependent regulation makes sense in the future, without digging too deeply into whether incorporating them in the past was simply a bad decision.

The US government has in some ways enhanced its capacity by devel-oping close relations with credit rating agencies. But there are also losers in this market. Given the effective duopoly maintained by Moody's and Standard & Poor's, European and Asian governments have no alternative but deal with agencies whose political views they do not always share. The relationship between the US government and the rating agencies has thus far been mutually supportive, although the severity of the 2008 credit crisis is likely to lead to further strains.

GOVERNANCE THROUGH BUSINESS?

At the beginning of this chapter we distinguished two strands in the dis-cussion about marketisation and state capacity. We have looked at the argument that states have lost control of the markets they have created.

Now we look at the argument that marketisation has resulted in the surrender of significant powers to private businesses operating independently of government control. As we have said, we are generally sceptical about viewing the relationship between the state and hierarchy on the one hand and markets on the other in zero-sum terms. We also doubt that markets – or major players within them, such as business interests – have replaced hierarchy as a key mode of governance. This section argues that the relationship between governments and business can be usefully understood from a state-centric relational perspective. States shape the environment in which business operates. States sometimes constrain and discipline business interests for wider purposes. But generally the state–business relationship should be understood as a productive, positive-sum relationship.

Businesses – whether small local businesses or giant transnationals – make decisions that affect the lives of millions of people. These decisions fall within the scope of governance because they contribute to the provision of such collectively valued goals as full employment, economic growth, sustainable development and rising wages. We cannot draw a line and say that governance has nothing to do with the activities of private firms. Neither can governments afford to ride roughshod over the interests of business, especially if this threatens a widespread loss of confidence or a substantial slowdown in private investment. In capitalist systems, in which investment decisions are primarily taken by private firms, governments are structurally dependent upon businesses for private investment and economic growth (Lindblom, 1977; Przeworski, 1985; Bell & Wanna, 1992).

Whether acting collectively or individually, businesses are often in a strong bargaining position when lobbying government. Chapter 2 noted that the American health insurance industry was widely blamed for derailing Hillary Clinton's proposals for health reform. This chapter has shown that private security firms sought to secure a favourable legal environment for their activities in Iraq. The examples of businesses using political processes for their own ends are legion. ExxonMobil was instrumental in persuading the US government to allow further oil exploration in Alaska. The defence firm BAE Systems was heavily implicated in the UK government's decision to terminate a police inquiry into the alleged payment of bribes to Saudi officials. The scandal over food-for-oil sanctions in Iraq revealed that the Australian Department of Foreign Affairs and Trade and the Wheat Export Authority had sought to maximise the export revenue of the privately owned Australian Wheat Board at the expense of fulfilling their regulatory duties (Bartos, 2006).

Examining governance through associations Chapter 8 looks more closely at the interactions between business associations and governments. Here we identify a number of reasons why the authority of business is limited. Chapter 1 explained that states possess key resources including legitimacy and a monopoly on the use of violence, so they cannot simply be rolled into submission by business. It is clear, though, that business possesses some preference-shaping power. Firms can persuade governments of the virtues of acting in certain ways and can seek to persuade consumers of the legitimacy of their behaviour. They can also help set government and media agendas. David Coen (1997) argues that business groups pressed for the creation of a European Single Market. Yet business lacks coercive power: the ability to impose its decisions against opposition. Sovereign governments can and have forced businesses to pay minimum wages, recognise trade unions, accept the welfare state, reduce pollution and pay taxes on windfall profits. Businesses can and do bargain and negotiate with governments, but they cannot force them to behave in certain ways.

Businesses may sometimes be more lucky than powerful. Here, power means being successful despite opposition, whereas luck means getting what you want without trying (Barry, 1989). Businesses sometimes get what they want because government *also* wants what they want: a classic positive-sum outcome. As we have seen, this is the case with credit rating agencies, which have been gifted a dominant market position because it is in the interest of government to require firms to gain a credit rating from an approved agency. Another example is the issue of nuclear power, which we touched on in Chapter 3. In recent years the governments of the United States, the United Kingdom, South Korea, Japan and China have committed themselves to expand the use of nuclear power. Some environmental critics have sought to account for this decision in terms of the power of large nuclear firms like EDF Energy. Yet we might alternatively describe these firms as the lucky beneficiaries of government's determination to be seen to be addressing problems of energy security and climate change without creating state-owned nuclear companies.

In capitalist systems governments rely on private firms to invest and spur the economy. Globalisation is argued to have given transnational firms an additional lever on national governments by making the threat to exit a national economy more plausible. However, Chapter 2 showed that the key determinants of investment decisions are market access, a skilled workforce, and other publicly provided infrastructure. Globalisation has not resulted in a qualitative shift in the power of business. Furthermore, as we have emphasised, states retain responsibility for the metagovernance of markets. Governments not only operate under established governance rules: they play a major role in choosing governance rules. Where a government believes that marketisation has resulted in a loss of effectiveness, accountability or legitimacy, it can assert hierarchical control. In 2001 several large American companies, including, most famously, Enron, collapsed shortly after revealing massive and previously undisclosed debts. One year later, Congress passed and the President approved a new law prohibiting audit firms from engaging in a variety of non-audit consultancy work, and requiring firms to protect whistleblowers and to establish genuinely independent audit boards with a legal responsibility to disclose any 'material weakness' in a company's internal control structures. These measures proved hugely controversial; many companies threatened to move overseas because of the increased cost of doing business in America. One study published by the right-wing American Enterprise Institute describes the legislation as a 'colossal failure, poorly conceived and hastily enacted during a regulatory panic' (quoted, *Economist*, 20 April 2006). Yet the survival of the law in the face of sustained business opposition ought to encourage scepticism about the ability of business or any other organisations to operate independently of national governments. In *Rupert's Adventures in China*, Bruce Dover (2008) provides an entertaining account of the limits of one transnational firm: Rupert Murdoch's News Corporation. Murdoch first tried to gain access to the Chinese market in 1993 with the purchase of Hong Kong's STAR TV. Murdoch saw the potential for a positive-sum relationship between the Chinese government and his company. He stood to gain access to the world's largest domestic market; in return the Chinese sought more 'objective' and 'balanced' coverage of China in the Western media. In 2001 a deal was struck: STAR TV programs were carried on a cable network in the Guangdong region, and in return Murdoch agreed to show the Chinese government's new 24-hour rolling news service, CCTV9, on his Fox cable network in the United States at no cost. The bargain was an unequal one. STAR TV broadcast programs in Mandarin, but most people in Guangdong speak Cantonese. Despite spending hundreds of millions of dollars on programming, STAR TV remained in a financially precarious position. Murdoch had been forced into the deal because the Chinese government had the coercive power to ban satellite dishes, prohibit joint ventures between overseas firms and local media companies, and censor programs. In the long term Murdoch hoped that he would secure access to more of the Chinese market. Following the appointment of a new leadership cadre in Beijing, News International hit, in Murdoch's words, a 'brick wall' in 2005. The government, fearing 'cultural pollution', affirmed its ban on satellite dishes and prohibited the further involvement of any foreign media company in China.

Nor have governments in Western democracies hesitated to take the kid gloves off and exert forceful authority over powerful business interests. Aggressive industry restructuring in the United Kingdom under the Thatcher government, for example, roused a hostile response from industry, with the leader of the Confederation of British Industry at one point promising a 'bare-knuckle fight with the government'. The government, however, prevailed in its plans for industry restructuring and marketisation. Similarly, in the United States in the 1930s, the Roosevelt administration successfully introduced new labour laws and welfare state policies that raised hostility from important business sectors (Skocpol, 1980; Block, 1980; Helleiner, 1994). In Australia as well, the Keating Labor government turned on big business during the 1990s, claiming (largely erroneously) that the peak business association, the Business Council of Australia, had been 'partisan' during the 1993 federal election. Keating publicly attacked CEOs, and ministers and senior bureaucrats were discouraged from active engagement with the Business Council. As a former director commented:

> the philosophy that informed government's attitude was if business put its head above the parapet then it'd be kicked in. And that had the effect of causing many in the business leadership to actually retreat. They ultimately had an obligation to their own shareholders not to expose the company to retaliation at the political level . . . and they backed off [Bell 2008a, 564].

CONCLUSION

In *Reinventing Government*, David Osborne and Ted Gaebler (1992) argue that governments can devolve responsibility for 'rowing' – delivering actual services to citizens – without compromising their ability to 'steer' – to raise resources and set priorities. Their book is written in the style of a can-do business manual complete with inspiring examples; at times it is quite galling. It has also been read as constituting an unqualified defence of the application of neo-liberal economic principles to the government sector (see Bevir, 2007, xxiii). Yet, while recognising that 'privatisation is one arrow in the government's quiver', Osborne and Gaebler (1992, 47) are clear that those who 'believe business is always superior to government are selling the American people snake oil'.

Privatization is simply the wrong starting point for a discussion of the role of government. Services can be contracted out or turned over to the public sector. But governance cannot. We can privatize discrete steering functions, but not the overall process of *governance*. If we did, we would have no mechanism by which to make collective decisions, no way to set the rules of the marketplace, no means to enforce rules of behaviour. [p. 47 emphasis in original]

The choice is not between markets and hierarchies. Markets are suffused with hierarchy. States not only create markets: they manage them. Privatisation, deregulation, contracting-out, PPPs and internal and external markets all require ongoing hierarchical intervention. Markets are managed and, as Michael Keating (2004, 6) argues, can be used to 'assist in the achievement of many of the state's policy directions and goals'.

7 | Governance through community engagement

Despite Trends Towards fragmentation and greater individualism in modern Western societies, there has been a growing interest in a wide range of governance engagements or partnerships between governments, citizens and communities. These arrangements vary from relatively inconsequential forms of public consultation to ambitious provisions for joint decision-making.

There is nothing new in the principle of community engagement, but this chapter describes precedents for apparently novel governance arrangements. The scale and scope of engagement efforts have increased over the last decade or more for several reasons.

- The development of the internet and the explosion in the ownership of home computers has made it easier and cheaper for governments to solicit citizens' opinions. (On the possibilities of e-governance, see Torres et al., 2006; Dunleavy et al., 2006; Budd & Harris, 2008.) In 2006, when the UK prime minister's office launched a website (http://petitions.pm.gov.uk/) that allowed visitors to create or sign on-line petitions, one petition, calling on the government to abandon proposals to introduce a road-pricing scheme, attracted almost 2 million signatures.
- At a normative level, democratic theorists have, in recent decades, championed the virtues of deliberation and civic engagement over established forms of representative democracy. It is now routinely argued that public deliberation in which citizens reflect carefully on and debate the merits of policies enhances the legitimacy of decisions (Barber, 1984; Elster, 1998; Dryzek, 2000; Besson & Marti, 2006).
- Civic engagement and the fostering of 'active citizens' are key policy principles of the 'communitarian' (Etzioni, 1995) and 'third way' (Giddens,

1998) philosophies that proved attractive to a number of centre-left governments in the 1990s. They are argued to lead to healthier and more prosperous societies, where rights are balanced with responsibilities.

- Perhaps most significantly, governments have learnt that community engagement can enhance their capacity to formulate and implement policies. Governments have sought to engage more thoroughly with citizens in order to inform themselves of potential discontent; to enhance the legitimacy of decisions and ease implementation; to broaden the base of responsibility for policy and thus help shield government from blame; and to incorporate wider inputs or participation in government decision-making (Irvin & Stansbury, 2004). The evidence is that citizens are more likely to conclude that policies are fair if they have been given the opportunity to participate in their formulation (Keating, 2004, 159). In promoting community engagement, governments have recognised – or have at least said that they recognise – that there are occasions when hierarchical governance unleavened by community engagement can be counterproductive. Community engagement is regarded as an antidote to a declining state legitimacy which manifests itself in growing mistrust of politicians and falling rates of political participation.

- Finally, governance through community engagement is sustained by a growing conviction that centralised forms of expert knowledge can be inappropriate or unreliable and that forms of knowledge garnered through dialogue and engagement with citizens or communities should be valued (Bell, 2004b).

This chapter explores the role of citizens and communities as partners in governance in national and local settings. We defer analysis of international governance until the next chapter, mainly because such activism is generally conducted through internationally based activist associations and NGOs rather than directly through citizens or communities. We start by distinguishing among the many different forms of community engagement and offer examples of particular governance arrangements. Advocates of community engagement argue that the state should share its power and resources and devolve governance functions to citizens and communities. In accordance with our broader state-centred relational approach to governance, we stress that governance processes involve a range of state–society links, but that the role of the state remains of central importance.

While recognising that there have been many useful experiments and initiatives, we emphasise the limitations of community engagement as a mode of governance. Three critical issues shape and potentially impede governance via community engagement. There are questions about:

- the willingness and capacity of citizens and communities to participate in such arrangements, especially on a sustained basis
- who exactly is being engaged, and how representative and legitimate such engagements are
- government motives and capacities, especially in relation to power sharing.

CITIZEN AND COMMUNITY ENGAGEMENT

Community engagement can be defined as 'the process of working collaboratively with and through groups of people affiliated by geographical proximity, special interest, or similar situations to address issues that affect them' (Lowe & Hill, 2005, 170). Community engagement can sometimes devolve responsibility for both the formulation and the implementation of policy to communities and, on this basis, has been celebrated as constituting an alternative to markets, hierarchies and pressure-group politics. Yet it is clear that the term community engagement can describe a variety of different arrangements.

Table 7.1 draws on work by the International Association for Public Participation (2005; see also Arnstein, 1969; Bishop & Davis, 2002; Head, 2007). It depicts a range of engagement alternatives distinguished in terms of the amount of authority shared between government and citizens. Towards one end of the spectrum is 'empowerment', which formally incorporates public input; at the extreme it places final decision-making authority in the hands of the public via community committees, citizens' juries, ballots and referendums. Here the claims of community engagement to constitute a distinct mode of governance are clearest. The other end of the spectrum is the simple sharing of information. Towards the middle are options such as 'consultation and collaboration', where the government solicits the views and input of citizens and communities in a spirit of partnership but reserves the right to take final policy decisions. In formal consultation processes governments listen to and acknowledge the public's concerns and aspirations and provide feedback on the extent to which their views influenced policy decisions. At its best, such consultation becomes an ongoing dialogue involving mutual learning and accommodation. At its worst, it is tokenistic and creates a sense of betrayal when communities believe that their views have been ignored. 'Standing' involves innovations such as formal participation in forums of review and decision. Examples include formal public engagement in processes

Table 7.1. Forms of public participation in governance

Form of participation	Goal	Promise to the public	Technique or instrument	Limitations
Inform	To provide the public with balanced and objective information to assist them in understanding the problem, alternatives, opportunities and/or solutions.	We will keep you informed.	Fact sheets Web sites Open homes	Limited public input One-way communication Passive communities
Consult or collaborate	To work or partner directly with the public throughout the process to obtain feedback or input and to ensure that public concerns and aspirations are consistently understood and considered.	We will keep you informed, listen to and acknowledge concerns and aspirations and provide feedback on how (or how not) public input or advice influenced the decision.	Workshops Deliberative polling Surveys Dialogue sessions Consensus forums Advisory bodies Public hearings Focus groups Public comment	Expensive and time-consuming for complex issues Communities feel betrayed if they do not like the decision Issue of who can speak or engage on behalf of the community Raises important questions about community commitment and capacity Power differentials, privileged access, and bias towards established community interests Possibility of co-option Legitimacy issues for those excluded

Involve	To work with communities in joint on the ground projects such as community development, environmental protection	We will work with you to help solve local problems and assist with resources and ideas	Joint task forces Co-management of resources Landcare groups Neighbourhood Watch groups	Heavy demands on local activists, burnout Limited resources and inputs from government
Collaborate	To allow third party involvement in formal review processes	We will ensure your right to legal standing in review processes and acknowledge input and detail our responses	Review courts and tribunals Statutory processes for social and environmental impact assessments	Only relevant to those issues that come to formal reviews or court, legalistic Expensive and time-consuming Bias towards well-funded interests
Empower	To devolve aspects of decision making to communities, parcel out authority, or place final decision-making in the hands of the public.	We will implement what you decide, although governments set the parameters, parcels of authority or questions for decision.	Devolved decisions to formal community committees, citizens' juries, ballots and referendums, e-democracy	Costly, time-consuming Raises legitimacy issues about representation Possibility of co-option Capacity questions re local communities Potentially divisive Are votes/referendums the best way to participation?

Source: Adapted from International Institute of Public Participation <http://iap2.org>.

such as environmental impact reviews (Glasson et al., 2005, 5–7). Such forms of engagement can be effective but also time-consuming, expensive and legalistic, requiring funding and specialised resources to operate effectively. Finally, in 'joint projects' the government helps or provides resources to community groups to implement policies. Examples include conservation groups or Neighbourhood Watch schemes performing tasks which, in other instances, might have been undertaken by government.

We will look at some examples of these arrangements. A good example of empowerment is the provision in nearly half of all the states in the United States to hold a public referendum on policy propositions which, through a petition, have attracted the support of a minimum number of citizens. Referendums have a long history. The Swiss federal constitution of 1891 permitted citizens to request a vote on constitutional provisions. In California ballot propositions have, for some time, been a staple part of the political process (Allswang, 2000). In 2004, 18 ballots were held on topics as varied as stem cell research, the collection of DNA samples, gambling, and additional taxation on personal incomes above $1 million to fund mental health care. Provisions for citizens' initiatives have recently been included in the French constitution and the constitution of the European Union. In 2004 British Columbia, Canada, created a Citizens' Assembly on Electoral Reform to explore options and make recommendations about a new electoral system. The assembly comprised 160 randomly selected citizens who were charged with receiving submissions, consulting with interested parties and experts, and discussing available options. In assessing the impact of the Assembly's efforts, Bob Goodin and John Dryzek (2006, 225) observe that British Columbia's legislature gave a commitment to put any recommendations to a formal referendum: 'the macro-political uptake of this mini-public's recommendation was hard wired'.

Danish consensus conferences are a good example of collaboration. Consensus conferences – which have subsequently been employed in Israel, the United States, Spain, Japan, Australia, Switzerland and New Zealand (http://www.loka.org/TrackingConsensus.html) – deal with techno-scientific topics of interest to the public whose character is uncertain, contested or controversial (Fixdal, 1997, 370). The Danish Board of Technology has organised consensus conferences on genetically modified food, gene therapy, electronic identity cards, food irradiation, fishing, road pricing and electronic surveillance. The conference consists of a broadly representative Citizen Panel of about 15 lay people and a Planning Committee of eight or so experts. Introductory material, often written by a science journalist, is reviewed by the Planning Committee and then distributed to the Citizen Panel. At the conference, experts answer questions in public sessions before the Citizen Panel submits a final report and recommendations to the government and parliament (Blok, 2007, 167; Bruun, 2005). Consensus conferences are a significant form of engagement, yet the government retains considerable power: it sets the agenda by deciding which issues to take to a conference, and it decides whether to accept the conference's recommendations.

The Pacific Northwest of the United States provides an example of a joint management arrangement in which about 20 Native American tribes co-manage the salmon fisheries with state and federal agencies. This arrangement grew out of a history of debilitating conflict between the relevant parties, who were finally forced to cooperate under court orders. The co-management arrangements have encouraged parties to cooperate to analyse and assess biological data and pursue initiatives to improve habitat and construct fish hatcheries. In what Sara Singleton (2000, 13) describes as a 'striking transformation', disputes between the parties now rarely go to adjudication by third parties or the courts.

Landcare projects in Australia provide an alternative example of a joint arrangement: the federal government has devolved partial responsibility for environmental restoration and conservation projects to more than 4000 community-based Landcare groups (Curtis & Lockwood, 2000). Another system of natural resource governance in Australia is the array of community-based regional bodies that co-manage regional projects and challenges with government, from bio-diversity and habitat protection to water quality and soil conservation (Head & Ryan, 2004).

Archon Fung and Erik Olin Wright (2003) bring together a range of fascinating examples in which communities have provided various inputs to policy-making, including joint decision-making, in areas as diverse as local public schooling policy in Chicago, worker training in Wisconsin, species protection and conservation policy in the United States, participatory local budgeting in Brazil, and local village empowerment in Kerala, India. In the case of species protection and conservation policy in the United States, a former state of conflict and gridlock between developers and conservationists over the protection of endangered species threatened by development projects has been ameliorated through the formation of local stakeholder management committees. Typically composed of government officials, developers, conservationists and local groups, they are charged with formulating Habitat Conservation Plans to balance development interests with acceptable levels of species protection. After the local committee has formulated a plan, it is submitted for approval (or not) by higher authorities within the state (see also Thomas, 2003).

These examples demonstrate successful experiments in governance through community engagement. We will now look at the features they share. On a cautionary note we then consider the governance capacities of citizens and communities before discussing the democratic legitimacy of. such governance arrangements.

THE FOUNDATIONS OF COMMUNITY ENGAGEMENT

What are the common features that underpin successful citizen or community engagement? In a study of watershed management in the United States, Thomas Koontz and Elizabeth Johnson (2004) found that successful community engagement required the broad participation of the full range of affected interests. Others have highlighted the importance of citizen skills and knowledge (Kellogg, 1998); the need to engage the public early in the decision-making process (Duram & Brown, 1998); careful selection of community representatives; transparent decision-making; and clear lines of authority (Irvin & Stansbury, 2004, 61). Singleton (2000, 4) lists a number of 'necessary conditions' that must be in place to underpin effective community engagement.

- Governments must exhibit a strong prior preference for collective action and effective community engagement.
- Citizens must be given sufficient information and data in order to reach a decision.
- The community must have the social and material capacity to overcome collective-action problems.

Singleton notes that small or close-knit communities in which people have existing social ties find themselves in a stronger position.

Along similar lines, Kenneth Kernaghan (1993, 62) has considered *genuine* collaboration between community organisations and government. Ideally, he says, it involves shared decision-making between parties; the mutual acceptance of a certain loss of autonomy; and a shared contribution of resources. He goes on to argue that collaborative forms of governance are most likely to prove successful when all significant stakeholders are involved; there is a mutual dependence between the partners and the potential for positive-sum cooperation; and arrangements are sustained through resource commitments and effective institutions.

In their review of the factors underpinning successful community engagement, Fung and Wright (2003, 15–24) outline three 'primary background conditions'.

- Engagements must cover specific areas of community concern, of sufficient magnitude to help mobilise communities.
- There should be 'involvement of ordinary people affected by these problems and officials close to them'.
- There should be genuine deliberation between participants in the sense that solutions are achieved through ongoing dialogue and negotiation.

Ideally, the power asymmetries between those who actually engage in such processes should not be too large because 'individuals [who] cannot dominate others to secure their first best preference are often more willing to deliberate' (Fung & Wright, 2003, 23).

Beyond these background conditions, Fung and Wright isolate three 'institutional design features' – metagovernance functions – common to the cases they examined. The necessary features are:

- Clear lines of responsibility with some devolution of authority to empowered local units charged with specific functions and responsibilities. In other words, governments must devolve specific and clearly articulated parcels of authority to local participants.
- Formal links between communities or local units and the state through shared resources and information flows and clear lines of responsibility and accountability (see also Singleton, 2000, 16).
- New state institutions designed to support and guide decentralised local units.

The conditions identified by Fung and Wright suggest that effective community engagement requires restructuring both of the state and of the incentives of state officials. This is why they describe their examples of deliberative democracy as state-centric; ideally, such governance arrangements are developed in intimate association with the state. Local participatory bodies need to be carefully linked to the state, which performs critical metagovernance functions: coordinating and distributing resources; solving problems that local units cannot deal with; rectifying incompetent decision-making in local units; diffusing learning and innovations across boundaries; and helping to build more equal access and power balances in local arenas to facilitate participation. Chapter 2 emphasised that the state often finds itself in a strong position in networks because it occupies a structurally 'central' position. If community engagement is to prove effective, governments must empower others.

These factors are a challenging list of ingredients and criteria. Community involvement makes potentially heavy demands on local citizens. It is also clear that the role of the state is central in successful institutional designs. We will now explore the requirements for successful public engagement in governance, starting with detailed questions about the governance capacities of citizens and communities.

WILLING AND CAPABLE CITIZENS AND COMMUNITIES?

Those who proclaim the merits of community engagement as a mode of governance sometimes assume an idealised vision of community, in which communities or citizens are eager activists, relatively homogenised, rich in social capital, well organised and led by capable leaders. But if we reverse or substantially qualify these assumptions, does the idea of community engagement look as potentially attractive?

One important issue relates to the willingness of citizens to engage in governance processes. Chapter 5 showed that high levels of social capital – 'those features of social organisation, such as networks, norms and social trust that facilitate coordination and cooperation for mutual benefit' (Putnam, 1993, 67) – are an important prerequisite of governance through persuasion. Governance through community engagement is also more likely to prove effective when there are high levels of social capital and a community is able and willing to engage in governance. Yet in the case of the United States Robert Putnam (2000) has documented a precipitous decline in levels of social capital since the 1960s as communities have been buffeted by job mobility, social fragmentation, long working hours and the dominance of home (rather than public) entertainment (see Chapter 5). Theda Skocpol (1996) offers an account of such developments based on changed processes of electoral and advocacy politics, which involve a shift away from local activism and grassroots activities towards nationally organised, poll-driven, top-down forums. She also charts a shift in the focus of civic elites and leaders, from local groups and participation to wider and more professionally organised processes and the marginalisation of civil elites and local leaders – upon whom processes of community engagement often depend – by professional lobbyists and party apparatchiks. As she argues:

> privileged Americans remain active in think tanks, advocacy groups, and trade and professional associations, jetting back and forth between manicured neighbourhoods and exotic retreats. Everyone else has been left to

work at two or three poorly paid jobs per family, coming home exhausted to watch TV and answer phone calls from pollsters and telemarketers [Skocpol, 1996, 24].

Even in the United States many citizens still wish to be informed and consulted and engage in governance activities. As we have emphasised, individuals are not exclusively self-interested and sometimes work for the public interest. Sidney Verba, Kay Schlozman and Henry Brady (1995) estimate that up to 10 per cent of the American population is politically active. This is a small proportion of the overall population but nevertheless amounts to more than 25 million people engaged in governance activities. On the other hand, one study of community responses to the local stock-piling of chemical weapons in the United States found that, although many expressed an interest in participation, only around one per cent of people followed through on this interest by phoning for information about how to become engaged (Williams et al., 2001). Looking at particular examples, Skocpol (1996) estimates that, in major civic associations such as the American Association of Retired Persons, no more than 5–10 per cent of members participate even in the most minimal ways in local affiliates or clubs.

We have noted that the rapid loss in social capital that has occurred in the United States seems not to have occurred in other countries. Yet there is plenty of evidence of limited willingness to engage in political activities elsewhere. In the late 1990s the UK government introduced a system called Best Value to replace, or at least augment, the system of compulsory competitive tendering in which local councils were required to contract-out certain activities. Under Best Value, local councils are required to compare their service provision with that found in other areas and consult with business and the local community about the quality of service delivery (Boyne, 2000). In reviewing the levels of community engagement councils were able to elicit, Paul Foley and Steve Martin (2000, 486) sound a note of caution:

> Only a fifth of residents living in Best Value pilot areas stated that they would like to have more of a say in the ways local services were run. Moreover, most of those who wanted to be more involved favoured passive forms of consultation such as postal surveys as opposed to more interactive approaches such as public meetings and citizens' juries.

Best Value consultations about service delivery are not, of course, the most glamorous or ambitious of governance activities. Proponents of community engagement might argue that limited exercises in consultation will not generate the same interest as genuine efforts to empower local communities. Yet, although generally supportive of governance through community engagement, Fung and Wright (2003, 37–8) recognise that ignorance about local political issues, when combined with an underlying sense of apathy and a predisposition to free-ride, can endanger effective governance. For these reasons Graham Pearce and John Mawson (2003, 63) conclude that 'devolved [governance] processes should not be too ambitious', while Renee Irvin and John Stansbury (2004, 58) indicate that 'where communities are complacent, there is a strong argument for top-down administration, simply on grounds of efficiency'.

A second problem is that civil society associations and communities may not have the organisational resources or capacities to engage effectively with government. In a study of the capacity of community organisations to work with government to deliver local housing services in the United States, Patricia Fredericksen and Rosanne London (2000) found that only one of the 18 organisations they studied could be described as well organised in terms of its service delivery functions.

A third problem arises when engagement processes are dominated by unrepresentative local elites who use engagement procedures to pursue their own interests (Irvin & Stansbury, 2004; Abel & Stephan, 2000; Smith & McDonough, 2001; Keating, 2004, 162; Halpin, 2006). As Fung and Wright (2003, 33) comment, 'perhaps the most serious potential weakness of [community engagement] experiments is that they pay insufficient attention to the fact the participants in these processes usually face each other from unequal positions of power'. Because of inequalities of income, gender, race or education, certain groups are able to mobilise and defend their interests at the expense of others. As Foley and Martin (2000, 486) reflect,

> community aspirations are nowhere near as homogeneous as government pronouncements frequently imply. Previous community-based initiatives have repeatedly demonstrated that local people rarely speak with one voice and their influence is not unambiguously positive. Communities can be deeply fragmented and many local people support policies which would exacerbate rather than combat social exclusion. Moreover, 'community representatives' are often atypical precisely because, unlike most local people, they are willing to become involved.

Encouraging local engagement while ensuring a basic level of equality in that engagement constitutes an important metagovernance function for the state. Community activists do not simply spring *de novo* from a voluntarist soil, but must be cultivated through public assistance. As Brian Head (2007, 444) says, 'The community sector (as with the business sector) comprises a shifting range of unorganised, partially organised and well organised stakeholders. Their capacity and interest in interaction and engagement will vary widely.' Accordingly, governments must continuously develop the capacities of weaker groups through programs that provide training or resources to encourage people to recognise and defend their mutual interests (Head, 2007; Keating, 2004; Wiseman, 2006). As Michael Marinetto (2003b, 110) points out, 'public authorities as the gatekeepers to executive power and as holders of significant resources are crucial to creating opportunities for active citizenship'. In one study, William Maloney and colleagues (2000) showed that Birmingham City Council in the United Kingdom achieved a tangible increase in the number and capacity of community-based voluntary associations through targeted financial grants and community development schemes. In other instances governments have attempted to deal with another problem of community activism, the burnout of activists. This has been a problem in the Landcare movement in Australia and has prompted government agencies to offer assistance and training to find and motivate new activists and leaders.

Citizens or groups may decline to be involved in formal governance arrangements for fear of being co-opted by the state. Many environmentalists, for example, worry about this; the danger is that 'incorporation' into consensus or deliberative forums might isolate group leaders from their communities or limit alternative forms of political mobilisation (Doyle, 2000). Whelan and Lyons (2005) document a case in Queensland, Australia, where conservation groups decided to boycott engagement that was seen as potentially co-optive or unproductive. 'By rejecting both hierarchical, centralised decision-making and the inadequate engagement practices proposed by the state, activist groups mobilised community opinion and action to bring about an historic win' (Whelan & Lyons, 2005, 596).

ACCOUNTABILITY AND LEGITIMACY

Traditional systems of representative democracy require only limited engagement of citizens through occasional elections. The Austrian economist Joseph Schumpeter (1942, 269) defines such 'competitive' forms of democracy as constituting an 'arrangement for arriving at political decisions in which individuals acquire the power to decide by means of a competitive struggle for the people's vote'. Schumpeter contrasts this modern, competitive notion of democracy with its 'classical' alternative, which requires direct, community-based, decision-making. In Ancient Greece major decisions were made by the Assembly, or *Ecclesia*, which met about 50 times a year, at which every (male) citizen was entitled to speak and vote (Hansen, 1991).[1] Schumpeter argues that in a world where millions of people living in cities must confront technically complex issues there is no alternative to the competitive model of democracy. John Mueller (1992) also defends limited concepts of democracy because they do 'not require more from the human spirit than apathy, selfishness, common sense, and arithmetic'.

The arguments for community engagement that have been developed over the last few decades draw upon and seek to promote broad-based 'participatory' or 'deliberative' systems of democracy in which decisions are taken directly by the people (see Goodin, 2003, 1–8). According to Eva Sorensen and Jacob Torfing (2008b, 32–3), governance arrangements involving such participatory schemes could potentially deal with several 'problems' encountered in representative democracies. They could enhance a vertical balance of powers through the establishment of sub-elites and governance networks; establish a link between top-down representative democracy and bottom-up participatory democracy; serve as a medium for enhancing political empowerment and mutual trust; widen the institutional and discursive sphere of the political and thus enlarge the space for political discussion and contestation; and improve governance efficiency and 'output legitimacy' in processes of public governance.

We encountered the distinction between input and output legitimacy in Chapter 2 (Scharpf, 1999). Input legitimacy may be strengthened where decisions are taken by politicians who are elected to office. But community engagement may lead to more output legitimacy if it results in better decisions being taken. In a similar vein, Michael Keating (2004, 159) has argued:

> Currently, increased public participation is widely seen as the best way to draw disaffected citizens back into the political mainstream and of overcoming increasing perceptions of a 'democratic deficit'. By involving citizens in some way in the decision-making process, governments then hope to bridge any 'legitimation gap'. Indeed, a representative body that has sought and considered the advice of constituents is on much stronger ethical ground, even if they subsequently reject that advice, than representatives whose judgment is formed without consultation.

Governance through community engagement requires a careful balancing of different modes of legitimacy. Where it is difficult to define the boundaries of a community affected by a decision, and where engagement processes are dominated by unrepresentative local elites, the state needs to exercise its metagovernance responsibilities by continuously monitoring, and perhaps curtailing, the authority devolved to local communities. Grace Skogstad (2003, 968) offers a solution to this dilemma of achieving a balance of the various forms of authority in society, from hierarchical state authority to popular authority: underline the centrality of representative democracy and the legitimate authority of the state. As she argues, popular authority, as manifested in community engagement strategies, can only ever be a potentially useful complement to formal systems of representative democracy. 'Mechanisms of participatory democracy . . . that give representatives of society formal or informal rights of participation cannot substitute for state-centred governing because of their representational inadequacies.' Still, such participatory schemes can help to boost 'input legitimacy'.

A WILLING AND ABLE STATE?

A central claim made in this book is that the state remains the major player in shaping and managing public governance. We have emphasised the state's role both as a direct participant in governance arrangements and as operating the crucial higher-level functions of metagoverning such arrangements. Now we consider the state's role in citizen and community engagement, looking at the institutional disjunctures and coordination problems that may damage links between governments and communities, and consider how much power governments or state agencies are actually willing or able to devolve to communities.

Our starting-point is a widely held view: governments do not like sharing power. In examining the Blair government's devolution of governance authority in the United Kingdom, Mike Marinetto (2003b, 116) concludes that 'for all its support for community involvement, the Labour government [retains] a predilection for strong central control'. Jonathan Murdoch and Simone Abram (1998, 49) found that central government strategies and objectives consistently limited community input into housing policy in the United Kingdom. Local groups were given some discretion in how best to meet objectives but were 'tied' into 'a set of calculations and relations that extend down a planning hierarchy from the central state'.

It might be objected that the UK state has always been reluctant to embrace 'horizontal inclusivity' (Wallington, Lawrence & Loechel, 2008). Yet in writing about community engagement experiments in the Netherlands, Geert Teisman and Eric-Hans Klijn (2002, 198) similarly conclude that, although 'there is intensified interaction between public and private partners, there is little joint decision-making and continuity in cooperation'. In the case of a commitment to ensure public participation in the redevelopment of Rotterdam Harbour, they conclude that public officials 'wanted to retain their primacy' and consistently thwarted engagement efforts (p. 204). Examining the development of community-based governance mechanisms in the United States, Singleton (2000, 16) also points to 'the depth of resistance among state managers to sharing regulatory authority'. Wallington, Lawrence and Loechel (2008, 17) reach a similar conclusion in their study of local input into regional governance in Queensland, implicating 'unequal power relationships'. The 'official framing of policy' remained the centrepiece of such governance arrangements, leading them to conclude: 'The reluctance of farmers and others to participate in what amounts to a co-option of regional participants serving a policy agenda in the interests of, and defined by, government is perhaps unsurprising.' Again in Australia, Brian Head (2007, 449), an academic with practical experience in community engagement, points out that:

> non-governmental organisations and community groups often report unhappy experiences of 'participation', owing to poor project management or even bad faith by governments; for example, in cases in which people enter an apparently participatory process, only to find there is an absence of genuine devolution or meaningful involvement because the government sector has been unwilling to forgo control over processes and the shaping of results.

Previous chapters argued that governance arrangements ought to be viewed in terms of an exchange relationship between governments and non-government actors. Governments may not like to share power but they may be required to do so where non-state actors possess valuable resources and there is a strong mutual dependency. The following chapter on associative governance describes the substantial power-sharing that occurs in corporatist arrangements where business, and perhaps trade unions, are in a position to negotiate access to the policy-making process. By contrast, community engagement is often a limited, sometimes symbolic, activity because communities do not generally possess the resources governments need, or at least not enough to encourage governments to devolve power or authority to them (Head, 2007, 450).

A case in point is the experience of what Jurian Edelenbos (2005) terms 'interactive governance' in urban redevelopment in the Dutch municipality of Enschede in the 1990s. Edelenbos (2005, 111) starts by depicting a shift 'from government to governance', that is, 'a shift from hierarchical and well institutionalised forms of government towards less formalised, bottom-up forms of governance in which state authority makes way for an appreciation of mutual interdependence with different stakeholders'. However, the details of this case reveal a different story. The activities of local participatory forums of deliberation and advice ran in parallel with, but did little to affect, traditional decision-making structures. Local councillors remained the final decision-makers and were largely disengaged from the participatory process. Furthermore, public servants who became involved used the participatory processes as little more than a 'sounding board' (p. 122) for their own ideas. Ultimately, the 'politicians and civil servants did not perceive the temporary organisational structure of the interactive process as having any authority'. As Edelenbos concludes, 'the case of Enschede has shown that institutional dissociation takes place between the interactive process and the existing administrative structures and procedures' (p. 123).

The experience of water resource planning in New South Wales, Australia, offers another telling example of the limits of community engagement (Bell & Park, 2006). The challenge was to devise plans to share water between rival users while leaving enough water in the drought-affected river system to maintain a sustainable environment. The New South Wales government established 36 catchment management committees across the state in 2002 which included representatives of the stakeholders. These committees were given the responsibility, but not the power, to create water-sharing plans. The legislation stated that the committees were *advisory* and that the relevant minister had the discretion to alter or change the plans. We can conceive of such a governance arrangement as the 'networks in the shadow of hierarchy' described by Scharpf (1994, 27). It seems clear that the government wanted stakeholders to negotiate among themselves, to 'sort things out', and then advise the government about an appropriate plan to share water based on local input and compromise; in other words to offer the product of what Scharpf (1994, 28) calls 'negotiated self-coordination'. Formally, this is not a power-sharing model. As we will see below, this highlights the dilemmas confronting governments who wish to reap the benefits of stakeholder commitment and negotiation but do not wish to relinquish power or authority (Teisman & Klijn, 2002).

In choosing to establish community engagement, the government must weigh up its potential benefits. These include the legitimacy derived from community involvement; information benefits arising from the coal-face knowledge of stakeholders; and the possibility of 'negotiated self-coordination'. However, in this case these benefits were not seen as outweighing the results of decisions made by the government on the basis of arm's-length stakeholder input. After a lengthy process of often painful negotiation, committees submitted their water-sharing plans to the state government in 2004. The minister then amended most of them. Clearly, the government either did not recognise or could not realise strong mutuality gains from stakeholder involvement, despite the creation of an extensive system of governance. By overruling the water-sharing plans developed by the management committees, the government left stakeholders feeling frustrated and ignored. As the Irrigation Association of Australia explained:

> It was quite contentious and it led to a number of sections of the industry feeling that they had been disenfranchised to some extent. There was a consultative process gone through, then the recommendations of that consultative process disappeared into the bureaucracy... The only thing worse than not consulting is to consult and then to ignore the results... Where that happened it has given those water sharing plans a difficult start in life because significant number of the stakeholders are feeling 'well, that wasn't agreed by us' [Bell & Park, 2006; see also Craig & Vanclay, 2005].

There is a general lesson to be learnt here about governance and the use of language. Rod Rhodes, whose notion of 'governance without government' we encountered in Chapter 1, suggests that, rather than simply defining governance in terms of particular institutional arrangements, we ought to look at the ways in which 'individuals construct governance' (Rhodes & Bevir, 2003, 195) and how governance 'arises from the bottom up' (Bevir & Rhodes, 2006, 99). Rhodes is right to emphasise that governance is not simply a piece of academic jargon 'divorced from [the language] of practitioners and commentators' (Riddell, 2000, quoted, Bevir & Rhodes, 2003, 9). Politicians and public servants discussing governance often pepper their speeches and policy documents with references to 'community engagement', 'partnership' and 'policy capacity'. Drawing upon such references, academics have documented what they describe as a transition from government to governance. In this self-reinforcing circle academics and practitioners feed off each other. Our suspicion is that many politicians and public servants have learnt to use the language of community engagement strategically; it becomes a presentation device to obscure, or at least make more palatable, the exercise of hierarchical control. Public servants, consciously or unconsciously, have adopted a new governance language in order to achieve certain goals without revising the underlying ideas, or indeed, power structures.

There is, however, an interesting question here. If people adopt language for essentially strategic reasons, will that language eventually come to constrain their actions? Does the language of networks and community engagement eventually lead to more networks and community engagement? Discussing deliberation and constitution-making, Jon Elster (1998) suggests that language can have this effect. In a legislative setting there is usually a strong expectation that politicians justify the demands they make in terms of an appeal to the public interest. But the existence of this norm gives politicians an incentive to alter their behaviour. A politician who wishes to avoid the appearance of obvious self-interest might, for example, demand a public subsidy or other allocation not simply for their constituents but for all the residents of the area where their constituency is located. Once having used a particular argument to justify a policy, politicians come under pressure to accept other applications of that argument so as not to appear incoherent or hypocritical.

It is easy to see how the language of networks, partnership and community engagement might similarly constrain politicians and public servants. Even if everyone in a room believes that everyone else is using language strategically, the ideas embedded within that language may nevertheless affect people's behaviour. A public servant who has learnt to assert the importance of community engagement will, for example, find it difficult to always and everywhere dismiss requests to consult about policies. There is one important difference between these settings. Elster focuses on the relatively short period of time in which proposals are debated and voted upon in a legislative assembly. Governments, however, have much more time to claw back any concessions their language leads them to make during the course of the policy process. At a stage when they are drafting proposals and seeking stakeholder support, policy-makers might litter their speeches and briefing documents with references to partnership, consultation and community engagement. And this may lead them to modify their behaviour. But, over time, governments can be expected to reassert hierarchical control, so exposing the limits of their rhetorical commitment to community engagement.

POWER-SHARING AND THE STATE

We have argued that the development of community engagement as an alternative mode of governance is often limited by the reluctance of state officials to share power. How might we account for this reluctance? The simplest explanation, to which public choice theorists might most easily subscribe, is that power is a valuable resource and that self-interested politicians will no more forfeit power than a private sector entrepreneur would pass up a profit opportunity. Yet there may be more principled reasons why state officials cling to their authority.

First, politicians may, rightly or wrongly, feel that community engagement is too time-consuming to undertake in situations where there are economic or political pressures to make – and be seen to be making – immediate decisions. Amidst a growing water shortage crisis in 2006–7 in south-east Queensland, the state government initially promised, then shelved, a community referendum on recycling waste water for human consumption, such was the sense of urgency. Second, politicians or officials may believe that community engagement processes would upset or contradict broader strategies or standards. A well-honed argument against the ballot initiatives employed in California is that they result in contradictory decisions that preclude strategic policy development. Voters find it too easy to approve both lower taxes and higher public expenditure, or improved environmental standards and lower vehicle taxes, when left to determine these issues separately. Third, as we have suggested, government officials may be reluctant to concede authority where they believe that engagement processes are likely to be dominated by unrepresentative local elites.

Fourth, governments may be reluctant to concede authority where they believe that community engagement is unlikely to result to in a deliberative consensus. As Skogstad (2003) suggests, there may be limits to what can be deliberatively handled, thrashed out or agreed upon in community engagement settings. Where significant interests are at stake and competition between groups takes a zero-sum form, bargaining and deliberation may not be enough to resolve differences. As we have seen, there are often dangers of parochialism and an inability to develop coherent links to strategic plans or concerns of wider groupings of state agencies or whole-of-government approaches (Keating, 2004, 168). Moreover, many decisions involve voting, and community groups are often not structured to accord with such processes of choice aggregation. Skogstad quotes Chambers (2001, 48), who argues that 'talking (understood as deliberation) and voting do not mix well'. In a contest for votes, deliberation can become 'strategic, competitive and adversarial'. Even when there *is* a shared commitment to partnership and the public interest, individuals and groups can fail to reach an agreement if they are committed, whether consciously or not, to inconsistent policy ideas or competing policy paradigms. Skogstad (2001, 968) cites the case of an attempt to develop a provincial land use strategy in British Columbia, Canada, where various community engagement processes failed to produce a consensus. The deadlock was eventually broken by the strategic use of state resources and authority, including more traditional forms of 'horse-trading', overseen by the then premier, Mike Harcourt.

> Members of the Harcourt team recognised that the path to land use consensus would have to be greased with dollars; forest workers threatened by change would have to be appeased. Most important, they recognised that, more often than not, the results generated by advisory processes would have to be massaged into final outcomes, through traditional behind the scenes bargaining [Skogstad, 2003, 908].

Finally, other scholars have suggested that fundamental institutional mismatches can inhibit community engagement. Eran Vigoda (2002) argues that in modern systems of public administration, serving citizens as clients clashes with collaborating with them in governance arrangements. The problem is that government bureaucracies are fashioned along classical Weberian lines, with steep hierarchies of authority, concentration of power among senior officials, professional specialisation, clear accountabilities, impersonal rule-based behaviour, an increased fascination with business models, and a fear of sanctions for poor performance and hence a risk-averse culture. Vigoda cites Dennis Thompson (1983, 235), who says: 'democracy does not suffer bureaucracy gladly . . . many values we associate with democracy – equality, participation, and individuality – stand sharply opposed to the hierarchy, specialisation and impersonality we ascribe to modern bureaucracy'. Other institutional problems arise when government structures attempt to mesh with local engagement. For example, in dealing with problems that cut across agency jurisdictions or traditional lines of responsibility, the separate 'silos' of government bureaucracies can create problems as agencies attempt to coordinate activities not just with each other but with a wide range of local groups and engagements (Head, 2007, 449; Boxelaar et al., 2006).

In institutional terms, the challenge for government is to understand how to better connect the state's administrative apparatus with quite different local organisational environments that feature flatter structures, deliberation and compromise. As Chapter 3 argued in relation to metagovernance, public administrators involved in community engagement need to develop skills in networking, negotiation, mediation, conflict resolution, and synthesising or reconciling diverse frames of knowledge while also focusing on broader strategic and accountability concerns (Hess & Adams, 2002; Davis & Rhodes, 2000). The case described by Edelenbos (2005), however, indicates that effectively linking hierarchical state structures with participatory forums can be difficult. Case research by Lucia Boxelaar, Mark Paine and Ruth Beilin (2006) suggests that reconciling diverse frames of knowledge is no easy task and that bureaucratic, positivist and expertise-based forms of knowledge tend to prevail in such participatory settings. Similarly, Gill Callaghan and Gerald Wistow (2006) demonstrate in a case study of participation in primary health care in the United Kingdom that hierarchical power relations were inscribed in different knowledge forms and this served to limit effective participation by the lay public.

If governments do attempt to share power, they must be clear about their intentions in order to avoid confusion and disappointment. As Irvin and Stansbury (2004, 59) conclude: 'Lack of representation and authority to make decisions appears to be the key reason for participatory processes backfiring and actually increasing public dissatisfaction.' Furthermore, as Keating (2004, 160) argues:

> disappointed expectations, leading to further alienation, are most common where the participants believe that they will have more power over the decision than is intended. It is therefore critical that government is clear at the outset about its purpose in seeking greater citizen participation, the means that will be employed to achieve that participation, and what that implies for the respective roles of the participating parties. [See also Kane & Bishop, 2002.]

Honestly stating the limits of its own willingness to share authority constitutes an important metagovernance responsibility of the state.

DO-IT-YOURSELF COMMUNITY ENGAGEMENT

Thus far this chapter has examined the governance potential of community engagement from a state–community relational perspective. This perspective fits our broader approach to governance, but it does not exhaust the potential opportunities for meaningful community engagement in governance practices. Indeed, the case we now examine comes close to one of 'governance without government', albeit on a small, localised scale and still in the shadow of hierarchy.

Our focus is on how communities might deal with collective-action problems. These are the problems that arise when individually advantageous behaviour leads to a sub-optimal collective outcome (Barry & Hardin, 1982). For example, it may be individually advantageous to drive to work, but when everyone does this in a large city, traffic gridlock and high levels of air pollution may be the (sub-optimal) collective result. Such problems have been a focus of public choice approaches to institutional analysis, which focuses on 'institutional design' (Goodin, 1996) or on working out how institutions – conceived of as sets of incentives and disincentives that shape behaviour – might be devised to deal with collective-action problems. One of the major puzzles in public choice theory, which always assumes selfish behaviour, is why individuals would rationally contribute to the solution of collective-action problems. The suspicion is that individuals will simply free-ride on the actions of others, hoping to gain benefits but not shoulder any costs.

For some time, scholars assumed that selfish behaviour would always win and that only strict, even authoritarian, hierarchical controls could deal with such problems (Hardin, 1968; Ophuls, 1977). However, in examining collective-action problems arising from the consumption of natural resources, using the principles of public choice analysis, Elinor Ostrom (1990; Dolsak & Ostrom, 2003) identified an alternative and seemingly non-hierarchical means of resolving such problems. Where the number of users is relatively small and it is possible to monitor behaviour, people can develop elaborate but informal rules, norms and conventions governing the allocation of resources that prevent free-riding.

> Some scholarly articles ... recommend that 'the state' control most natural resources to prevent their destruction; others recommend that privatizing these resources will resolve the problem. What one can observe in the world, however, is that neither state nor the market is uniformly successful in enabling individuals to sustain long-term, productive use of natural resource systems. Further, communities of individuals have relied on institutions resembling neither the state nor the market to govern some resource systems with reasonable degrees of success over long periods of time [Ostrom, 1990, 1].

In the village of Alanya, Turkey, about 100 fishermen traditionally competed for access to the best fishing in local waters. As a result fishing stocks were being depleted while fishermen spent much of their time fighting for the best spots. In the 1970s the fishermen agreed to allocate fishing spots randomly and to rotate among them in an agreed sequence. As Ostrom (1990, 19) observes, this system has the effect of spacing each fishing boat far enough apart to maximise overall returns and gives each fisherman an equal chance of fishing at the best spots at the best times. This institutional solution is not entirely independent of the state, however. The calendar allocating fishermen to spots is deposited each year with the mayor and the local police. The implication is that hierarchy might be deployed if the collective agreements fail, and this knowledge may spur efforts at cooperation. Normally, however, the fishermen themselves monitor the agreement; they have every reason to notice if someone is occupying their allocated space.

CONCLUSION

This chapter has outlined a range of possible options and design principles regarding citizen or community engagement in governance. In line with our overall argument, it has highlighted the state-centred control and oversight of such arrangements. Apart from a few exceptional cases, such as the fishermen of Alanya, community engagement typically occurs in the shadow of hierarchy. As Head (2007, 449) suggests, 'if community engagement is largely at the discretion of the state – and indeed, is largely organised, shaped and subsidised by the state – there must be questions raised about the robustness and independent strength of community engagement'. Such views underline the importance of adopting a state-centred relational approach to the discussion of governance. Community engagement promises benefits but needs to be carefully managed. The key site of such management must be within the state itself, given its preponderance in such engagements. Governments choose when to engage communities and what to engage them about. Even when governing in partnership with communities, governments retain the authority to revise governance rules and abandon engagement processes.

In light of the range of limitations and concerns described above, ambitions about community engagement should probably be limited. Active power-sharing is unusual in such settings; it occurs under tightly prescribed conditions where the government has the whip hand. Moreover, in practice, according to Patrick Bishop and Glyn Davis (2002, 22), 'most citizen participation takes the form of consultation, which begins with the acknowledgment that governments decide'. They suggest, however, that such consultation assumes some degree of reciprocity, with those being consulted having at least some capacity to influence decisions. Whether such reciprocity or influence occurs, however, may be another matter and, as usual, is mainly at the discretion of authoritative decision-makers within the state. Governments tend to commit themselves rhetorically to community engagement. This may be, in part, because community engagement offers governments a means of enhancing their legitimacy. Community engagement, like governance through persuasion, is attractive because it is non-coercive. Yet this rhetorical commitment to community engagement is not always realised in practice.

8

Governance through associations

ASSOCIATIVE GOVERNANCE OCCURS when governments or state agencies form governing partnerships with societal organisations or NGOs. In this chapter we explore associative governance in two loosely categorised forms: corporatism, where governments jointly make and implement public policy in cooperation with major interest associations; and private-interest government, where governments or state agencies sanction or encourage the use of private authority in governance arrangements. A good example of corporatism is when governments formally negotiate with labour associations to establish and jointly implement wage moderation policies in a national economy. An example of private-interest government is when governments allow firms or business associations to set codes of practice or self-regulate their activities in certain sectors.

Political scientists have always debated how influential interest-groups are within the policy process and how defensible that influence is. Two contrasting positions are offered by pluralists and public choice theorists. Although tracing its intellectual origins back to John Locke's theory of consent and Montesquieu's 18th-century celebration of the separation of powers, pluralist theory was developed mostly by American political scientists in the 1950s and 1960s. At the core of pluralist theory is a belief that power ought to be dispersed throughout society; that public participation in political processes should be encouraged; and that government policy should command the consent of the public. Pluralists have argued that interest-groups enhance the democratic process because they limit the power of the state by checking and balancing any excessive concentrations of political power that may arise (Truman, 1951; Dahl, 1956). In contrast, public choice theorists challenge the involvement of organised private interests in governance arrangements. Since the 1970s they have argued that interest-groups pursue their own narrowly defined concerns, lobbying for special privileges or 'rents'; and that, cumulatively, this undermines economic efficiency (Tullock, 1989; 1993; 2005). On this basis public choice theorists argued that the post-war proliferation in interest-group politics had 'overloaded' the state and even led to the 'decline of nations' (Olson, 1982).

Our own account of the dynamics of governance through association differs in two respects from such arguments. In the first place, rather than being inherently attractive or unattractive, the costs and benefits of governance through association depend, in particular, on prevailing institutional arrangements, especially on the capacities of associations and on the strength and capacity of the state. Where the associations representing private interests have a high membership density or coverage, effective internal procedures for mediating member interests, and selective incentives to help mobilise members in collective action, interest-group politics need not lead to rent-seeking or economic catastrophe. Second, far from being a handmaiden for private interests, the state can enhance its policy capacity by establishing associative governance arrangements with non-state actors and by effectively metagoverning such relationships. Chapter 2 anticipated parts of this argument by challenging the notion that governance networks operate with substantial autonomy from the state. Here, we provide more examples of the ways in which states can metagovern associative governance relationships.

This chapter explores examples of associative governance in terms of corporatism and private-interest government. We then probe the role of the state in associative governance. The final section shifts the focus of the argument, examining so-called 'non-state market-driven' governance arrangements, in which private firms and associations work collaboratively with campaign groups or NGOs to develop codes of conduct regulating the behaviour of firms. Such codes of conduct are entirely voluntary. Firms have an incentive to embrace these codes if they calculate that by doing so they can avoid adverse publicity or attract additional customers. From our state-centric relational approach to governance, the most significant feature of such governance arrangements is that they seem to operate independently of governments and perhaps even constitute an example of 'governance without government'. The chapter concludes by examining the limits to the significance of such arrangements. Codes of conduct are not always followed; they cover only a small fraction of business activity; and for campaign groups generally they remain an inferior alternative to state regulation.

FORMS OF ASSOCIATIVE GOVERNANCE

As we said at the beginning of the chapter, associative governance can be divided into two types, corporatism and private-interest government. We will look at them in turn.

CORPORATISM

Most introductory textbooks recognise that interest-groups are important political actors and that governments often adopt particular policies after lobbying by such groups. Chapter 2 pointed to academic work on 'policy networks' composed of interest-groups and government actors. Chapter 5 showed how the National Farmers Union persuaded the UK government to adopt a particular policy in relation to an outbreak of foot-and-mouth disease. However, the presence of powerful interest-groups with ready access to government officials is not necessarily evidence of an alternative form of governance. Governance through hierarchy is entirely consistent with the presence of powerful interest-groups and their lobbying activities.

What we have called associative governance (see Hirst, 1994; Hirst & Veit, 2001) requires interest-groups to play a formal partnership role in governance and even perhaps in the development and implementation of public policy. The lead candidate for this form of governance is corporatism, an arrangement in which government works with major interest associations, usually peak bodies representing the collective interests of a particular group, granting them a formal role in policy formulation and securing their cooperation in implementing policy (Schmitter, 1974; Lehmbruch & Schmitter, 1982; Cawson, 1986). Of course, the degree of power-sharing under such relationships varies, but in the more robust forms of corporatism, major interest associations acquire a quasi-public status, becoming virtually an arm of the state's policy-making and implementation apparatus. Claus Offe (1981) explores the conditions for such an 'attribution of public status'. Important associative capacities include representing or speaking for key functional interests, such as business or labour; and the ability to aggregate interests, to act as a source of support for government policy, to act as a key bargaining interlocutor, or to help shape member or sector compliance.

Probably the most prominent examples of corporatist policy-making are bipartite or tripartite arrangements in which business associations and/or peak union organisations bargain with government over wage moderation or industrial restructuring, either at a sectoral or national level. Peak union organisations, for example, may accept wage moderation and work to encourage wage restraint as part of an anti-inflationary policy in return for concessions from the state, such as tax relief or social policy or other benefits. In this respect, discussions about corporatism ought to be understood in the context of more general debates about how, at a sectoral or national level, differing mixes of governance modes and sets of institutional relations have produced different 'varieties of capitalism' (Hall & Soskice, 2001). Institutional configurations and relations between markets, states and associations help govern and shape processes and preferences at the level of the firm, such as investment, corporate governance, inter-firm clustering, labour–management relations, training and skill formation, and research, development and innovation (Morgan et al., 1999). Because of institutional differences and varying modes of economic governance, capitalist economies have markedly different capacities for growth, innovation and productivity, as well as methods of sharing the proceeds of economic growth (Hall & Soskice, 2000; Berger & Dore, 1996).

In 'liberal market' systems such as those of the United States and the United Kingdom, economic coordination and governance occurs mainly through market processes, with clear boundaries between the public and private sectors. Such a system can be compared, at the other end of this ideal-typical spectrum, to 'coordinated market' systems in Japan, Germany and much of Northern Europe, which feature much higher levels of deliberative and collaborative activity within the private sector and between the public and private sectors. In such systems the emphasis is on long-term planning and investment strategies through the development of close relationships between state and non-state actors. Corporatist forms of governance are a defining feature of such coordinated market systems. Northern European countries in particular have for decades engaged in such corporatist forms of governance. For example, the Danish 'negotiated economy' features patterns of wide social dialogue and bargained consensus between major associations in the economy and with government (Nielsen & Pedersen, 1993; Amin & Thomas, 1996). There are similar corporatist arrangements in the Netherlands (Visser & Hemerijck, 1997). In recent years the Irish economy has also been managed through ongoing coordination and bargaining between key state, business and union organisations who have worked together to secure wage moderation and other goals as part of a strategy to manage inflation and economic development (House & McGrath, 2004).

There have also been some counter corporatist trends. In the United Kingdom in the early 1980s corporatist decision-making procedures were dismantled by a neo-liberal government intent on reducing trade union power (Crouch & Dore, 1990). Even once avowedly corporatist Sweden has seen a conceptual shift among many businesses, which led in the 1990s to the repudiation of corporatist governance and the collapse of norms of social partnership (Lindvall & Sebring, 2005). Yet as Jurgen Grote and Phillipe Schmitter (1999) observe, there has, for the most part, been a 'renaissance' of corporatism in those European countries with collectivist political cultures and established traditions of social partnership charac-terised by power-sharing and the search for consensus (Lijphart, 1999). In these countries the economic pressures of globalisation and economic restructuring have been interpreted as affirming the need for greater coop-eration with the state. In exploring the importance of ideas and ideology in shaping governing practices, research by Peter Katzenstein (1985; 2003) on European corporatism shows that the social construction of perceived threats and a sense of external economic vulnerability have prompted coop-eration between potentially hostile groups. As he concludes, 'perceived vul-nerability generated an ideology of social partnership that acted like glue for corporatist politics' (2003, 11). Hence, a favourable conceptual envi-ronment constitutes one important prerequisite for corporatist governance arrangements.

Of equal importance are the institutional capacities of the private organ-isations drawn into corporatist arrangements. Private-interest government roles, and especially corporatist governance arrangements, make substan-tial organisational demands on civil society associations. Under associa-tive forms of governance, associations must be able to draw resources from members, such as funds or information, as well as loyalty and com-mitment. Organisational capacity also implies aggregating and analysing information, acting as a forum for deliberation and negotiation, building trust and reciprocity among members, and perhaps fostering new or wider definitions of interests and goals. In this way associations may help over-come collective action problems and other organisational challenges posed by participating in governance relationships with governments. Associa-tions can also be seen as sources of private authority. This may inhere in a past history of contributions to governing, the ability of the organisation to represent and speak for its membership or constituency, and the social or economic importance or reputation of its members.

If corporatism is to work effectively, peak associations must be able to coherently represent particular sectors and bargain authoritatively in closed forums with governments. In particular, associational elites must be able to deliver the cooperation and compliance of group members, since groups are required to play an active role in implementing centrally agreed policies. In France, the fragmentation of the labour movement into competing associations has been partly responsible for non-corporatist labour arrangements; in the United Kingdom and the United States, the prevalence of liberal views about competition and the desirability of maintaining an arm's-length relationship between business, unions and government has also limited corporatist policy-making (Gordon, 1998).

To see how normative ideas about the appropriate limits of state authority and institutional capacities interact to determine the efficacy and durability of corporatist arrangements, we will examine the rise and fall of corporatist governance in Australia. Within a generally liberal and confrontational political culture, the kind of corporatist arrangements common in Western Europe had traditionally found little favour in Australia. However, a new Labor government elected in 1983 forged an initially very successful corporatist wages policy via formal, ongoing negotiations with the peak union organisation, the Australian Council of Trade Unions (ACTU). The unions agreed to exercise wage moderation, while successive Accords (as they were called) committed the government to providing tax cuts and other social benefits such as improved health care in return. During a period in which the Labor government was, in other areas, deregulating markets, the Accords helped to control wage inflation and achieve sustained economic growth (Kelly, 1992, 54–75; Matthews, 1994; Bell, 1995).

How can we account for the apparently sudden emergence of corporatism in Australia? The election of a social democratic government led by an instinctive corporatist deal-maker, Bob Hawke, was clearly important, as was Hawke's union background as president of the ACTU (Kelly, 1984). More generally, the Labor government needed the cooperation of the trade union movement to help contain wage-push inflation, which at the time was the major macroeconomic policy challenge facing the country. Earlier confrontations with the unions under the conservative Fraser government had failed, so a fresh approach was desired. The Accords were popular with the electorate and helped promote industrial peace, which encouraged the corporatist partners to support such deals.

The introduction of corporatism into Australia required a favourable institutional environment. The established tradition of formal, centralised wage negotiation provided a backdrop to Labor's new approach. Throughout the 20th century industrial relations in Australia had been managed through a series of quasi-judicial tribunals, most importantly the Commonwealth Court of Conciliation and Arbitration, with legal authority to set binding minimum pay levels and conditions of work and to impose solutions in the event of industrial disputes (Bell, 1997, 183–4). One reason Australian unions were prepared to accept the introduction of corporatism in the 1980s is because of this centralised institutional tradition. Government involvement in the industrial system was an established normative frame and institutional reality. Of equal importance in preparing the ground for corporatism was the development of the ACTU into a powerful peak body by the late 1970s with sufficient organisational capacity and representational coverage to effectively lead the union movement. In the face of political pressure from a threatening conservative government in the 1970s, the ACTU, under Bob Hawke, became much more of an 'encompassing association'; one able to negotiate and deliver on centrally negotiated wage deals (Keating & Dixon, 1989; Matthews, 1994).

Corporatist political arrangements can be difficult to maintain in liberal political systems that emphasise freedom of association and the voluntary nature of group membership. Peak associations are also vulnerable to defections from their member units. Over time, the Accords slowly weakened in the face of countervailing neo-liberal pressures and moves by strong unions for collective bargaining to gain wage rises beyond the restrictions of the Accords (Hampson, 1996). The unions became wary of the Accords' promise to sustain economic growth, especially after the devastating recession induced by monetary policy in the early 1990s. Business interests began pushing for more liberal arrangements under the banner of so-called enterprise bargaining. By the late 1980s, both the government and unions were offering qualified support to the new enterprise bargaining agenda. The government increasingly recognised that such a move was the natural corollary of its 'competitiveness' agenda and earlier financial and product market deregulation.

The reluctance of peak business organisations – especially the body representing big business, the Business Council of Australia (BCA) – to embrace the Accords also weakened the system. Hawke had sought a formal alliance with the BCA at the inception of the Accord system. The BCA, reflecting entrenched liberal sentiments, flatly rejected such overtures, preferring instead to maintain a cordial but arm's-length relationship with the government (McLaughlin, 1991). As a former BCA insider put it:

> Hawke thought the creation of the Business Council in 1983 was a marvellous opportunity to shore up corporatism, but he was sadly disappointed because the Council position was: 'this is our policy and we are not going to negotiate with you on policy. We'll advocate our position. You'll have to take a decision in government' [interview, 25 November 2003, Melbourne, quoted Bell, 2008b].

The BCA's steadfast refusal to embrace corporatism caused ongoing tensions with the government. Yet the BCA would have found itself in an extremely difficult position if it had behaved otherwise. The corporate sector was, on the whole, opposed to close 'collaboration' with government, and especially to back-room corporatist deal-making. Moreover, the BCA lacked the institutional capacity to negotiate on behalf of all businesses in Australia, let alone to guarantee their compliance with any deals struck (Bell, 1995).

PRIVATE-INTEREST GOVERNMENT

As it is usually defined, corporatism represents a particular form of governance through association: one in which relations between the state and key interests are mediated through peak organisations. In their work on private-interest government Phillipe Schmitter and Wolfgang Streeck (1985) demonstrate that a broad range of private associations do not simply lobby governments for particular policies but come to exercise measures of delegated authority on behalf of the state. Private-interest government thus refers to the role played by private associations as either formal or informal interlocutors with governments in helping to govern (Schmitter & Streeck, 1985). The main governance relations typically include associations or organisations lending expert authority to governments, operating under delegated authority, acting as regulatory partners with governments, or working to 'organise' non-state roles in wider governance processes. Operating locally or at the national or international level, the associations in question act as sources of organisational capacity and private authority in such governance processes. Examples of such associations include business associations, trade unions, expert panels, and NGOs such as human rights, consumer or environmental organisations.

Chapter 4 discussed a good example of private-interest government, where industry associations work with government in systems of 'responsive regulation'. Another example is the role of business associations in facilitating worker training and skills formation. Training workers within a firm confronts employers with a serious problem of collective action: why devote resources to training workers who can be poached by other employers in a competitive market? Firms have strong incentives to free-ride on any training provided by other firms. Governments can attempt to overcome this source of market failure with incentive payments or subsidies or other assistance to firms: that is, through a form of hierarchical governance. But in a study of training regimes in France and East Germany, Pepper

Culpepper (2001) shows that business associations can potentially play an important governance role by organising 'decentralised cooperation' among firms.

States retain the significant capacity to sanction behaviour and offer incentives. But because they lack detailed knowledge of skills shortages within particular industries, they cannot tailor their policies with precision. Culpepper argues that business associations can assist governments to implement policy, especially in targeting assistance to firms with the greatest 'cooperative propensities' (p. 284). Cooperation is possible and mutually beneficial because the 'state is strong where private associations are weak, but it is also weak where they are strong' (p. 281). In France and East Germany in some instances associations helped overcome cooperation dilemmas among firms by drawing on their views and information, acting as a deliberative and learning forum for them, and mobilising them in favour of agreed positions. In this way business associations helped develop and stabilise the expectations of firms and provided important inputs for policy-makers. After studying a range of regional cases in each country, Culpepper confirmed one of the key hypotheses of his study: that 'the presence of employers' associations with capacities of information, deliberation, and mobilisation is a necessary condition for reforms premised on securing decentralised cooperation to succeed' (p. 286).

Culpepper's study shows the sorts of roles that associations can potentially play as sources of 'private governance' working in partnership with state agencies in a positive-sum relationship. Private associations representing individual firms can bargain over the details of policy and so save the government the need to strike separate deals. Just as importantly, private associations give firms the chance to talk to and learn from other firms in a non-competitive setting. By building trust, reducing uncertainty and resolving problems of collective action, private associations are crucial in many countries in overcoming micro-level 'coordination problems' in capitalist economies. Peter Hall and David Soskice (2001, 11), whose work on the varieties of capitalism we introduced in our discussion of corporatism, argue that in such settings: 'deliberative proceedings in which participants engage in extensive sharing of information about their interest and beliefs can improve the confidence of each in the strategies likely to be taken by others'.

Another example of business associations playing a role in associative governance was the development and implementation of the goods and services tax in Australia from the late 1990s. Peter Hendy, a former chief executive of the Australian Chamber of Commerce and Industry, recounts this role:

> The federal government worked closely with and leaned very heavily, much more so than most people would realise, on business associations to help educate companies on how to transition to the new tax system. Because it was a new system the feedback to government was critical. As part of the new system, there was initially a huge fuss about issues such as Business Activity Statements and their administrative complexity. It should be noted that the government threw large amounts of money at this problem. For example, I recall that there was about $250 million in grants direct to business associations to run the education campaign and another $250 million to fund vouchers to small businesses to buy software etc. This is therefore not just a market issue responding to an announced government policy, but a policy implementation issue requiring (in the public interest) further government involvement than normal. The government took this path because it simply didn't have the administrative infrastructure to get to hundreds of thousands of small businesses. If they hadn't utilised business associations, the government would have had to otherwise spend large amounts of resources creating that infrastructure for a one off administrative event. The government simply doesn't have the tentacles into the business sector that a binocular view of the modern welfare state suggests. They don't even have a consolidated mailing list for small business to send out political messages [Peter Hendy, personal communication, 10 June 2008].

There are many other examples of private associations playing a formal governance role in ways which benefit government. For example, Gerald Berk and Marc Schneiberg (2005) examine the role of business associations in 'organising markets' in the early 20th century in the United States. A number of sectoral business associations used research into cost accounting, deliberation, learning, and benchmarking to manage markets and conclude a period of mutually destructive cut-throat competition. Associations in industries such as printing, bridge-building, textiles, and iron and steel production, among others, also used associative collaboration to improve productivity and reduce excessive costs and prices. As Berk and Schneiberg (2005, 73) argue, 'developmental associations perturbed habits, invited firms to reflect upon background cost conditions, and used information, deliberation, and benchmarking to foster discovery, experimentation and productivity improvement'. Similarly, Kelly Kollman and Aseem Prakash (2002) look at the varying uptake in Europe of a voluntary compliance regime on environmental factors, of the sort examined in Chapter 5. They find that German firms are far more likely than British or American ones to join, and then to comply, with these arrangements. Why? Compliance with environmental codes is potentially costly because it requires additional employee training, the collection of data and preparations for certification. In Germany well-developed industry associations and local chambers of commerce have reduced these costs because they have 'provided checklists to help firms carry out internal audits' (p. 47) and assisted with certification procedures.

In further examples of governance through associations, governments often allow private associations to establish national accounting standards for companies. In the United States the authority to set such standards has for some time been delegated to the Federal Standards Accountancy Board, a private association that is overseen by the Securities and Exchange Commission but operates independently of it on a day-to-day basis. For governments, the expertise provided by such private associations and the close links they maintain with individual firms provide an important governance resource (Mattli & Buthe, 2005). Similarly, the Australian federal government gave responsibility for the implementation of an export promotion program, Export Access, to a number of national industry associations in the 1990s. It did so in the belief that such bodies have strong networks and possess more detailed knowledge of the circumstances of individual firms and so would be able to implement the program effectively (Bell, 1995).

In the international arena, Claire Cutler, Virginia Haufler and Tony Porter (1999) and Rodney Hall and Thomas Biersteker (2002) provide a range of examples of the exercise of private authority in international regulation. Walter Mattli and Tim Buthe (2003) show how the International Organisation for Standards (ISO) and similar organisations promulgate thousands of product standards covering areas such as health and safety and environmental protection.[1] The ISO is composed of representatives of more than 150 national standards bodies and has a secretariat based in Switzerland. Operating largely on a deliberative basis, delegations of national organisations meet under the auspices of the ISO to debate and argue about appropriate standards. Among the standards promulgated by the ISO in 2007 are those relating to greenhouse gas validation and verification; drinking water; the sustainable development of fisheries; biofuels; and food safety. The ISO typically works by consensus and has no legal coercive power to enforce the agreed standards. However, in the case of standards relating to, for example, the dimensions of freight containers and the format of bank cards, the use of ISO standards is enforced via national regulatory bodies.

Other examples of associations shaping governance practices can be found in the realm of ideas and their impact on defining interests and identifying problems; knowledge-based organisations, groups of experts or 'epistemic communities' can shape policy outlooks (Hass, 1992; Finnemore, 1996). The Intergovernmental Panel on Climate Change (IPCC, for example, which operates under the auspices of the United Nations Environmental Program, is a scientific intergovernmental organisation whose main decisions are taken in plenary sessions by national representatives. The IPCC has no coercive power. National governments are under no obligation to accept or even directly respond to the recommendations in assessment reports published in 1990, 1995, 2001 and 2007. Yet the IPCC has used its reputation for scientific expertise and political impartiality to set agendas and shape preferences. Similarly, in a mammoth analysis of *Global Business Regulation* John Braithwaite and Peter Drahos (2000) show how private authority plays an important regulatory role in international arenas, from aviation to food standards to labour standards to finance.

An important potential institutional issue relating to associational governance is the problem of organisational elitism. This raises again the issues of accountability and legitimacy that were canvassed in relation to community engagement. If anything, such problems become potentially more serious under associative governance arrangements that involve the substantial devolution of power to private associations. Early studies by Robert Michels (1915) and others in the tradition of elite theory found that professional administrators and organisational leaders, even in social democratic settings, often tended to dominate the rank-and-file membership, which results in attenuated democratic processes and outcomes.

A recent case in point is analysed by Knut Mikalsen and colleagues (2006). The Norwegian Fisheries Association, as a result of a partnership with the Norwegian government to manage fisheries, shifted over time from a bottom-up organisation to one pursuing 'the economic interests of its most powerful members' (p. 201). While the organisation 'pays lip service to the goals of social responsibility and the broader mission of the association as the voice of all fishers, there is – in practice – a growing emphasis on protecting the privileges and investments of a much narrower group of "professionals"' (p. 206). On a similar though broader scale, Paul Magnette (2003) argues that new participatory forms of governance in the European Union aimed at curbing the EU's 'democratic deficit' are highly problematic, largely because the systems in place tend to be dominated by narrowly organised and 'elitist' interests in policy-making. Other studies point to similar problems of limited democracy and limited internal accountability in a range of civil society associations (Warleigh, 2001; Lyons, 2001; McLaverty, 2002; Halpin, 2006).

THE ROLE OF THE STATE WITHIN ASSOCIATIVE GOVERNANCE

Governance through associations often requires the state to share power to a greater degree than any of the other modes of governance we have examined. In the case of corporatist arrangements, the state commits itself to a measure of joint decision-making with partner organisations. In the case of private-interest government the state agrees to delegate authority for the creation and implementation of regulatory rules to non-state actors. The previous chapter argued that states are usually reluctant to share power: there must be clearly perceived payoffs or relationships of dependency to push governments down this path. In relation to strong associative forms such as corporatism, it seems clear that such arrangements are most likely to emerge when the state is sufficiently autonomous to avoid capture by major interest associations, but not sufficiently authoritative to rule by decree and hence reject cooperation with affected groups. Therefore states might share power with associations which possess valuable resources, such as expertise and legitimacy, and which can frustrate efforts by the state to implement policy unilaterally. As Trevor Matthews (1988) suggests, associations can be 'vitally important allies' in helping governments govern.

Yet the state remains a major actor within associative governance arrangements. First, we stress that the corporatist and private-interest government arrangements that we have discussed are created and maintained by the state. A case in point is the study by George Christou and Seamus Simpson (2006, 43) of the development of a 'new European transnational private governance' arrangement for the internet. In the late 1990s the European Commission recognised a need to create a top-level domain name of 'eu' as an alternative to national names like 'dk' (Denmark) or 'hu' (Hungary). In deference to the participatory culture of the internet and the expertise of commercial interests, the European Commission recognised that it could not manage the domain system unilaterally. Instead, it created a private, transnational, not-for-profit company, the European Registry for Internet Domains (Eurid), to administer the dot-eu registry. The resulting arrangements, while containing elements of self-regulation and private governance, gave the European Union 'all rights' relating to the registry databases, including the 'right to re-designate the registry itself'. The authors conclude that 'the shadow of hierarchy looms large' over governance arrangements because Eurid is subject to a 'time-limited and renewable agreement' (p. 53).

Governments can revise governance rules, and any authority given to private associations can potentially be withdrawn. For example, the activities of rating agencies in credit markets and devolved forms of self-regulation in industry are artefacts of state strategic choices in allocating and overseeing such roles. In the United Kingdom in the early 1980s and in Australia in the mid-1990s, incoming neo-liberal governments changed the rules of governance and simply dissolved corporatist arrangements. Furthermore, it is through the imprimatur of the state that these governance arrangements acquire legitimacy. According to Ian Hurd (1999), to the extent that a state accepts some rule or body as legitimate that rule or body becomes an authority. In this respect, some accounts of the role of private associations or firms risk confusing largely private functions with collective arrangements. For example, the analysis by Cutler (2002) of 'private coordination' and 'private international regimes' blurs private organisational arrangements in markets – informal agreements, production alliances, cartels and joint research initiatives – with more publicly oriented arrangements such as standards-setting and regulation.

Governance through association does not emerge spontaneously. States must provide private actors with sufficient incentives to involve themselves in governance activities. Governments and state agencies often place heavy demands on associations to report data, comment on draft proposals, and sit on consultative committees. There are demands for information; for advice, often at short notice; for appearances before hearings; for participation on consultative bodies or corporatist forums; and the need to keep members informed of the steady stream of new rulings and policy decisions emanating from the state. One associational respondent in a study conducted by Bell (1995) likened his role to that of an 'unpaid public servant'. A key metagovernance requirement for governments is to ensure that private associations have sufficient incentives to undertake these governance activities.

Typical was the largely unsuccessful attempt to implant corporatist practices at a sectoral level by the government of Ontario between the mid-1980s and mid-1990s. The government's objective was to encourage organised labour and business interests to work together to negotiate and help implement a set of policies on industry, training, and occupational health and safety across industry sectors. In his account of this experiment,

Neil Bradford (1998) points out that in a neo-liberal institutional and conceptual setting this was always an ambitious strategy. One major problem was that business interests mostly resisted collectivist engagements. As Bradford points out, 'the viability and durability of such reforms depends on the willingness of organised business interests to share power responsibly with other social actors'. On the whole such cooperation was not forthcoming, because business saw the incentives, largely provided by the state, as insufficient; and because, more broadly, business interests distrusted such 'incorporationist' governance strategies, preferring instead to maintain the 'autonomy of the firm'. Only in the case of industrial policy were the 'inducements to business large enough and the threats small enough to convince corporate managers that partnership did not mean making unwarranted concessions' (p. 568).

Once the rules of the game have been established, the state remains a pivotal actor within associative governance arrangements. Although the basic relationship in such arrangements is one of exchange, the roles of government and associations are not equal. Chapter 2 pointed out that the central position of governments in associational networks allows them to 'dominate the exchange' (Chhotray & Stoker, 2009, 22). As an example of the ways in which states can dominate governance arrangements that appear to involve a substantial measure of power-sharing, consider Mexico's approach to the North American Free Trade Agreement (NAFTA). The decision to seek membership of NAFTA was made centrally by Mexico's political leaders. Having made this decision, the Mexican government sought to win support for this agenda from the business community. It created a new body, the Business Coordinating Council for Foreign Trade, whose selected members were invited to discuss the trade deal with the government. Before the first meeting of this corporatist body the Mexican government revealed its hand through a political marketing campaign which framed a free trade agreement as one in which businesses and social groups would all gain. To limit any dissent, the government indicated that business leaders would be invited to discussions and allowed to lobby for temporary concessions only if they accepted the principle of NAFTA membership. 'The provision of these concessions gave potential opponents an incentive to work for the best possible terms rather than against the initiative in general. While the Mexican state allowed businesspeople to participate in shaping NAFTA's terms, that opportunity came with strings attached' (Fairbrother, 2007, 284).

In this case the central position of the government allowed it to set the agenda, determining the key issues to be resolved through associational governance. Yet governments can also exert control by setting agendas *within* governance relationships. Consider the Open Method of Coordination (OMC) introduced in the European Union in 2000. The OMC seeks to encourage mutual learning between national governments, the supra-national institutions of the European Union, and interest-groups across a range of policy issues. As described by Helen Wallace (2000, 33), the aim of the OMC is 'not to establish a single common framework, but rather to share experience and encourage the spread of best practice'. Whereas hierarchical governance results in coercive rules and regulations, the OMC results in recommendations and regulations which actors are *encouraged* to implement. These recommendations are negotiated between 'public and private actors at different levels of decision-making', meaning that 'no distinction is made between steering subjects and steering objects' (Kohler-Koch & Rittberger, 2006, 36–7). The OMC has been lauded as a 'new mode of governance' and a retreat from centralised decision-making in the European Union (Heritier, 2003). The European Commission, however, has shown that it can steer the OMC process from behind the scenes. It can decide whether to use the OMC to address a particular policy problem. It frames policy problems, sets the sequence of consultation, drafts recommendations, and monitors their implementation. As Burkard Eberlein and Dieter Kerwer (2004, 126) conclude: 'Although the OMC should be a combination of bottom-up participation and top-down guidance, in reality it is often dominated by the centre.'

Governments can also dominate governance arrangements in situations where actors possess very different empirical and normative ideas about the appropriate policies to pursue. Conceptual differences can sometimes be resolved through processes of deliberation or policy learning such as the OMC, but they are often embedded in organisational cultures that resist change (Alvesson & Sveningsson, 2008). This is partly because organisations are, from the moment of their inception, given differing mandates, responsibilities and lines of accountability. Where organisations possess very different cultures, attempts to govern through associational partnerships are likely to generate misunderstandings, conflict and paralysis. Even when organisations are genuinely committed to working together in partnership, 'the shadow of hierarchy' may be needed to ensure the smooth functioning of governance arrangements. In some cases the conceptual differences among organisations in a network may even prompt the government to reassert control and govern through hierarchy.

The treatment of drug addicts in the United Kingdom offers a good example of this governance dynamic. In a 10-year strategy document,

Tackling Drugs to Build a Better Britain, published in 1998, the government identified drug addiction as a 'wicked problem' that required government and non-government organisations to deliver 'joined-up' solutions within a 'network governance' approach (Acevedo & Common, 2006). The institutional expression of the government's joined-up approach was to create about 150 local Drug Action Teams (DATs). These teams were charged with 'bringing together representatives of local agencies involved in delivery of the Drug Strategy, such as health services, social services, police, probation services, local education authorities, youth services, social housing providers and voluntary sector providers' (http://drugs. homeoffice.gov.uk/dat/). Initially, DATs were given the responsibility to commission services, monitor and report on performance, communicate with stakeholders and oversee the development of coordinated 'street-level' services.

Yet conceptual differences between the agencies involved in drug treatment undermined the value of the partnership approach and the smooth running of the DATs (Parker, 2004, 381). The criminal justice agencies, principally the police and probation services, tended to frame addiction in terms of criminal enforcement and the protection of the community. In contrast, many of the voluntary workers in drug treatment charities favoured harm minimisation. A second difference emerged within the health sector between mental health workers who believed that addiction was a symptom of underlying mental health problems that had to be treated first and those working in health clinics who favoured immediate treatment for the addiction itself. Finally, a third difference emerged between youth justice workers, who tended to favour minimal intervention for fear of stigmatising and so alienating drug addicts, and drug workers in non-statutory agencies, who advocated long-term care relationships. According to one senior official working within a DAT:

> the cultural aspects [of working] were the key, particularly as . . . the main ethos of the youth justice system is to divert youngsters from the criminal justice system and very much based on minimal interventions. Whereas the needs of a drugs worker in that system are much more intense and it's not minimal intervention, it's about developing a relationship and getting into a lot of the problems. So those two approaches didn't work together, they were contrary to how people worked [quoted Newburn, 2003, 616].

Over time, as the full extent of the differences between agencies and the limits of a partnership approach became apparent, the government started to metagovern the DATs more actively. In 2001 the Home Office was given overall responsibility for the delivery of drug services in England, while regional Government Offices, composed of representatives of the major central government departments, were charged with monitoring the performance of the DATs. In 2002 much of the remaining discretion that DATs had been given to implement policy was eliminated when the newly created National Treatment Agency was charged with determining local treatment plans. Within three or four years the rhetorical commitment to a network approach gave way to what was, in effect, hierarchical control.

While acknowledging the extent to which governance through association requires states to share power, we once again emphasise the ways in which states can enhance their policy capacities by developing these relations. Recall the argument of Michael Atkinson and William Coleman (1989) in Chapter 3 that different forms of structured interaction between the state and society are linked to different styles of policy-making. Long-term, strategic and 'anticipatory' policy styles in industrial policy typically require the existence of state-directed or corporatist policy networks. Governments concede policy-making authority to trade unions and business leaders when they commit their authority to corporatist governance arrangements. But in doing so, government can enhance their capacity in achieving, for example, higher economic growth at a lower inflationary cost.

In arguing that there is a positive-sum relationship between states and private associations, we must return to the critique of public choice in Chapter 2. The basic claim is that in a competitive economic market setting the pursuit of self-interest leads (as if by an 'invisible hand') to the collective good, but that in a competitive political market the pursuit of sectional interests may be economically and politically destructive. Friedrich Hayek (1982) argues that sectional interest-groups undermine the legitimacy of the state and, in the case of trade unions, the rule of law. Mancur Olson (1982) argues that interest-group politics leads to institutional sclerosis and economic decline. Economists have estimated the costs of 'rent-seeking' by interest-groups to be as high as 50 per cent of American gross domestic product (Laband & Sophocleus, 1988); 20 to 40 per cent of Indian gross domestic product (Mohammad & Whalley, 1984); and 12 per cent of American domestic consumption expenditure (Lopez & Pagoulatos, 1994). For a critical assessment of such figures see Hindmoor (1999).

Whether or not private associations have an incentive to pursue a narrow, rent-seeking, agenda depends upon their institutional configuration.

As Mancur Olson (1982, 74–110) actually recognises, interest-groups that form peak associations representing the interests of large numbers of members have less incentive to pursue economically destructive rent-seeking policies. Using evidence from Latin America, Richard Doner and Ben Schneider (2000) seek to identify the factors that encourage business associations to play a constructive political role. In their view, 'progressive' associations have a high membership density or coverage, effective internal procedures for mediating member interests, and selective incentives to help mobilise members in collective action. In addition to these institutional attributes, associations are more likely to play a progressive rather than rent-seeking role in the presence of 'external drivers'. Doner and Schneider emphasise the role of perceived threats of economic vulnerability in mobilising business cooperation. Finally, and most crucially, they stress the role of the state in providing incentives for appropriate forms of behaviour, particularly supportive incentives such as subsidies or institutionalised access to policy deliberation within the state.

This final point is worth underlining. The relationship between the state and private associations is most likely to take a positive-sum form when the state intervenes *hierarchically* to secure the authoritative position of the associations. This is a form of metagoverning or 'steering'. Governments or state agencies can bolster the strength of associations by offering financial or other supporting resources. Furthermore, state leaders can actively shape patterns of interaction between groups and the state, and act as brokers among competing interests. Governments and their administrative agencies may block the access of certain groups to forums of policy-making while giving others a monopoly on representation. In Austria, for example, membership in major business and union associations is compulsory under law, thus strongly enhancing the associative capacity of key interests. And as Streeck (1983, 270) points out in relation to Germany:

> Ministerial departments tend to discourage individual firms from contacting them directly on matters that can be dealt with by their associations . . . by urging firms to go through established associational channels, state officials increase the functional importance and the prestige of associations in relation to their members [and] they help interest groups speak with one voice.

Such corporatist proclivities resonate with the state capacity literature, where the term 'embeddedness' describes the ability of state leaders and policy-makers to forge positive, collaborative and change-oriented relations with key groups or sectors (Evans, 1995). This capacity for positive state–society collaboration, or what Linda Weiss (1998) terms 'governed interdependence', in turn depends on the organisational and associative capacity and outlook of major social or economic groupings and interest associations.

GOVERNANCE WITHOUT GOVERNMENT?

The governance arrangements we have been examining so far in this chapter consist of partnership arrangements between state and private associations. Yet during the last decade academics have identified new forms of non-state market-driven (NSMD) governance arrangements, in which private firms, under pressure from consumers and non-governmental campaign groups, develop and voluntarily abide by codes of conduct in the apparent absence of any state involvement. David Vogel (2008, 262) reports that there are now more than 300 codes, primarily addressing either labour or environmental practices, with a particular focus on such high-profile political issues as child labour, sweatshops, diamond mining and fair-trade coffee and cocoa production.

One of the most successful and intensely studied NSMD arrangements relates to forestry (Cashore, 2002; Bartley, 2003; Conroy, 2007; Tollefson, Gale & Haley, 2009). The Forest Stewardship Council (FSC) was created in 1993 and is managed through a general assembly and board of directors on which environmental and social groups and forestry firms are equally represented. The FSC has developed 10 principles of responsible forestry management, including reduction of the environmental impact of logging activities and maintenance of the ecological functions and integrity of the forest; maintenance of forests of high conservation value, having outstanding significance or critical importance; equitable use and sharing of benefits derived from the forest; and recognition and respect of indigenous people's rights. Forest owners apply to the FSC for certification and, if successful, can then display the FSC logo in an effort to attract customers. Based in Bonn, Germany, the FSC now has national offices in more than 50 countries, including Burkina Faso, the Congo, Ghana, Brazil and Papua New Guinea.

NSMD arrangements resemble some of the governance arrangements we have already discussed. Chapter 6 showed how NGOs like the Terrence Higgins Trust and firms like McDonald's have attempted to persuade people to change their behaviour in ways that contribute to the achievement of collectively valued goods. In these cases NSMD governance results in pressure upon firms to change their *own* behaviour. Chapter 4 examined the proliferation of systems of self-regulation, showing that it occurs in the shadow of hierarchy. In relation to NSMD arrangements, self-regulation is apparently undertaken voluntarily in the absence of the state.

We finally seem to have encountered a credible example of 'governance without government'. Cutler and her colleagues (1999, 2) describe NSMD systems as amounting to the 'privatisation' of governance. Benjamin Cashore (2002, 504) suggests that NSMD 'governance systems' derive their 'policy-making authority not from the state, but from the manipulation of global markets and attention to consumer preferences'. Virginia Haufler (2006, 92) suggests that 'one of the most significant changes in recent years is that the "who" in "who governs" must now be expanded to include the participation of nongovernmental and non-corporate actors'. Similarly, Steven Bernstein (2005, 60) argues that the civil regulations contained within NSMD systems 'represent an innovative form of governance'. Archon Fung (2002, 150), whose work on community engagement we examined in Chapter 7, describes the 'social markets' contained within NSMD systems as 'creating distinctive areas of governance'. Reviewing the literature on what he calls 'private transnational governance' within international relations, Phillip Pattberg (2005, 591) similarly points to the way in which 'the locus of authoritative problem solving does not rest with governments and their international organisations alone' and how 'authority is indeed relocated in many different settings, involving public-private as well as purely private actor constellations'.

We recognise that NSMD systems constitute a separate and innovative governance arrangement, and that the continued development of a global civil society centred on campaigning organisations – Greenpeace, Amnesty International, Human Rights Watch, the World Wide Fund for Nature (instrumental in the creation of the FSC), World Vision, Oxfam, and the fair trade movement – is likely to result in more of them. It is no surprise that we doubt some of the claims made on behalf of NSMD arrangements, especially the notion that they operate in isolation from governments.

First, it is clear that firms often work through associations to establish NSMD systems with the explicit intention of forestalling government regulation. Vogel (2008, 268), for example, points to the example of Responsible Care, a code of conduct governing the behaviour of chemical firms, which was adopted by a number of national chemical associations in order to reduce demands for further government regulation following the explosion at a chemical plant in Bhopal, India, in 1984 which ultimately killed over 13 000 people. As Mathias Koenig-Archibugi (2005, 122) observes, the distinction between voluntary and state-imposed codes of conduct 'is best thought of not as a dichotomy, but as the ends of a continuum'. NSMD systems may not operate directly under the shadow of hierarchy in the same way as conventional systems of self-regulation, but they do operate under the threat of hierarchy.

Second, the history of the FSC shows that, behind the scenes, national governments can play an effective metagovernance role in supporting the activities of campaign groups. Fred Gale (2008) shows how the UK government supported the Friends of the Earth's early interest in forest certification by funding a series of consultancy projects to investigate the possibility of using market incentives to ensure sustainable forest management. In Australia, Gale (2008) shows how forest certification was kick-started by the Department of Agriculture, Fisheries and Food: it hosted a conference in Queensland in 1996, which resolved that 'certification and labelling are potentially useful tools among many others to promote sustainable forest management'.

Third, it is not always clear what impact NSMD systems actually have on firms' behaviour and thus on the achievement of collectively valued goals. The FSC system rests on rigorous external auditing which requires firms to demonstrate to independently accredited auditors that they are adhering to each of the 10 principles of responsible forestry management on an ongoing basis (Cashore, 2002, 513). Yet in this respect the FSC is something of an exception. 'Relatively few' industry and corporate codes are independently monitored, and some contain absolutely no monitoring provisions at all (Vogel, 2008, 269). Fervent hopes have been expressed that NSMD arrangements represent a 'civilising influence' that can give 'globalisation a human face' (Cutler, 2006, 200). Yet these governance arrangements are unlikely to do so in the absence of metagovernance to ensure their effectiveness or accountability.

Fourth, while more than 300 business codes have been promulgated, these cover only a tiny fraction of all business activity. The firms that are most likely to adopt stringent codes of conduct are those with global brand names who can afford the costs of certification processes and whose reputation is most likely to be tarnished by allegations that they are acting unethically. Codes of conduct have now been developed to regulate the activities of industries that have previously attracted unwelcome newspaper headlines. Firms in other industries have less incentive to develop codes of conduct. The growth in NSMD governance arrangements may therefore be subject to rapidly diminishing returns. Even within the forestry industry, which has the most successful NSMD arrangement, the FSC has certified only about three per cent of the world's forests.

Because of inadequacies in the monitoring of their implementation and limitations in their reach, NSMD systems remain a second-best alternative for campaign groups. The World Wide Fund for Nature did not press for the creation of the FSC until the manifest inadequacies of the International Tropical Timber Agreement became apparent and national governments had failed to develop an effective international forestry treaty during the 1992 UN Conference on Environment and Development in Rio de Janeiro. It is worth noting that nearly all of the codes of conduct govern the behaviour of private firms, often transnational corporations, operating in developing countries with weak or non-existent systems of national regulation. If, over time, NGOs can persuade national governments to develop international regulatory regimes that incorporate higher environmental or labour standards and constrain the activities of multinational firms, the demand for NSMD governance will probably fall.

CONCLUSION

This chapter has offered examples of associations playing a key role in governance arrangements, showing that state and non-state actors can benefit from these partnerships. A central argument is that associative governance reveals the state making substantial use of private associative resources. In some cases, states may come to depend heavily on these resources. Such dependence implies reciprocity and a willingness on the part of the state to provide incentives for cooperation, even to the point of explicitly sharing authority with non-state actors. These state-sponsored selective incentives are an important condition for successfully soliciting associational cooperation.

Successful associative governance also depends on the willingness of associations to cooperate or be incorporated in governance partnerships. This willingness might be linked to incentives offered by the state, but it is also associated with a favourable conceptual environment in which actors trust each other and are prepared to cooperate for mutual gain. Associations must overcome difficult organisational or institutional challenges in order to be effective partners, including issues related to membership coverage and loyalty, resources and authority. Such arrangements may be unstable: changes in government and changes in the state's governing strategy can easily weaken or undermine them. As we have seen, in the United Kingdom, Canada and Australia corporatist experiments were brought to an abrupt end by the election of new governments. We have also argued that the ingredients for successful associative governance vary across different countries and policy arenas. In the final analysis, major associative governance arrangements are chosen by states. Such choices are shaped by ideological dispositions and by assessments of the institutional capacity and resources of non-state associations and their ability to deliver.

9 | Conclusion

To be governed is to be watched, inspected, spied upon, directed, law-driven, numbered, regulated, enrolled, indoctrinated, preached at, controlled, checked, estimated, valued, censured, commanded.... It is, under pretext of public utility, and in the name of the general interest, to be placed under contribution, drilled, fleeced, exploited, monopolized, extorted from, squeezed, hoaxed, robbed; then, at the slightest resistance, the first word of complaint, to be repressed, fined, vilified, harassed, hunted down, abused, clubbed, disarmed, bound, choked, imprisoned, judged, condemned, shot, deported, sacrificed, sold, betrayed.... That is government; that is its justice; that is its morality.

Pierre-Joseph Proudhon, *General Idea of the Revolution in the Nineteenth Century*, 1851.

States form a part of the backdrop to everyday life. They register births, deaths and marriages. They control immigration, collect taxes, provide public goods and regulate what people can eat, watch and buy. It is true that in some countries communities of people have effectively opted out of the state for religious or political reasons – the Amish in the United States, for example. It is also true that states have sometimes collapsed. Yet for most people in most countries the state remains as central (although perhaps not as objectionable) an actor today as it was for Pierre-Joseph Proudhon in 19th-century France.

Yet those writers who advocate a society-centred perspective on governance argue that governments have lost power and are no longer the 'cockpit from which society is governed' (Klijn & Koppenjan, 2000, 136). Lester Salamon (2002, 1–2), for example, argues that 'problems have become too complex for government to handle on its own, because disagreements exist about the proper ends of public action, and because government increasingly lacks the authority to enforce its will on other crucial actors without giving them a meaningful seat at the table'. Similarly, Donald Kettl (2002, 161) says:

> to rule effectively, government must first attain and then exercise sovereignty. It must be able to chart its course and ensure that that course is followed. Hyperpluralism, policy networks, devolution, and globalization have all greatly diffused power. Government might retain its legal position, but exercising political sovereignty amidst such diffused power represents a major challenge.

One way of analysing these arguments about the power of governments is in terms of a long-standing debate within political science about the 'faces', or dimensions, of power (see Hay, 2002, 171–82). Power is most obviously manifested when one actor can force another actor to behave in a certain way. Writing about the distribution of power in the United States, Robert Dahl (1957; 1961) offered an 'intuitive' definition of power in which 'A has power over B to the extent that he can get B to do something that B would otherwise not do'. In this case we can observe the exercise of power by looking at who triumphs when actors disagree with each other. This conception of power brings to mind the definition by Theda Skocpol (1985, 9) of state autonomy in Chapter 3 as the ability of government to 'implement official goals, especially over the actual or potential opposition of powerful social groups or in the face of recalcitrant socioeconomic circumstances'.

There is, however, more to power than coercion. As Peter Bachrach and Morton Baratz (1962; 1963) pointed out in a critique of Dahl's argument, a second face of power is manifested in the capacity of some actors to keep issues off policy agendas. A classic example was identified by Matthew Crenson (1971). In the town of Gary, Indiana, the largest local employer, US Steel, succeeded in keeping clean-air laws off the local political agenda despite the obvious health problems being caused by air pollution. There was no obvious political conflict in Gary, no legislative tussles or interest-group marches, and so no behavioural sign of power being exercised. Yet this non-issue, far from demonstrating the absence of dominating power relations, was actually testimony to US Steel's power and the dependence of the city upon the jobs it provided. Here, the exercise of power meant keeping an issue off the agenda. But agenda-setting can also, of course, mean putting issues on the agenda (Kingdon, 1984) and, less obviously, determining the sequence in which options are discussed or voted on (Riker, 1982, 169–92).

Finally, as Steven Lukes (1974) argues, a third face of power is manifested in the capacity of some actors to shape the preferences of others:

> A may exercise power over B by getting him to do what he does not want to do, but he also exercises power over him by influencing, shaping or determining his very wants. Indeed is it not the supreme exercise of power to get another or others to have the desires you want them to have – that is, to secure their compliance by controlling their thoughts and desires?

In challenging the society-centred account of governance, we have argued that governments continue to exercise considerable power. In terms of the first, coercive, face of power, governments in nation-states continue to possess legal sovereignty and a monopoly on the legitimate use of violence, and this underpins the exercise of hierarchical authority. Governments are not simply one actor within 'pluricentric' networks (Sorensen & Torfing, 2008a, 3). Governments do not simply operate within exogenously given sets of governance rules. They also have authority, not possessed by any other actor, to choose the governance rules and, as we explained in our discussion of metagovernance, act as a court of appeal for disputes between other actors. Chapter 4 makes the case that, far from fading into obscurity, hierarchical, top-down governance is resurgent. Governments can nationalise failing banks, suspend share trading, ban certain food products, introduce traffic congestion charges, detain suspected terrorists and ban the export of basic foodstuffs. Through their capacity to introduce taxes or subsidies, governments can raise or lower the costs of a wide range of activities.

Governments also retain considerable powers to set agendas. By exploiting their marketing expertise and resources, as well as their democratic legitimacy, governments identify policy problems, frame debates and advance policy solutions. In recent years Western governments have identified weapons of mass destruction, energy dependence and the costs of an ageing population as items for the policy agenda, thus preparing the ground for the eventual invasion of Iraq, decisions on the future of nuclear power, and pension reform. Of course governments do not have a monopoly on setting agendas. The media, think-tanks, political parties, international organisations, private firms, community organisations and interest-groups can all bring forward topics for agendas in the policy process (Majone, 2006). In recent years the campaign group Landmine Action, having inspired public debate about the use of landmines, has been instrumental in persuading governments to sign a moratorium on the production, stockpiling, use or export of cluster bombs. Oxfam and War on Want have primed public opinion about debt relief (Busby, 2007) and, more recently, raised concerns about the link between the use of biofuels and world food prices.

But governments can also exert control by setting agendas *within* governance relationships. In the case of governance through community engagement, governments can decide which issues to consult a community about, how to structure consultation processes and how to set the boundaries of the community to be consulted. Governments can decide whether to promise a referendum on the results of any consultation or simply promise to take note of views expressed. In the case of associative governance relationships, governments can use their central location in networks to set the objectives of any partnership arrangement, the issues to be decided, the way in which those issues are framed, the sequence in which issues are to be addressed, and the procedures to be followed in the case of any disagreement. Chapter 8 showed the European Union exploiting its agenda-setting powers to steer outcomes achieved through the Open Method of Coordination and the Mexican government securing support for the North American Free Trade Agreement by requiring businesses to express in-principle support for a treaty before being able to negotiate concessions within it. The lesson is that governments do not always need to 'enforce their will' (Salamon, 2002, 1–2) in order to achieve their goals.

Finally, as emphasised in Chapter 5, governments retain a considerable power to shape people's preferences. Where it would be too economically or politically costly to impose policies, governments can exploit their legitimacy and marketing budgets to persuade people to change their behaviour to protect either their own long-term interests or, in the case of collective goods, those of the society in which they live. Governments are not the only actors who can govern through persuasion, but their capacity to combine persuasion with the exercise of hierarchical authority gives them a great advantage over non-state actors. Of course, governance through persuasion is not always successful. After the failure of a campaign to persuade shoppers to use fewer plastic bags, the Irish government was forced to introduce a tax, levied at the point of sale, upon consumers. Yet particularly in societies with high levels of social capital, persuasion can prove a surprisingly effective governance strategy. Richard Thaler and Cass Sunstein (2008, 60–1) describe how a Texan television campaign in which local football players collected litter, smashed beer cans in their bare hands, and growled 'don't mess with Texas' was credited with achieving a 72 per cent reduction over six years in roadside littering. In our own city of Brisbane, Australia, which is suffering the effects of years of drought, a long-standing campaign to persuade people to use less water has been combined with threats to fine or reduce water pressure to households using more than 800 litres of water a day; there has been a 30 per cent fall in average household water consumption.

Power is a useful concept with which to analyse the limitations of the society-centred account of governance. As Michael Lister and David Marsh (2006, 255) argue: 'modern governance involves the state in more complex relationships with other governmental and societal actors, but it doesn't inevitably reduce its role or power'. Yet in talking about the faces of power there is a danger of adopting a zero-sum conception in which the power of governments is equated with the (relative) powerlessness of interest-groups, businesses and other non-state actors. In our view power is 'conditional and relational', and therefore an adequate theory of the state can only be produced as part of a 'wider theory of society' (Jessop, 2001). As governments have experimented with a range of governance arrangements, the boundaries between the state and society have blurred (McLennan, 1989; Cammock, 1989; Mitchell, 1991). This blurring does not mean that governments have forfeited the 'ability to steer society' (Jordan, Wurzel & Zito, 2005, 480). Indeed a new wave of statist theorists – whose work we reviewed in Chapter 3 – have emphasised that governing capacity is a product *both* of the state's institutional and other resources, and of the *relations* it constructs with non-state actors. 'Embedded' states (Evans, 1992; 1995) are not undermined by close links with powerful economic actors, but rely on them. On this revisionist account, the 'strong state is one with the political support to be strong' (Gourevitch, 1986, 238). As Cathie Jo Martin (1989, 191) suggests, this revised and relational statist theory suggests the need for rethinking Theda Skocpol's definition of autonomy, 'since in this view state elites achieve their agendas by working with private-sector groups rather than by insulating themselves from them. The autonomy question as traditionally posed allows for neither mutuality of interests nor reciprocity of influence.' This theme of expanding governance capacities through partnerships is endorsed by John Braithwaite (2008, 26) when he writes that the 'state's capacity to govern is actually extended by capacities to enlist through negotiation the governance capacities of other actors'.

These revisionist statist approaches resonate with the state-centric relational approach to governance developed in this book. Governance through markets, associations, community engagement and, potentially at least, persuasion, requires governments to enter into exchange relationships with non-state actors. But governance has not replaced government. This is partly because, as we demonstrated in Chapter 5, the total amount of governance has risen. Governance through markets, associations and community engagement has increased, but so too has governance through hierarchy. It is also because governments have *enhanced* their capacity to achieve their goals by developing closer governance relationships with non-state actors. Finally, governance has not replaced government because governments are not simply actors in governance relationships. They also metagovern those arrangements by overseeing, steering and coordinating them; selecting and supporting the key participants; mobilising resources; ensuring that wider systems of governance are operating fairly and efficiently; and taking prime carriage of democracy and accountability issues. This is why existing accounts which encourage us to think about a spectrum of possible governance arrangements running from society-centred to state-centred are flawed. By seeing government as one point on a governance continuum, we lose sight of the integral role governments play in *all* governance relationships and the strength that governments potentially derive from their relationships with non-state actors.

Precisely because it has become all-pervasive, the term governance attracts suspicion. As Guy Peters (2000, 35) observes, 'the real danger is that governance becomes meaningless and a tautology; something happened and therefore governance occurred'. It is true that governance has been defined in many different ways. But this is true of just about any interesting concept in the social sciences – including, of course, terms like democracy, power and justice. In this book we have defined governance as the tools, strategies and relationships used by governments to help govern, and identified a number of different modes of governance. Our state-centric relational approach offers a useful way of understanding the contemporary importance of the state, the adaptations of the state in the face of new policy challenges, and the ways in which states across the world are attempting to enhance their governing capacities.

Notes

5 GOVERNANCE THROUGH PERSUASION

1 The World Values Survey – cited in Table 2.3 – asks respondents how much confidence they have in major companies as well as in governments and public servants. People in the United States, Japan and South Africa have more confidence in major companies than in government. In the United States 53% of respondents had either 'a great deal' or 'quite a lot' of confidence in major companies and only 37% the same level of confidence in government in 1999. Yet people in most OECD countries trust government more than companies. The most striking result is for Iceland, where 70% have confidence in the government but only 39% have confidence in major companies. At the time of writing it is unclear how the implosion of the Icelandic economy caused by the global credit crisis will affect trust. The Icelandic prime minister's reported comments that 'there will always be fish' seem unlikely to inspire confidence.

2 On 19 February 2001 a vet working at an abattoir in Essex reported a suspected case of foot-and-mouth disease to the State Veterinary Service, which rolled out contingency plans requiring the slaughter of animals on infected farms, a ban on all animal movements near infected farms, and the tracing of 'dangerous contacts'. Over the next 221 days more than 2000 animals contracted the disease in the United Kingdom, and over four million were slaughtered to limit its spread. As the crisis developed, the central argument became whether the policy of slaughter should be abandoned in favour of preventive vaccination.

3 In his most recent work Putnam has detected signs of a dramatic turnaround in American social attitudes. Research indicates that the generation of Americans currently in their teens and twenties – whose attitudes, it is suggested, may have been most affected by 9/11 – will be the most engaged citizens for over 60 years. The evidence is that electoral participation among this group is increasing and that college students are more interested in talking about and taking part in politics (*Economist*, 10 July 2008).

6 GOVERNANCE THROUGH MARKETS AND CONTRACTS

1 In the case of privatisation see Megginson & Netter, 2001; Kikeri, Nells & Shirley, 1992; and OECD, 2005a. Assessments of the savings accrued through contracting-out can be found in Mueller, 2003, 373–80; Miranda & Lerner, 1995; and Lavery, 1999.

Debates on the performance of public–private partnerships can be found in English, 2005; Akintoye, Beck & Hardcastle, 2003; and Freeman, 2003. For an introduction to writing on the economic consequences of globalisation see Brady, Beckfield & Zhao, 2007; Stiglitz, 2002; and, for developing countries, Wade, 2005.

2 States have not always succeeded in suppressing illegal markets. At a recent World Health Organization conference, one participant reported that in some remote Pakistani villages up to half of the residents had sold one kidney at a going rate of around $2500 (*USA Today*, 30 March 2007).

7 GOVERNANCE THROUGH COMMUNITY ENGAGEMENT

1 Participation in Athenian democracy was in other respects limited. As well as women, slaves and those lacking in property were excluded from the democratic process.

8 GOVERNANCE THROUGH ASSOCIATIONS

1 ISO is not an acronym. Because the acronym for 'International Organisation for Standardisation' would vary in different languages, its founders chose ISO, derived from the Greek *isos*, meaning 'equal'.

Bibliography

Abel, T. D. and Stephan, M. (2000), 'The Limits of Civic Environmentalism', *American Behavioural Scientist*, 44, 614–28.

Acevedo, B. and Common, R. (2006), 'Governance and the Management of Networks in the Public Sector', *Public Management Review*, 8, 395–414.

Akintoye, A., Beck, M., and Hardcastle, C. (2003), *Public–Private Partnerships: Managing Risks and Opportunities* (Oxford: Blackwell).

Alesina, A. and Perotti, R. (1996), 'Fiscal Adjustments in OECD Countries – Composition and Macroeconomic Effects', *IMF Working Papers*, 96/70 (Washington, DC: IMF).

Alesina, A. and Summers, L. (1993), 'Central Bank Independence and Macroeconomic Performance: Some Comparative Evidence', *Journal of Money, Credit and Banking*, 25, 151–62.

Allswang, J. (2000), *The Initiative and Referendum in California, 1898–1998* (Stanford University Press).

Alvesson, M. and Sveningsson, S. (2008), *Organizational Culture: Cultural Change Work in Progress* (London: Routledge).

Amin, A. and Hausner, J. (eds) (1997), *Beyond Market and Hierarchy: Interactive Governance and Social Complexity* (Cheltenham: Edward Elgar).

Amin, A. and Thomas, D. (1996), 'The Negotiated Economy: State and Civic Institutions in Denmark', *Economy and Society*, 25, 255–81.

Andersen, H. (2004), 'Governance and Regime Politics in Copenhagen', Eurez Lecture 16 (University of Copenhagen, Department of Geography).

Anderson, K. and Winters, A. (2008), *The Challenge of Reducing International Trade and Migration Barriers* (Copenhagen: Consensus Project).

Arnstein, S. (1969), 'A Ladder of Participation', *Journal of the American Institute of Planners*, 35, 216–24.

Arnull, A. and Wincott, D. (2003), *Accountability and Legitimacy in the European Union* (Oxford University Press).

Arrow, K. and Debreu, G. (1954), 'Existence of an Equilibrium for a Competitive Economy', *Econometrica*, 22, 265–90.

Atkinson, M. and Coleman, W. (1989), 'Strong States and Weak States: Sectoral Policy Networks in Advanced Capitalist Economies', *British Journal of Political Science*, 19, 47–67.

Australian National Audit Office (2003), *Management of the Detention Centre Contracts* (Canberra: Commonwealth of Australia).

Avant, D. (2005), *The Market for Force: Private Security and Political Change* (Washington: George Washington University).

Ayres, I. and Braithwaite, J. (1992), *Responsive Regulation* (Oxford University Press).

Bache, I. (2000), 'Government Within Governance: Steering Economic Regeneration Policy Networks in Yorkshire and Humberside', *Public Administration*, 78, 575–92.

—— (2003), 'Governing Through Governance: Education Policy Control under New Labour', *Political Studies*, 51, 300–14.

—— and Flinders, M. (eds) (2005), *Multi-Level Governance* (Oxford University Press).

Bachrach, P. and Baratz, M. (1962), 'The Two Faces of Power', *American Political Science Review*, 56, 941–52.

—— (1963), 'Decisions and Non-decisions: An Analytical Framework', *American Political Science Review*, 57, 641–51.

Baker, W. (1984), 'The Social Structure of a National Securities Market', *American Journal of Sociology*, 89, 775–811.

Baldwin, R. (2004), 'The New Punitive Regulation', *Modern Law Review*, 67, 351–83.

Barber, B. (1984), *Strong Democracy: Participatory Politics for a New Age* (Berkeley: University of California Press).

Barlett, W. and Le Grand, J. (1993), *Quasi-Markets and Social Policy* (Basingstoke: Palgrave).

Barrados, M., Mayne, J. and Wileman, T. (2000), 'Accountability for Collective Programme Delivery Arrangements in Canada's Federal Government: Some Consequences of Sharing the Business of Government', *International Review of Administrative Sciences*, 66, 495–551.

Barroso, M. (2008), 'Globalization and Europe: Prospering in the New Whirled Order. Address to the American Chamber of Commerce to the European Union', Brussels, 28 February 2008.

Barry, B. (1989), 'Is it Better to be Powerful than Lucky?', in B. Barry, *Democracy, Power and Justice: Essays in Political Theory* (Oxford: Clarendon Press).

—— and Hardin, R. (eds) (1982), *Rational Man and Irrational Society?* (London: Sage).

Bartle, I. and Vass, P. (2007), 'Self-Regulation within the Regulatory State: Towards a New Regulatory Paradigm', *Public Administration*, 85, 885–905.

Bartley, T. (2003), 'Certifying Forests and Factories: State, Social Movements and the Rise of Private Regulation in the Apparel and Forest Products Fields', *Politics and Society*, 31, 453–64.

Bartos, S. (2006), *Against the Grain: The AWB Scandal and Why it Happened* (Sydney: UNSW Press).

Basinger, S. and Hallerberg, M. (2004), 'Re-modeling the Competition for Capital: How Domestic Politics Erases the Race to the Bottom', *American Political Science Review*, 98, 261–76.

Beck, U. (1992), *Risk Society: Towards a New Modernity* (London: Sage).

Beeson, M. and Bell, S. (2009), 'The G20 and International Economic Governance: Hegemony, Collectivism or Both?', *Global Governance*, 15, 67–86.

Bell, S. (1989), 'State Strength and Capitalist Weakness: Manufacturing Capital and the Tariff Board's Attack on McEwenism', *Australian Journal of Political Science*, 24, 23–38.

—— (1995), 'Between the Market and the State: The Role of Business Associations in Public Policy: Evidence from Australia', *Comparative Politics*, 28, 25–53.

—— (1997), *Ungoverning the Economy* (Oxford University Press).

—— (2002), 'The Limits of Rational Choice: New Institutionalism in the Test Bed of Central Banking Politics in Australia', *Political Studies*, 50, 477–96.

—— (2004a), *Australia's Money Mandarins: The Reserve Bank and the Politics of Money* (Cambridge University Press).

—— (2004b), 'Appropriate Policy Knowledge and Institutional and Governance Implications', *Australian Journal of Public Administration*, 63, 22–30.

—— (2005), 'How Tight Are the Policy Constraints? The Policy Convergence Thesis, Institutionally Situated Actors and Expansionary Monetary Policy in Australia', *New Political Economy*, 10, 67–92.

—— (2008a), 'A Victim of its Own Success: Internationalization, Neo-liberalism and Organisational Involution at the Business Council of Australia', *Politics and Society*, 34, 543–70.

—— (2008b), 'The Limits of Statism: Explaining Business Collective Action at the Business Council of Australia', *Polity*, 40, 464–87.

—— and Park, A. (2006), 'The Problematic Metagovernance of Networks: Water Reform in New South Wales', *Journal of Public Policy*, 26, 63–83.

Bell, S. and Quiggin, J. (2008), 'The Limits of Markets and the Politics of Water Management in Rural Australia', *Environmental Politics* (forthcoming).

Bell, S. and Wanna, J. (1992), *Business-Government Relations in Australia* (Sydney: Harcourt Brace Jovanovich Group).

Bellamy, R. and Castiglione, D. (1997), 'Constitutionalism and Democracy – Political Theory and the American Constitution', *British Journal of Political Science*, 27, 595–618.

Bemelmans-Videc, M., Rist, R. and Vedung, E. (eds) (1998), *Carrots, Sticks and Sermons: Policy Instruments and their Evaluation* (New Brunswick: Transaction Publishers).

Benyon, J. and Edwards, A. (1999), 'Community Governance of Crime Control', in G. Stoker (ed.), *The New Management of British Local Governance* (London: Macmillan).

Berg, C. (2008), *The Growth of Australia's Regulatory State: Ideology, Accountability and the Mega-Regulators* (Melbourne: Institute of Public Affairs).

Berger, S. and Dore, R. (eds) (1996), *National Diversity and Global Capitalism* (Ithaca: Cornell University Press).

Berk, G. and Schneiberg, M. (2005), 'Varieties *in* Capitalism, Varieties *of* Association: Collaborative Learning in American Industry, 1900–1925', *Politics and Society*, 33, 46–87.

Bernstein, S. (2005), 'Legitimacy in Global Environmental Governance', *Journal of International Law and International Relations*, 1, 39–66.

Bernstein, W. (2008), *A Splendid Exchange: How Trade Shaped the World* (New York: Atlantic Monthly Press).

Besson, S. and Marti, J. (eds) (2006), *Deliberative Democracy and its Discontents* (Cheltenham: Ashgate).

Bevir, M. (2002), 'A Decentered Theory of Governance', in H. Bang (ed.), *Governance, Governmentality, and Community* (Manchester University Press).

—— (ed.) (2007), *Public Governance: Volume 1* (London: Sage).

—— and Rhodes, R. (2003), *Interpreting British Governance* (Basingstoke: Routledge).

—— and —— (2006), 'Interpretive Approaches to British Government and Politics', *British Politics*, 1, 84–112.

Bevir, M. and Rhodes, R. A. W. (2008), 'Decentred Theory, Change and Network Governance', in E. Sorensen and J. Torfing. (eds), *Theories of Democratic Network Governance* (London: Palgrave).

Birch, A. (1984), 'Overload, Ungovernability and Delegitimation: The Theories and the British Case', *British Journal of Political Science*, 14, 136–56.

Bishop, P. and Davis, G. (2002), 'Mapping Public Participation in Policy Choices', *Australian Journal of Public Administration*, 6, 14–29.

Blair, T. (2006), 'The Future of Europe', speech, 2 February 2006, http://www.number-10.gov.uk/output/Page9003.asp

Blinder, A. (1996), 'Central Banking in a Democracy: Federal Reserve Bank of Richmond', *Economic Quarterly*, 82, 1–14.

Block, F. (1980), 'Beyond Relative Autonomy: State Managers as Historical Subjects', in R. Miliband and J. Saville (eds), *The Socialist Register* (London: Merlin Press).

Blok, A. (2007), 'Experts on Public Trial: On Democratizing Expertise Through a Danish Consensus Conference', *Public Understanding of Science*, 16, 163–82.

Bloomfield, P. (2006), 'The Challenging Business of Long-Term Public–Private Partnerships: Reflections on Local Experience', *Public Administration Review*, 66, 400–11.

Blyth, M. (2002), *Great Transformations: Economic Ideas and Institutional Change in the Twentieth Century* (Cambridge University Press).

Borkley, P. and Leveque, F. (1998), *Voluntary Approaches for Environmental Protection in the European Union* (Paris: OECD).

Borzel, T. (1999), 'Towards Convergence in Europe? Institutional Adaptation to Europeanization in Germany and Spain', *Journal of Common Market Studies*, 37, 573–96.

Borzel, T. A. and Panke, D. (2008), 'Network Governance: Effective and Legitimate?', in E. Sorensen and J.Torfing (eds), *Theories of Democratic Network Governance* (London: Palgrave).

Botterill, L. (2005), 'Policy Change and Network Termination: The Role of Farm Groups in Agricultural Policy Making', *Australian Journal of Political Science* 40, 207–219.

Bottomore, T. (1989), 'Max Weber and the Capitalist State', in G. Duncan (ed.), *Democracy and the Capitalist State* (Cambridge University Press).

Bovens, M. and Hart, P. (1996), *Understanding Policy Fiascos* (London: Transaction).

Bowden, M. (2001), *Killing Pablo: The Hunt for the World's Greatest Outlaw* (New York: Simon & Schuster)

Boxelaar, I., Paine, M. and Beilin, R. (2006), 'Community Engagement and Public Administration: Of Silos, Overlays and Technologies of Government', *Australian Journal of Public Administration*, 65, 113–26.

Boyne, G. (2000), 'External Regulation and Best Value in Local Government', *Public Money and Management*, 20, 7–12.

Bradford, N. (1998), 'Prospects for Associative Governance: Lessons from Ontario, Canada', *Politics and Society*, 26, 539–73.

Brady, D., Beckfield. J. and Seeleib-Kaiser, M. (2005), 'Economic Globalisation and the Welfare State in Affluent Democracies: 1975–2001', *American Sociological Review*, 70, 921–48.

Brady, D., Beckfield, J. and Zhao, W. (2007), 'The Consequences of Economic Globalization for Affluent Democracies', *Annual Review of Sociology*, 33, 313–34.

Braithwaite, J. (2008), *Regulatory Capitalism: How it Works, Ideas for Making It Work Better* (Cheltenham: Edward Elgar).

—— and Drahos, P. (2000), *Global Business Regulation* (Cambridge University Press).

Brewer, G. and DeLeon, P. (1983), *The Foundations of Policy Analysis* (Pacific Grove: Brooks).

Brewer, G., Selden, S. and Facer, R. (2000), 'Individual Conceptions of Public Service Motivation', *Public Administration Review*, 60, 254–64.

Brittan, S. (1975), 'The Economic Contradictions of Democracy', *British Journal of Political Science*, 5, 129–59.

Brown, T. and Potoski, M. (2004), 'Managing the Public Service Market', *Public Administration Review*, 64, 656–68.

Bruner, C. and Abdelal, R. (2005), 'To Judge Leviathan: Sovereign Credit Ratings, National Law, and the World Economy', *Journal of Public Policy*, 25, 191–217.

Bruun, J. (2005), 'Citizen Projects and Consensus Building at the Danish Board of Technology: On Experiments in Democracy', *Acta Sociologia*, 48, 221–35.

Buchanan, J. (1997), 'The Balanced Budget Amendment: Clarifying the Arguments', *Public Choice*, 90, 117–38.

—— (1999), 'Politics without Romance', in *The Collected Works of James Buchanan*, vol. 1: *The Logical Foundations of Constitutional Liberty* (Indianapolis: Liberty Fund).

—— and Wagner, R. (1977), *The Consequences of Mr Keynes* (London: IEA).

Budd, L. and Harris, L. (2008), *E-Governance: Managing or Governing?* (London: Routledge).

Bull, H. (1977), *The Anarchical Society: A Study of Order in World Politics* (Basingstoke: Macmillan).

Burney, E. (2005), *Making People Behave: Anti-Social Behaviour, Politics and Policy* (Devon: Willan Publishing)

Burns, J. and Sorenson, G. (1999), *Dead Centre: Clinton–Gore Leadership and the Perils of Moderation* (New York: Scribner).

Busby, J. (2007), 'Bono Made Jesse Helms Cry: Jubilee 2000, Debt Relief, and Moral Action in International Politics', *International Studies Quarterly*, 51, 247–75.

Business Council of Australia (1999), *Avoiding Boom/Bust: Macroeconomic Reform for a Globalised Economy* (Melbourne: BCA).

Butler, D., Adonis, A. and Travers, T. (2004), *Failure in British Government: The Politics of the Poll Tax* (Oxford University Press).

Caldart, C. C. and Ashford, N. A. (1999), 'Negotiation as a Means of Developing and Implementing Environmental and Occupational Health and Safety Policy', *Harvard Environmental Law Review*, 23, 141–202.

Callaghan, G. and Wistow, G. (2006), 'Publics, Patients, Citizens, Consumers? Power and Decision Making in Primary Health Care', *Public Administration*, 84, 583–601.

Cammock, P. (1989), 'Bringing the State Back In', *British Journal of Political Science*, 19, 261–90.

Campbell, J. (2004), *Institutional Change and Globalization* (Princeton University Press).

Caplan, B. (2007), *The Myth of the Rational Voter: Why Democracies Choose Bad Policies* (Princeton University Press).

Capoccia, G. (2002), 'Anti-system Parties: A Conceptual Reassessment', *Journal of Theoretical Politics*, 14, 9–35.

Cashore, B. (2002), 'Legitimacy and the Privatisation of Environmental Governance: How Non-State Market Driven (NSMD) Governance Systems Gain Rule Making Authority', *Governance*, 15, 503–29.

Castells, M. (1996), *The Rise of the Network Society* (Oxford: Blackwell).

Castles, F. (2004), *The Future of the Welfare State* (Oxford University Press).

—— (ed.) (2007), *The Disappearing State? Retrenchment Realities in an Age of Globalisation* (Cheltenham: Edward Elgar).

Cawson, A. (1986), *Corporatism and Political Theory* (Oxford: Blackwell).

Cerny, P. (1995), 'Globalisation and the Logic of Collective Action', *International Organisation*, 49, 595–625.

Chambers, S. (2001), 'Constitutional Referenda and Democratic Deliberation', in M. Mendelsohn and A. Parkin (eds), *Referendum Democracy* (London: Palgrave).

Cherry, J. (2005), 'Big Deal or Big Disappointment?: The Continuing Evolution of the South Korean Developmental State', *Pacific Review*, 18, 327–54.

Chhotray, V. and Stoker, G. (2009), *Governance Theory: A Cross-Disciplinary Approach* (Basingstoke: Palgrave Macmillan).

Christiano, T. (2004), 'Is Normative Rational Choice Theory Self-Defeating?', *Ethics*, 115, 122–41.

Christou, G. and Simpson, S. (2006), 'The Internet and Public–Private Governance in the European Union', *Journal of Public Policy*, 26, 43–61.

Cini, M. (2003), *European Union Politics* (Oxford University Press).

Cioffi, J. (2006), 'Building Finance Capitalism: The Regulatory Politics of Corporate Governance Reform in the United States and Germany', in J. Levy (ed.), *The State after Statism* (Cambridge, Mass: Harvard University Press).

Clegg, D. and Clasen, J. (2007), 'Levels and Levers of Conditionality: Measuring Change within Welfare States', in J. Clasen and N. Siegel (eds), *Investigating Welfare State Change* (Cheltenham: Edward Elgar).

Coen, D. (1997), 'The Evolution of the Large Firm as a Political Actor in the European Union', *Journal of European Public Policy*, 4, 91–108.

—— and Thatcher, M. (2005), 'The New Governance of Markets and Non-Majoritarian Regulators', *Governance*, 18, 329–346.

Cole, D. H. and Grossman, P. Z. (1999), 'When is Command and Control Efficient? Institutions, Technology, and the Comparative advantage of Alternative Regulatory Regimes for Environmental Protection', *Wisconsin Law Review*, 887–938.

Collins, J., Thomas, G., Willis, R. and Wilsdon, J. (2003), *Carrots, Sticks and Sermons: Influencing Public Behaviour for Environmental Goals* (London: Demos).

Connell, D. (2007), *Water Politics in the Murray–Darling Basin* (Sydney: Federation Press).

Conroy, M. (2007), *Branded! How the 'Certification Revolution' is Transforming Global Corporations* (Galbriola Island: New Society).

Considine, M. (2003), 'Governance and Competition: The Role of Non-profit Organisations in the Delivery of Public Services', *Australian Journal of Political Science*, 38, 63–77.

——— and Lewis, J. (2003), 'Bureaucracy, Network, or Enterprise? Comparing Models of Governance in Australia, Britain, the Netherlands, and New Zealand', *Public Administration Review*, 63, 131–40.

Conway, P. and Nicoletti, G. (2006), 'Product Market Regulation in the Non-Manufacturing Sectors of OECD Countries: Measurement and Highlights', Economics Department Working Papers No. 530 (Paris: OECD).

Cowhey, P. and Richards, J. (2006), 'Building Global Service Markets: Economic Structure and State Capacity', in J. Levy (ed.), *The State After Statism: New State Activities in the Age of Liberalisation* (Cambridge, Mass.: Harvard University Press).

Craig, A. and Vanclay, F. (2005), 'Questioning the Potential of Deliberativeness to Achieve "Acceptable" Natural Resource Management Decisions', in R. Eversole and J. Martin (eds), *Participation and Governance in Regional Development* (London: Ashgate).

Craig, C. and McCann, J. (1978), 'Assessing Communication Effects on Energy Conservation', *Journal of Consumer Research*, 5, 82–8.

Crawford, A. (2006), 'Networked Governance and the Post-Regulatory State?', *Theoretical Criminology*, 10, 449–79.

Crenson, M. (1971), *The Un-politics of Air Pollution: A Study of Non-Decision Making in the Cities* (Baltimore: Johns Hopkins University Press).

Crouch, C. and Dore, R. (1990), *Corporatism and Accountability: the Role of Organized Interests in British Public Life* (Oxford University Press).

Crozier, M., Huntington, S. P. and Watanuki, J. (eds) (1975), *The Crisis of Democracy* (New York University Press).

Culpepper, P. D. (2001), 'Employers, Public Policy and the Politics of Decentralised Cooperation in Germany and France', in P. A. Hall and D. Soskice (eds), *Varieties of Capitalism: The Institutional Foundations of Comparative Advantage* (Oxford University Press).

Cunningham, N. and Grabosky, P. (1998), *Smart Regulation, Designing Environmental Policy* (Oxford: Clarendon Press).

Cunningham, N. and Rees, J. (1997), 'Industry Self regulation: An Institutional Perspective', *Law and Policy*, 19, 363–414.

Curtis, A. and Lockwood, M. (2000), 'Landcare and Catchment Management in Australia: Lessons for State-Sponsored Community Participation', *Society and Natural Resources*, 13, 61–73.

Cutler, C. A. (2002), 'Private International Regimes and Inter-firm Cooperation', in R. B. Hall and T. J. Biersteker (eds), *The Emergence of Private Authority in Global Governance* (Cambridge University Press).

Cutler, C. (2006), 'Transnational Business Civilization, Corporations, and the Privatization of Global Governance', in C. May. (ed.), *Global Corporate Power* (Boulder: Lynne Rienner).

——— Haufler, V. and Porter, T. (eds) (1999), *Private Authority in International Politics* (New York: SUNY Press).

Dahl, R. (1956), *A Preface to Democratic Theory* (University of Chicago Press).

——— (1957), 'The Concept of Power', *Behavioural Science*, 2, 201–15.

——— (1961), *Who Governs? Democracy and Power in an American City* (New Haven: Yale University Press).

——— (1974), *Polyarchy: Participation and Opposition* (New Haven: Yale University Press).

Damgaard, B. (2006), 'Do Policy Networks Lead to Network Governance?', *Public Administration*, 84, 673–91.

Danziger, R. (1997), 'HIV Prevention in Hungary', *Health Policy*, 40, 231–6.

Darnall, N. and Carmin, J. (2005), 'Greener and Cleaner? The Signalling Accuracy of U.S. Voluntary Environmental Programs', *Policy Sciences*, 38, 71–90.

Davies, J. S. (2000), 'The Hollowing-Out of Local Democracy and the "Fatal Conceit" of Governing Without Government', *British Journal of Politics and International Relations*, 2, 414–28.

Davis, G. and Rhodes, R. A. W. (2000), 'From Hierarchy to Contracts and Back Again: Reforming the Australian Public Service', in M. Keating, J. Wanna and P. Weller (eds), *Institutions on the Edge* (Sydney: Allen & Unwin).

Deacon, D. and Golding, P. (1994), *Taxation and Representation: The Media, Political Communication and the Poll Tax* (London: John Libbey).

De Bruijn, H. and Dicke, W. (2006), 'Strategies for Safeguarding Public Values in Liberalized Utility Sectors', *Public Administration*, 84, 717–35.

De Hart, J. and Dekker, P. (1999), 'Civic Engagement and Volunteering in the Netherlands', in J. Van Deth, K. Mraffi, K. Newton and P. Whiteley (eds), *Social Capital and European Democracy* (London: Routledge).

DeLeon, P. (1999), 'The Missing Link Revisited: Contemporary Implementation Research', *Policy Studies Review*, 16, 31–8.

DELG (Department of the Environment and Local Government) (2002), *Plastic Bag Environmental Levy* <http://www.mindfully.org/Plastic/Laws/Plastic-Bag-Levy-Ireland4mar02.htm>.

Della Porta, D. (2001), 'A Judges' Revolution? Political Corruption and the Judiciary in Italy', *European Journal of Political Research*, 39, 1–21.

Delmas, M. and Keller, A. (2005), 'Free Riding in Voluntary Environmental Programs: The Case of the U.S. EPA WasteWise Program', *Policy Sciences*, 38, 91–106.

Dika, S. and Singh, L. (2002), 'Applications of Social Capital in Educational Literature: A Critical Synthesis', *Review of Educational Studies*, 72, 31–60.

Dolsak, N. and Ostrom, E. (eds) (2003), *The Commons in the New Millenium: Challenges and Adaptation* (Cambridge, Mass.: MIT Press).

Doner, F. D. and Schneider, B. R. (2000), 'Business Associations and Economic Development: Why Some Associations Contribute More than Others', *Business and Politics*, 2, 261–88.

Dover, B. (2008), *Rupert's Adventures in China: How Murdoch Lost a Fortune and Found a Wife* (New York: Random House).

Dowding, K. (1995), 'Model or Metaphor? A Critical Review of the Policy Network Approach', *Political Studies*, 43, 136–58.

Doyle, T. (2000), *Green Power: The Environmental Movement in Australia* (Sydney: UNSW Press).

Drezner, D. (2007), *All Politics is Global: Explaining International Regulatory Regimes* (Princeton University Press).

Dryzek, J. (2000), *Deliberative Democracy and Beyond* (Oxford University Press).

—— (2001), 'Legitimacy and Economy in Deliberative Democracy', *Political Theory*, 29, 651–99.

Dunleavy, P., Margetts, H., Bastow, S., and Tinkler, J. (2006), *Digital Era Governance: IT Corporations, the State and E-Government* (Oxford University Press).

Duram, L. A. and Brown, K. G. (1998), 'Assessing Public Participation in US Watershed Planning Initiatives', *Society and Natural Resources*, 12, 455–67.

Dyson, K. (1980), *The State Tradition in Western Europe* (Oxford University Press).

Eberlein, B. and Kerwer, D. (2004), 'New Governance in the European Union: A Theoretical Perspective', *Journal of Common Market Studies*, 42, 121–42.

Edelenbos, J. (2005), 'Institutional Implications of Interactive Governance: Insight from Dutch Practice', *Governance*, 18, 111–34.

Elgie, R. (2006), 'Why Do Governments Delegate Authority to Quasi-Autonomous Agencies? The Case of Independent Administrative Agencies in France', *Governance*, 19, 207–27.

Elster, J. (1979), *Ulysses and the Sirens: Studies in Rationality and Irrationality* (Cambridge University Press).

—— (1983), *Sour Grapes: Studies in the Subversion of Rationality* (Cambridge University Press).

—— (1989), *Solomonic Judgments: Studies in the Limits of Rationality* (Cambridge University Press).

—— (1998), 'Deliberation and Constitution Making', in J. Elster (ed.), *Deliberative Democracy* (Cambridge University Press).

English, L. (2005), 'Using Public–Private Partnerships to Achieve Value for Money in the Delivery of Healthcare in Australia', *International Journal of Public Policy*, 1, 91–121.

Epstein, P. (1997), 'Beyond Policy Community: French Agriculture and the GATT', *Journal of European Public Policy*, 4, 355–72.

Etzioni, A. (1995), *The Spirit of Community: Rights, Responsibilities and the Communitarian Agenda* (London: Fontana).

European Parliament (2002), *Foot and Mouth Disease: 2001 Crisis* <http://www.europarl.europa.eu/omk/omnsapir.so>.

Evans, P. (1992), 'The State as Problem and Solution: Predation, Embedded Autonomy and Structural Change', in S. Hoggard and R. Kaufman (eds), *The Politics of Economic Adjustment* (Princeton University Press).

—— (1995), *Embedded Autonomy: States and Industrial Transformation* (Princeton University Press).

—— (1997), 'The Eclipse of the State? Reflections on Stateness in an Era of Globalisation', *World Politics*, 50, 62–87.

—— and Rauch, J. (1999), 'Bureaucracy and Economic Growth', *American Sociological Review*, 64, 748–65.

Fairbrother, M. (2007), 'Making Neo-liberalism Possible: The State's Organization of Business Support for NAFTA in Mexico', *Politics and Society*, 35, 265–300.

Featherstone, K. and Radaelli, C. (eds) (2003), *The Politics of Europeanization* (Oxford University Press).

Feigenbaum, H., Samuels, R. and Weaver, R. (1993), 'Innovation, Coordination, and Implementation in Energy Policy', in R. Weaver and B. Rockman. (eds), *Do Institutions Matter?* (Washington, DC: Brookings Institution).

Finnemore, M. (1996), *National Interests in International Society* (Ithaca: Cornell University Press).

Fischer, F. (2003), *Reframing Public Policy: Discursive Politics and Deliberative Practices* (Oxford University Press).

Fixdal, J. (1997), 'Consensus Conferences as Extended Peer Groups', *Science and Public Policy*, 24, 366–76.

Fligstein, N. (1996), 'Markets as Politics: A Political-Cultural Approach to Market Institutions', *American Sociological Review*, 61, 656–73.

—— (2001), *The Architecture of Markets* (Princeton University Press).

Flinders, M. (2002), 'Governance in Whitehall', *Public Administration*, 80, 51–75.

—— (2004), 'Distributed Public Governance in Britain', *Public Administration*, 82, 883–909.

—— (2006), 'Public/Private: The Boundaries of the State', in C. Hay, M. Lister and D. Marsh (eds), *The State: Theories and Issues* (Basingstoke: Palgrave Macmillan).

Foley, P. and Martin, S. (2000), 'A New Deal for the Community: Public Participation in Regeneration and Local Service Delivery', *Policy and Politics*, 28, 479–91.

Foucault, M. (1979), *Discipline and Punish: The Birth of the Prison* (Harmondsworth: Penguin).

—— (1991), 'Governmentality', in G. Burchell, C. Gordon and P. Miller (eds), *The Foucault Effect* (University of Chicago Press).

Fredericksen, P. and London, R. (2000), 'Disconnect in the Hollow State: The Pivotal Role of Organisational Capacity in Community-Based Development Organisation', *Public Administration Review*, 60, 230–39.

Fredriksson, P. and Millimet, D. (2002), 'Is There a California Effect in US Environmental Policymaking?', *Regional Science and Urban Economics*, 6, 737–64.

Freeman, M. (2003), *Critical Choices: The Debate over Public–Private Partnerships and What it Means for America's Future* (Washington, DC: National Council for Public–Private Partnerships).

Friedman, J. (ed.) (1996), *The Rational Choice Controversy* (New Haven: Yale University Press).

Friedman, T. L. (1999), *The Lexus and the Olive Tree* (New York: Straus & Giroux).

Fung, A. (2002), 'Making Social Markets: Dispersed Governance and Corporate Account-ability', in J. Donahue and J. Nye (eds), *Market-Based Governance* (Washington: Brookings Institution).

—— and Wright, E. O. (2003), *Deepening Democracy: Innovations in Empowered Partici-patory Governance* (London: Verso).

Funk, C. (2000), 'The Dual Influence of Self-Interest and Societal Interest in Public Opinion', *Political Research Quarterly*, 50, 317–42.

Gains, F. (2003), 'Executive Agencies in Government: The Impact of Bureaucratic Networks on Policy Outcomes', *Journal of Public Policy*, 23, 55–79.

Gale, F. (2008), 'Global Democratic Corporatism: Earth Governance Beyond States', Presentation to the Third Oceania Conference for International Studies (OCIS), University of Queensland, Brisbane, Australia, 2–4 July.

Gambetta, D. (1993), *The Sicilian Mafia: The Business of Private Protection* (Cambridge, Mass.: Harvard University Press).

Gamble, A. (1998), *The Free Economy and the Strong State: The Politics of Thatcherism* (London: Macmillan).

Gandy, O. (1982), *Beyond Agenda Setting: Information Subsidies and Public Policy* (Norwood: Ablex).

Garland, D. (1990), *Punishment and Modern Society: A Study in Social Theory* (Oxford: Clarendon).

Garrett, G. (1998), 'Global Markets and National Politics: Collision Course or Virtuous Circle?', *International Organisation*, 52, 787–824.

Giddens, A. (1998), *The Third Way: The Renewal of Social Democracy* (Cambridge: Polity Press).

Gilardi, F. (2002), 'Policy Credibility and Delegation to Independent Regulatory Agencies: A Comparative Empirical Analysis', *Journal of European Public Policy*, 9, 873–93.

Gill, G. (2003), *The Nature and Development of the Modern State* (Basingstoke: Palgrave).

Gittell, R. and Vidal, A. (1998), *Community Organization: Building Social Capital as a Development Strategy* (Thousand Oaks: Sage).

Glasson, J., Therivel, R. and Chadwick, A. (2005), *Introduction to Environmental Impact Assessment* (London: UCL Press).

Goffman, E. (1968), *Asylums* (Harmondsworth: Penguin).

Goggin, M., Bowman, A., Lester, J., and O'Toole, L. (1990), *Implementation Theory and Practice: Towards a Third Generation* (Glenview: Scott Foresman).

Goodin, B. (ed.) (1996), *The Theory of Institutional Design* (Cambridge University Press).

Goodin, R. (2003), *Reflective Democracy* (Oxford University Press).

Goodin, R. E. and Dryzek, J. (2006), 'Deliberative Impacts: The Macro-Political Uptake of Mini-Publics', *Politics and Society*, 34, 219–44.

Gordon, C. (1998), 'Why No Corporatism in the United States? Business Disorganisation and Its Consequences', *Business and Economic History*, 27, 29–46.

Gourevitch, P. (1986), *Politics in Hard Times* (Ithaca: Cornell University Press).

Gowan, P. (1999), *The Global Gamble* (London: Verso).

—— (2001), 'Explaining the American Boom: The Roles of "Globalisation" and the United States Global Power', *New Political Economy*, 6, 359–74.

Granovetter, M. (1985), 'Economic Action and Social Structure: The Problem of Embeddedness', *American Journal of Sociology*, 91, 481–510.

Green, D. and Shapiro, I. (1994), *Pathologies of Rational Choice Theory* (New Haven: Yale University Press).

Greer, A. (2002), 'Policy Networks and Policy Change in Organic Agriculture: A Comparative Analysis of the UK and Ireland', *Public Administration*, 80, 453–73.

Greve, C. (2004), 'Public Sector Reform in Denmark: Organizational Transformation and Evaluation', *Public Organization Review*, 3, 1573–86.

—— and Jespersen, K. (1999), 'New Public Management and its Critics: Alternative Roads to Flexible Service Delivery to Citizens?', in L. Rouban (ed.), *Citizens and the New Governance, Beyond New Public Management* (Amsterdam: IOS Press).

Grote, J. R. and Schmitter, P. C. (1999), 'The Renaissance of National Corporatism: Unintended Side-Effect of European Economic and Monetary Union or Calculated Response to the Absence of European Social Policy?', *Transfer*, 1, 34–63.

Hajer, M. (1995), *The Politics of Environmental Discourse: Ecological Modernization and the Policy Process* (Oxford University Press).

—— (2003), 'Policy without Polity: Policy Analysis and the Institutional Void', *Policy Sciences*, 36, 175–95.

Hall, P. (1999), 'Social Capital in Britain', *British Journal of Political Science*, 29, 418–61.

—— and Soskice, D. (eds) (2001), *Varieties of Capitalism: The Institutional Foundations of Comparative Advantage* (Oxford University Press).

—— and Taylor, R. (1996), 'Political Science and the Three New Institutionalisms', *Political Studies*, 44, 936–57.

Hall, R. and Biersteker, T. (eds) (2002), *The Emergence of Private Authority in Global Governance* (Cambridge University Press).

Hall, S. (1985), 'Authoritarian Populism: A Reply to Jessop et al.', *New Left Review*, 151, 115–24.

Halpin, D. R. (2006), 'The Participatory and Democratic Potential and Practice of Interest Groups: Between Solidarity and Representation', *Public Administration*, 84: 919–40.

Hampsher-Monk, I. and Hindmoor, A. (2009), 'Rational Choice and Interpretive Evidence: Caught Between a Rock and a Hard Place?' *Political Studies* (forthcoming).

Hampson, I. (1996), 'The Accord: A Post-Mortem', *Labour and Industry*, 7, 55–77.

Hansen, M. (1991), *The Athenian Democracy in the Age of Demosthenes: Structure, Principles and Ideology* (Oxford: Blackwell).

Hardin, G. (1968), 'The Tragedy of the Commons', *Science*, 162, 1243–8.

Hass, P. (1992), 'Epistemic Communities and International Policy Coordination', *International Organisation*, 46, 1–35.

Haufler, V. (2006), 'Global Governance and the Private Sector', in C. May (ed.), *Global Corporate Power* (Boulder: Lynne Rienner).

Hay, C. (2002), *Political Analysis* (London: Palgrave).

—— (2005), 'Globalization's Impact on States', in J. Ravenhill (ed.), *Global Political Economy* (Oxford University Press).

Hayek, F. (1945), *Individualism and Economic Order* (London: Routledge).

—— (1982), *Law, Legislation and Liberty: A New Statement of the Liberal Principles of Justice and Political Economy* (London: Routledge & Kegan Paul).

Head, B. (2007), 'Community Engagement: Participation on Whose Terms?', *Australian Journal of Political Science*, 42, 441–54.

—— and Ryan, N. (2004), 'Can Co-Governance Work? Regional Natural Resource Management in Queensland, Australia', *Society and Economy*, 26, 361–82.

Held, D., McGrew, A., Goldblatt, D. and Perraton, J. (1999), *Global Transformations: Politics, Economics and Culture* (Cambridge: Polity).

Helleiner, E. (1994), *States and the Reemergence of Global Finance: From Bretton Woods to the 1990s* (Ithaca: Cornell University Press).

Heritier, A. (2002a), 'New Modes of Governance in Europe: Policy-Making Without Legislating?', in A. Heritier (ed.), *Common Goods: Reinventing European and International Governance* (Lanham: Littlefield & Roman).

—— (2002b), 'Public-Interest Services Revisited', *Journal of European Public Policy*, 9, 995–1019.

—— (2003), 'New Modes of Governance in Europe: Increasing Political Capacity and Policy Effectiveness', in T. Borzel and R.Cichowski (eds), *The State of the European Union* (Oxford University Press).

Hess, M. and Adams, D. (2002), 'Knowing and Skilling in Contemporary Public Administration', *Australian Journal of Public Administration*, 61, 65–87.

Hibbs, D. (1977), 'Political Parties and Macroeconomic Policy', *American Political Science Review*, 71, 1467–87.

Hill, C. J. and Lynn, L. E. (2005), 'Is Hierarchical Governance in Decline? Evidence from Empirical Research', *Journal of Public Administration Research and Theory*, 15, 173–95.

Hindmoor, A. (1999), 'Rent Seeking Evaluated', *Journal of Political Philosophy*, 7, 434–52.

—— (2006a), *Rational Choice* (Basingstoke: Palgrave Macmillan).

—— (2006b), 'Public Choice Theory', in C. Hay, M. Lister and D. Marsh (eds), *The State: Theories and Issues* (Basingstoke: Palgrave Macmillan).

—— (2008), 'Public Policy', in P. Giddings and M. Rush (eds), *The Palgrave Review of British Politics* (Basingstoke: Palgrave Macmillan).

—— (2009), 'Explaining Networks through Mechanisms: Vaccination, Priming and the 2001 Foot and Mouth Disease Crisis', *Political Studies* (forthcoming).

Hinsley, F. (1986), *Sovereignty* (Cambridge University Press).

Hirsch, F. (1978), *Social Limits to Growth* (London: Routledge Kegan Paul).

Hirst, P. (1994), *Associative Democracy: New Forms of Economic and Social Governance* (Amherst: University of Massachusetts Press).

—— and Thompson, G. (1996), *Globalization in Question: The International Economy and the Possibilities of Governance* (Cambridge: Polity).

Hirst, P. and Veit, B. (eds) (2001), *Associative Democracy: The Real Third Way* (London: Frank Cass).

Hobsbawm, E. (1990), *Nations and Nationalism Since 1780: Program, Myth and Reality* (Cambridge University Press).

Hobson, J. (2000), *The State and International Relations* (Cambridge University Press).

Hocking, J. (2005), 'Liberty, Security and the State', in P. Saunders and J. Walter (eds), *Ideas and Influence: Social Science and Public Policy in Australia* (Sydney: UNSW Press).

Hoffman, S. (1987), *Janus and Minerva: Essays in the Theory and Practice of International Politics* (Boulder: Westview Press).

Holliday, I. (2000), 'Is the British State Hollowing Out?', *Political Quarterly*, 71, 167–76.

Hood, C. (1991), 'A Public Management for All Seasons?', *Public Administration*, 69, 3–19.

—— (2007), 'Intellectual Obsolescence and Intellectual Makeovers: Reflections on the Tools of Government after Two Decades', *Governance*, 20, 127–44.

—— Scott, C., James, O., Jones, G. and Travers, T. (1999), *Regulation inside Government: Waste-Watchers, Quality Police and Sleaze-Busters* (Oxford University Press).

House, J. D. and McGrath, K. (2004), 'Innovative Governance and Development in the New Ireland: Social Partnership and the Integrated Approach', *Governance*, 17, 29–58.

Hurd, I. (1999), 'Legitimacy and Authority in International Politics', *Review of International Studies*, 17, 67–85.

Industry Commission (1996), *Competitive Tendering and Contracting by Public Service Agencies* (Melbourne: Australian Government Publishing Service).

Inoguchi, T. (2000), 'Broadening the Basis of Social Capital in Japan', in R. Putnam (ed.), *Democracies in Flux: The Evolution of Social Capital in Contemporary Society* (Oxford University Press).

Intergovernmental Panel on Climate Change (2007), *Climate Change 2007: Mitigation. Contribution of Working Group III to the Fourth Assessment Report of the IPCC* (Cambridge University Press).

Irvin, R. A. and Stansbury, J. (2004), 'Citizen Participation in Decision Making: Is It worth the Effort?', *Public Administration Review*, 64, 55–65.

James, O. (2004), 'The UK Core Executive's Use of Public Service Agreements as a Tool of Governance', *Public Administration*, 82, 397–419.

Jayasuriya, K. (2001), 'Beyond Institutional Fetishism: From the Developmental to the Regulatory State', *New Political Economy*, 10, 381–7.

Jessop, B. (1997), 'The Governance of Complexity and the Complexity of Governance: Preliminary Remarks on Some Problems and Limits of Economic Governance', in A. Amin and J. Hausner (eds), *Beyond Market and Hierarchy: Interactive Governance and Social Complexity* (Cheltenham: Edward Elgar).

—— (1997a), 'Capitalism and its Future: Remarks on Regulation, Government and Governance', *Review of International Political Economy*, 4, 561–81.

—— (2001), 'Bring the State Back In (Yet Again): Reviews, Revisions, Rejections, and Redirections', *International Review of Sociology*, 1, 149–73.

—— (2002), *The Future of the Capitalist State* (Cambridge: Polity Press).

Johnson, C. (1995), *Japan, Who Governs? The Rise of the Developmental State* (New York: W. W. Norton).

Joppke, C. (1993), Decentralisation of Control in United States Nuclear Energy Policy', *Political Science Quarterly*, 107, 709–25.

Jordan, A. (1999), 'The Implementation of EU Environmental Policy: A Policy Problem without a Political Solution?', *Environment and Planning: Government and Policy*, 17, 69–90.

—— Wurzel, R. and Zito, A. (2005), 'New Environmental Policy Instruments (NEPIs) in the European Union. From Government to Governance?', *Political Studies*, 53, 477–96.

Jordana, J. and Levi-Faur, D. (eds) (2004), *The Politics of Regulation* (London: Edward Elgar).

Kane, J. and Bishop, P. (2002), 'Consultation and Contest: The Danger of Mixing Modes', *Australian Journal of Public Administration*, 61, 87–94.

Katzenstein, P. (1985), *Small States in World Markets: Industrial Policy in Europe* (Ithaca: Cornell University Press).

—— (2003), 'Small States and Small States Revisited', *New Political Economy*, 8, 9–30.

Kaufmann, C. (2004), 'Threat Inflation and the Failure of the Marketplace of Ideas: The Selling of the Iraq War', *International Security*, 29, 5–48.

Kaufmann, D. (2005), '10 Myths about Governance and Corruption', *Finance and Development*, 42, 41–63.

Kawabata, E. (2001), 'Sanction Power, Jurisdiction, and Economic Policy Making: Explaining Contemporary Telecommunications Policy in Japan, *Governance*, 14, 399–427.

Kay, A. (2006), *The Dynamics of Public Policy: Theory and Evidence* (Cheltenham: Edward Elgar).

Keating, M. (2004), *Who Rules? How Government Retains Control of a Privatised Economy* (Sydney: Federation Press).

—— and Dixon, P. (1989), *Making Economic Policy in Australia* (Melbourne: Longman).

Keele, L. (2007), 'Social Capital and the Dynamics of Trust', *American Journal of Political Science*, 51, 241–54.

Keeler, J. (1987), *The Politics of Neo-Corporatism in France: Farmers, the State and Agricultural Policy-Making in the Fifth Republic* (Oxford University Press).

Kellogg, W. A. (1998), 'Adopting an Ecosystem Approach: Local Variability in Remedial Action Planning', *Natural Resources and Environmental Issues*, 11, 465–83.

Kelly, J. (2006), 'Central Regulation of English Local Authorities: An Example of Meta-Governance?', *Public Administration*, 84, 603–21.

Kelly, P. (1984), *The Hawke Ascendancy: A Definitive Account of its Origins and Climax, 1975–1983* (London: Angus & Robertson).

—— (1992), *The End of Certainty: The Story of the 1980s* (Sydney: Allen & Unwin).

Kenworthy, L. (1997), 'Globalisation and Economic Convergence', *Competition and Change*, 2, 1–64.

Keohane, R. (2002), 'Ironies of Sovereignty: The European Union and the United States', *Journal of Common Market Studies*, 40, 743–65.

Keren, M. (2000), 'Political Perfectionism and the "Anti-System" Party', *Party Politics*, 6, 107–16.

Kernaghan, K. (1993), 'Partnership and Public Administration', *Canadian Public Administration*, 36, 57–76.

Kerwer, D. (2002), 'Rating Agencies: Setting a Standard for Global Financial Markets', *Economic Sociology*, 3, 40–6.

—— (2005), 'Holding Global Regulators Accountable: The Case of Credit Rating Agencies', *Governance*, 18, 453–75.

Kettl, D. (2002), *The Transformation of Governance: Public Administration for Twenty-First Century America* (Baltimore: Johns Hopkins University Press).

Kickert, W. (1993), 'Complexity, Governance and Dynamics: Conceptual Explorations of Public Network Management', in J. Kooiman (ed.), *Modern Governance* (London: Sage).

Kikeri, S., Nells, J. and Shirley, M. (1992), *Privatisation: The Lessons of Experience* (Washington, DC: World Bank).

Kim, K. and Nofsinger, J. (2007), *Corporate Governance* (Upper Saddle, NJ: Prentice Hall).

King, A. (1975), 'Overload: Problems of Governing in the 1970s', *Political Studies*, 23, 162–174.

—— (1988), 'Margaret Thatcher as a Political Leader', in R. Skidelsky (ed.), *Thatcherism* (Oxford: Blackwell).

Kingdon, J. (1984), *Agendas, Alternatives and Public Policy* (Boston: Little, Brown).

Kirkpatrick, I., Kitchener, M. and Whipp, R. (2001), 'Out of Sight, Out of Mind: Assessing the Impact of Markets for Children's Residential Care', *Public Administration*, 79, 49–71.

Kirzner, I. (1973), *Competition and Entrepreneurship* (University of Chicago Press).

Kitschelt, H. (1986), 'Political Opportunity Structures and Political Protest: Anti-Nuclear Movements in Four Democracies', *British Journal of Political Science*, 16, 57–86.

Kjaer, A. (2004), *Governance* (Cambridge University Press).

Klein, B. (1996), 'Why Hold-ups Occur: The Self-enforcing Range of Contractual Relationships', *Economic Enquiry*, 34, 444–63.

Klijn, E. and Koppenjan, J. (2000), 'Public Management and Policy Networks: Foundations of a Network Approach to Governance', *Public Management*, 2, 135–58.

Knack, S. and Keefer, P. (1997), 'Does Social Capital Have an Economic Pay-off?' *Quarterly Journal of Economics*, 111, 1251–88.

Knill, C. and Lehmkuhl, D. (2002), 'Private Actors and the State: Internationalization and Changing Patterns of Governance', *Governance*, 15, 41–63.

Knoke, D. (1990), *Political Networks: The Structural Perspective* (Cambridge University Press).

—— (2001), *Changing Organizations: Business Networks in the New Political Economy* (Boulder: Westview Press).

Koenig-Archibugi, M. (2005), 'Transnational Corporations and Public Accountability', in D. Held and M. Koenig-Archibugi (eds), *Global Governance and Public Accountability* (Oxford: Blackwell).

Kohler-Koch, B. and Rittberger, B. (2006), 'The Governance Turn in EU Studies', *Journal of Common Market Studies*, 44, 27–49.

Kollman, K. and Prakash, A. (2002), 'EMS-Based Environmental Regimes as Club Goods: Examining Variations in Firm-Level Adoption of ISO14001 and EMAS in UK, US and Germany', *Policy Sciences*, 35, 43–67.

Kooiman, J. (1993), 'Socio-Political Governance: Introduction' in J. Kooiman (ed.), *Modern Governance: New Government–Society Interactions* (London: Sage).

Koontz, T. M. and Johnson, E. M. (2004), 'One Size Does fit All: Matching Breadth of Stakeholder Participation to Watershed Group Accomplishments', *Policy Sciences*, 37, 185–204.

Koppenjan, J. F. M. (2008), 'Consensus and Conflict in Policy Networks', in E. Sorensen and J. Torfing (eds), *Theories of Democratic Network Governance* (London: Palgrave).

Krasner, S. (1984), 'Approaches to the State: Alternative Conceptions and Historical Dynamics', *Comparative Politics*, 16, 223–46.

Kymlika, W. (2002), *Contemporary Political Philosophy* (Oxford University Press).

Laband, D. and Sophocleus, J. (1988), 'The Social Cost of Rent Seeking: First Estimates', *Public Choice*, 58, 269–75.

Laffont, J. and Tirole, J. (1991), 'The Politics of Government Decision-Making: A Theory of Regulatory Capture', *Quarterly Journal of Economics*, 106, 1089–127.

Lalman, D., Oppenheimer, J. and Swistak, P. (1993), 'Formal Rational Choice Theory: A Cumulative Science of Politics', in A. Finifter (ed.), *Political Science: The State of the Discipline II* (Washington, DC: APSA).

Lampinen, R. and Uusikyla, P. (1998), 'Implementation Deficit – Why Member States Do Not Comply with EU Directives', *Scandinavian Political Studies*, 21, 231–51.

Lavery, K. (1999), *Smart Contracting for Local Government Services: Processes and Experience* (Westport: Praeger).

Le Grand, J. (2003), *Motivation, Agency, and Public Policy* (Oxford University Press).

Lehmbruch, G. and Schmitter, P. (eds) (1982), *Patterns of Corporatist Policymaking* (London: Sage).

Levi, G. and Vetoria, M. (2002), 'Fighting Against AIDS: the Brazilian Experience', *AIDS: Official Journal of the International AIDS Society*, 16, 2373–83.

Levy, J. (2006), 'The State also Rises: The Roots of Contemporary State Activism', in J. Levy (ed.), *The State after Statism* (Cambridge, Mass.: Harvard University Press).

Lijphart, A. (1999), *Patterns of Democracy: Government Forms and Performance in Thirty-Six Countries* (New Haven: Yale University Press).

Lilleker, D. (2007), *Key Concepts in Political Communication* (London: Sage).

Lindblom, C. (1977), *Politics and Markets: The World's Political-Economic Systems* (New York: Basic Books).

Lindvall, J. and Sebring, J. (2005), 'Policy Reform and the Decline of Corporatism in Sweden', *West European Politics*, 28, 1057–74.

Lipsky, M. (1980), *Street-Level Bureaucracy: Dilemmas of the Individual in Public Services* (New York: Russell Sage Foundation).

Lister, M. and Marsh, D. (2006), 'Conclusion', in C. Hay, M. Lister and D. Marsh (eds), *The State: Theories and Issues* (Basingstoke: Palgrave Macmillan).

Lonsdale, C. (2005), 'Contractual Uncertainty, the Problem of Power and Public Contracting', *Journal of Public Policy*, 25, 219–240.

Lopez, R. and Pagoulatos, E. (1994), 'Rent Seeking and the Welfare Cost of Trade Barriers', *Public Choice*, 79, 149–60.

Loughlin, M. and Scott, C. (1997), 'The Regulatory State', in P. Dunleavy. et al. (eds), *Developments in British Politics 5* (Basingstoke: Macmillan).

Lowe, J. and Hill, E. (2005), 'Closing the Gap Between Government and Community', in A. Rainnie and M. Grobbelaar (eds), *New Regionalism in Australia* (Aldershot: Ashgate).

Lowi, T. (1969), 'The Public Philosophy: Interest-Group Liberalism', in W. Connolly (ed.), *The Bias of Pluralism* (New York: Atherton).

Lukensmeyer, C. and Torres, L. (2000), *Public Deliberation: A Manager's Guide to Citizen Engagement* (IBM Centre for the Business of Government).

Lukes, S. (1974), *Power: A Radical View* (London: Macmillan).

Lundqvist, L. (2001), 'Implementation from Above: The Ecology of Power in Sweden's Environmental Governance', *Governance*, 14, 319–37.

Lundsgaard, J. (2002), *Competition and Efficiency in Publicly Funded Services* (Paris: OECD).

Lurie, I. (1997), 'Temporary Assistance for Needy Families: A Green Light for the States', *Publius: The Journal of Federalism*, 27, 73–87.

Lyons, M. (2001), *Third Sector: The Contribution of Non-profit and Co-operative Enterprise in Australia* (Sydney, Allen & Unwin).

Mackendrick, N. (2005), 'The Role of the State in Voluntary Environmental Reform: A Case Study of Public Land', *Policy Sciences*, 38, 21–44.

Magennis, S. (1999), 'Immunisation and Prevention: An Up-to-Date Perspective', in K. Booth and K. Luker (eds), *A Practical Handbook for Community Nurses* (Oxford: Blackwell).

Magnette, P. (2003), 'European Governance and Civic Participation: Beyond Elitist Citizenship?', *Political Studies*, 51, 144–60.

Majone, G. (1994), 'The Rise of the Regulatory State in Europe', *West European Politics*, 17, 77–101.

—— (1996), *Regulating Europe* (London: Routledge).

—— (1997), 'From the Positive to the Regulatory State: Causes and Consequences of Changes in the Mode of Governance', *Journal of Public Policy* 17, 139–67.

—— (2006), 'Agenda-Setting', in M. Moran, M. Rein, and R. Goodin (eds), *The Oxford Handbook of Public Policy* (Oxford University Press).

Mallin, C. (2007), *Corporate Governance* (Oxford University Press).

Maloney, W., Smith, G. and Stoker, G. (2000), 'Social Capital and Urban Governance: Adding a More Contextualised Top-Down Perspective', *Political Studies*, 48, 802–20.

Maltese, J. (2003), 'The Presidency and the News Media', in M. Rozell (ed.), *Media Power, Media Politics* (Lanham: Rowman & Littlefield).

Mameli, P. (2001), 'Splitting the Difference: Partnering with Non-Governmental Organizations to Manage HIV/AIDS Epidemics in Australia and Thailand', *Human Rights Review*, 2, 1524–89.

Mann, M. (1988), *States, War and Capitalism* (Oxford: Basil Blackwell).

—— (ed.) (1990), *The Rise and Decline of the Nation-State* (Oxford: Blackwell).

Marglin, S. (2008), *The Dismal Science: How Thinking Like an Economist Undermines Community* (Cambridge, Mass.: Harvard University Press).

Marinetto, M. (2003a), 'Governing Beyond the Centre: A Critique of the Anglo-Governance School', *Political Studies*, 51, 592–608.

—— (2003b), 'Who Wants to be an Active Citizen? The Politics and Practice of Community Involvement', *Sociology*, 37, 103–20.

Marks, G., Hooghe, L. and Blank, K. (1996), 'European Integration from the 1980s: State-Centric v. Multi-Level Governance', *Journal of Common Market Studies*, 34, 341–78.

Markusen, A. (2003), 'The Case Against Privatizing National Security', *Governance*, 16, 471–501.

Marsh, D. (1991), 'Privatization Under Mrs. Thatcher: A Review of the Literature', *Public Administration*, 69, 459–80.

—— (1992), *The New Politics of British Trade Unionism* (London: Macmillan).

—— (ed.) (1998), *Comparing Policy Networks* (Buckingham: Open University Press).

—— and Rhodes, R. (eds) (1992a), *Policy Networks in British Government* (Oxford: Clarendon).

—— and —— (eds) (1992b), 'New Directions in the Study of Policy Networks', *European Journal of Political Research*, 21, 181–205.

—— and —— (eds) (1992c), *Implementing Thatcherite Policies: Audit of an Era* (Buckingham: Open University Press).

Marsh, D., Richards, D. and Smith, M. J. (2003), 'Unequal Plurality: Towards an Asymmetric Power Model of British Politics', *Government and Opposition*, 38, 306–32.

Martin, C. (1989), 'Business Influence and State Power: The Case of US Corporate Tax Policy', *Politics and Society*, 17, 189–223.

Martin, H. and Schumann, H. (1996), *The Global Trap: Globalization and the Assault on Prosperity and Democracy* (London: Zed Books).

Matthews, T. (1988), 'Vitally Important Allies: The Role of Interest Groups in Government Decision Making', *Australian Journal of Public Administration*, 47, 147–63.

—— (1994), 'Employers Associations, Corporatism and the Accord', in S. Bell and B. Head (eds), *State, Economy and Public Policy in Australia* (Melbourne: Oxford University Press).

Mattli, W. and Buthe, T. (2003), 'Setting International Standards: Technological Rationality or Primacy of Power', *World Politics*, 56, 1–42.

—— and —— (2005), 'Accountability in Accounting? The Politics of Private Rule-Making in the Public Interest', *Governance*, 18, 399–429.

Maynard-Moody, S. and Musheno, M. (2003), *Cops, Teachers, Counsellors: Stories from the Front Lines of Public Service* (University of Michigan Press).

Mayntz, R. (1993), 'Governing Failure and the Problem of Governability', in J. Kooiman., (ed.), *Modern Governance* (London: Sage).

—— (1998), 'New Challenges to Governance Theory', European University Institute, Jean Monet Chair Paper, 98/50.

McGowan, F. and Wallace, H. (1996), 'Towards a European Regulatory State', *Journal of European Public Policy*, 4, 560–76.

McKeen-Edwards, H., Porter, T. and Roberge, I. (2004), 'Politics or Markets? The Determinants of Cross-Border Financial Integration in the NAFTA and the EU', *New Political Economy*, 9, 325–340.

McLaughlin, P. A. (1991), 'How Business Relates to the Hawke Government: The Captains of Industry', in B. Galligan and G. Singleton (eds), *Business and Government Under Labor* (Melbourne: Longman).

McLaverty, P. (2002), 'Civil Society and Democracy', *Contemporary Politics*, 8, 303–18.

McLennan, G. (1989), *Marxism, Pluralism and Beyond* (Cambridge: Polity).

Mead, L. M. (2001), 'Implementing Work Requirements in Wisconsin', *Journal of Public Policy*, 21, 239–64.

Megginson, W. and Netter, J. (2001), 'From State to Market: A Survey of Empirical Studies on Privatisation', *Journal of Economic Literature*, 39, 321–89.

Menahem, G. (2008), 'The Transformation of Higher Education in Israel Since the 1990s: The Role of Ideas and Policy Paradigms', *Governance*, 21, 499–526.

Menkhaus, K. (2007), 'Governance without Government in Somalia: Spoilers, State Building, and the Politics of Coping', *International Security* (31), 74–106.

Michels, R. (1915) [1959], *Political Parties: A Sociological Study of the Oligarchical Tendencies of Modern Democracy* (New York: Dover Publications).

Mikalsen, K. H., Hernes, H. C. and Jentoft, S. (2006), 'Leaning on User-Groups: The Role of Civil Society in Fisheries Goverance', *Marine Policy*, 31, 201–9.

Miller, D. (1989), *Market, State and Community: Theoretical Foundations of Market Socialism* (Oxford University Press).

Milward, H. and Provan, K. (2000), 'Governing the Hollow State', *Journal of Public Administration Research and Theory*, 10, 359–79.

—— and —— (2003), 'Managing the Hollow State: Collaboration and Contracting', *Public Management Review*, 5, 1–18.

Milward, H., Provan, K. and Else, B. (1993), 'What Does the Hollow State Look Like?', in B. Bozeman (ed.), *Public Management: The State of the Art* (San Francisco: Jossey-Bass).

Milward, H., Provan, K. and Isett, K. (2002), 'Collaboration and Integration of Community-Based Health and Human Services in a Nonprofit Managed Care System', *Health Care Management Review*, 27, 21–32.

Miranda, R. and Lerner, A. (1995), 'Bureaucracy, Organisational Redundancy, and the Privatisation of Public Services', *Public Administration Review*, 55, 193–200.

Mitchell, T. (1991), 'The Limits of the State: Beyond Statist Approaches and Their Critics', *American Political Science Review*, 85, 77–96.

Mohammad, S. and Whalley, J. (1984), 'Rent Seeking in India: Its Costs and Significance', *Kyklos*, 37, 387–413.

Moore, G. (2004), 'The Fair Trade Movement: Parameters, Issues and Future Research', *Journal of Business Ethics*, 53, 73–86.

Moran, M. (2002), 'Review Article: Understanding the Regulatory State', *British Journal of Political Science*, 32, 391–413.

—— (2003), *The British Regulatory State: High Modernism and Hyper-Innovation* (Oxford University Press).

—— (2006), 'The Transformation of the British State: From Club Government to State-Administered High Modernism', in J. Levy (ed.), *The State After Statism: New State Activities in the Age of Liberalisation* (Cambridge, Mass.: Harvard University Press).

Moravcsik, A. (1993), 'Preferences and Power in the European Community: A Liberal Intergovernmentalist Approach', *Journal of Common Market Studies*, 31, 473–524.

—— (2005), 'The European Constitutional Compromise and the Neofunctionalist Legacy', *Journal of European Public Policy*, 12, 349–86.

Morgan, K., Rees, G. and Smith, M. J. (1999), 'Networking for Local Economic development', in G. Stoker (ed.), *The New Management of British Local Governance* (Basingstoke: Macmillan).

Mosley, L. (2000), 'Room to Move: International Financial Markets and National Welfare States', *International Organisation*, 54, 737–73.

—— (2003), *Global Capital and National Governments* (Cambridge University Press).

Mueller, D. (2003), *Public Choice III* (Cambridge University Press).

Mueller, J. (1992), 'Democracy and Ralph's Pretty Good Grocery Store: Elections, Equality and the Minimal Human Being', *American Journal of Political Science*, 36: 983–1003.

Mulgan, R. (2002), 'On Ministerial Resignations (and the Lack Thereof)', *Australian Journal of Public Administration*, 61, 121–7.

—— (2002a), 'Accountability: An Ever-Expanding Concept', *Public Administration*, 78, 555–73.

—— (2006), 'Government Accountability for Outsourced Services', *Australian Journal of Public Administration*, 65, 48–58.

Muller, W. C. and Wright, V. (1994), 'Re-Shaping the State in Europe: The Limits to Retreat', *West European Politics*, 17, 1–11.

Murdoch, J. and Abram, S. (1998), 'Defining the Limits of Community Engagement', *Journal of Rural Studies*, 14, 41–50.

Murphy, C. (2000), 'Good Governance: Poorly Done and Poorly Understood', *International Affairs*, 76, 789–803.

Newburn, T. (2003), 'Drug Prevention and Youth Justice', *British Journal of Criminology*, 39, 609–24.

Newman, A. and Back, D. (2004), 'Self-Regulatory Trajectories in the Shadow of Hierarchy: Resolving Digital Dilemmas in Europe and the United States', *Governance*, 17, 387–413.

Newman, J. (2005), 'Introduction', in J. Newman. (ed.), *Remaking Governance* (Bristol: Policy Press).

Nielsen, K. and Pedersen, O. (1993), 'The Negotiated Economy: General Features and Theoretical Perspectives', in J. Hausner et al. (eds), *Institutional Frameworks of Market Economies* (London: Avebury).

Niskanen, W. (1971), *Bureaucracy and Representative Government* (Chicago: Aldine Atherton).

Nordhaus, W. (1975), 'The Political Business Cycle', *Review of Economic Studies*, 42, 169–90.

North, D. C. (1990), *Institutions, Institutional Change and Economic Performance* (Cambridge University Press).

Nye, J., Zelikow, P. and King, D. (eds) (1997), *Why People Don't Trust Government* (Cambridge, Mass.: Harvard University Press).

Obinger, H. and Zohlnhofer, R. (2007), 'The Real Race to the Bottom: What Happened to Economic Affairs Expenditure after 1980?', in F. Castles (ed.), *The Disappearing State? Retrenchment Realities in an Age of Globalisation* (Cheltenham: Edward Elgar).

O'Brien, R. (1992), *Global Financial Integration: The End of Geography* (London: Royal Institute of International Affairs).

O'Connor, J. (1973), *The Fiscal Crisis of the State* (New York: St Martin's Press).

OECD (2001), *The Well-Being of Nations: The Role of Human and Social Capital* (Paris: OECD).

OECD (2005a), *Modernising Government: The Way Forward* (Paris: OECD).

OECD (2005b), *Privatising State-Owned Enterprises: An Overview of Policies and Practices in OECD Countries* (Paris: OECD).

OECD (2005c), *Scale and Scope of State-owned Enterprises in OECD Countries* (Paris: OECD).

OECD (2007), *Can Policies Boost Birth Rates?* (Paris: OECD).

OECD (2008), *OECD Tax Revenue Trends, 1965–2006* (Paris: OECD).

Offe, C. (1981), 'The Attribution of Public Status to Interest Groups', in S. Berger (ed.), *Organized Interests in Western Europe* (Cambridge University Press).

—— (1984), *Contradictions of the Welfare State* (London: Hutchinson).

Okimoto, D. (1989), *Between MITI and the Market: Japanese Industrial Policy for High Technology* (Stanford University Press).

Olson, M. (1982), *The Rise and Decline of Nations: Economic Growth, Stagflation and Social Rigidities* (New Haven: Yale University Press).

Onis, Z. (1991), 'The Logic of the Developmental State', *Comparative Politics*, 24, 109–26.

Ophuls, W. (1977), *Ecology and the Politics of Scarcity* (San Francisco: Freeman).

Orcalli, G. (2007), 'Constitutional Choice and European Immigration Policy', *Constitutional Political Economy*, 18, 1–20.

Osborne, D. and Gaebler, T. (1992), *Reinventing Government: How the Entrepreneurial Spirit is Transforming the Public Sector* (Reading: Addison-Wesley).

Ostrom, E. (1990), *Governing the Commons: The Evolution of Institutions for Collective Action* (Cambridge University Press).

Parker, C. (2002), 'Regulating Self-Regulation: The ACCC, ASIC, Competition Policy and Corporate Regulation', in S. Bell (ed.), *Economic Governance and Institutional Dynamics* (Melbourne: Oxford University Press).

Parker, H. (2004), 'The New Drugs Interventions Industry: What Outcomes Can Drugs/Criminal Justice Treatment Programs Realistically Deliver?', *Probation Journal*, 51, 379–86.

Parker, R. (2007), 'Networked Governance or Just Networks? Local Governance of the Knowledge Economy in Limerick (Ireland) and Karlskorna (Sweden)', *Political Studies*, 55, 113–32.

Parsons, T. (1963), 'On the Concept of Power', *Proceedings of the American Philosophical Society*, 107, 232–62.

Pattberg, P. (2005), 'The Institutionalization of Private Governance: How Business and Non-profit Organizations Agree on Transnational Rules', *Governance*, 18, 589–610.

Pearce, G. and Mawson, J. (2003), 'Delivering Devolved Approaches to Local Governance', *Policy and Politics*, 31, 51–67.

Peters, G. (2000), 'Globalization, Institutions, and Governance', in. G. Peters and D. Savoie (eds), *Governance in the Twenty-first Century: Revitalizing the Public Service* (Buffalo: McGill–Queen's University Press).

Pierre, J. and Peters, G. (2000), *Governance, Politics and the State* (Basingstoke: Macmillan).

—— and —— (2005), *Governing Complex Societies* (Basingstoke: Palgrave Macmillan).

Pierre, J. and Peter, B. G. (2006), 'Governance, Government and the State', in C. Hay, M. Lister and D. Marsh (eds), *The State: Theories and Issues* (Basingstoke: Palgrave Macmillan).

Pierson, C. (1996), *The Modern State* (London: Routledge).

Pierson, P. (ed.) (2001), *The New Politics of the Welfare State* (Oxford University Press).

Poguntke, T. and Webb, P. (eds) (2005), *The Presidentisation of Politics: A Comparative Study of Modern Politics* (Oxford University Press).

Polanyi, K. (1957), *The Great Transformation* (Boston: Beacon Press).

Pollitt, C. and Bouckaert, G. (2000), *Public Management Reform: A Comparative Analysis* (Oxford University Press).

Porter, T. (1995), *Trust in Numbers: The Pursuit of Objectivity in Science and Public Life* (Princeton University Press).

Potoski, M. and Prakash, A. (2004), 'The Regulation Dilemma: Co-operation and Conflict in Environmental Governance', *Public Administration Review*, 64, 152–63.

Power, M. (1994), *The Audit Explosion* (London: Demos).

—— (1997), *The Audit Society: Rituals of Verification* (Oxford University Press).

Pressman, J. and Wildavsky, A. (1973), *Implementation: How Great Expectations in Washington are Dashed in Oakland: Or, Why It's Amazing that Federal Programs Work at All, This Being a Saga of the Economic Development Administration as Told by Two Sympathetic Observers who Seek to Build a Foundation on Ruined Hopes* (Berkeley: University of California Press).

Pressman, S. (2006), *Alternative Theories of the State* (Basingstoke: Palgrave Macmillan).

Productivity Commission (2003), *Social Capital: Reviewing the Concept and its Policy Implications* (Canberra: AusInfo).

Przeworski, A. (1985), *Capitalism and Social Democracy* (Cambridge University Press).

Putnam, R. (1993), *Making Democracy Work* (Princeton University Press).

—— (2000), *Bowling Alone: The Collapse and Revival of American Community* (New York: Touchstone).

Ranald, P. (1997), *The Contracting Commonwealth: Service Citizens or Consumers? Public Accountability, Service Quality and Equity Issues in the Contracting and Competitive Tendering of Government Services* (Public Sector Research Centre, University of New South Wales).

Reitbergen, W., Breukels, M. and Blok, K. (1999), *Voluntary Agreements – Implementation and Efficiency: Case Studies in the Sectors of Paper and Glass Manufacturing* (Utrecht: Department of Science, Technology and Society).

Rhodes, R. (1986), *The National World of Local Government* (London: Allen & Unwin).

—— (1995), 'The Institutional Approach', in D. Marsh and G. Stoker (eds), *Theory and Methods in Political Science* (Basingstoke: Macmillan).

—— (1996), 'The New Governance: Governing Without Government', *Political Studies*, 44, 652–67.

—— (1997), *Understanding Governance: Policy Networks, Governance, Reflexivity and Accountability* (Buckingham: Open University Press).

—— (2000), 'Governance and Public Administration', in J. Pierre (ed.), *Debating Governance* (Oxford University Press).

—— (2007), 'Understanding Governance: Ten Years On', *Organization Studies*, 28, 1243–64.

—— and Bevir, M. (2003), *Interpreting British Governance* (London: Routledge).

Richards, D. and Smith, M. (2004), 'Central Control and Policy Implementation in the UK: A Case Study of the Prime Minister's Delivery Unit', *Journal of Comparative Policy Analysis: Research and Practice*, 8, 325–45.

Riddell, P. (2000), *A Portrait of the Whitehall Program, Report to the Economic and Social Research Council on 'Future Whitehall'* (London: Church House).

Rieger, E. and Leibfried, S. (2003), *The Limits of Globalisation* (Cambridge: Polity Press).

Riker, W. (1982), *Liberalism Against Populism: A Confrontation Between the Theory of Democracy and the Theory of Social Choice* (San Francisco: W. H. Freeman).

Rittberger, B. and Richardson, J. (2003), 'Old Wine in New Bottles? The Commission and the Use of Environmental Policy Instruments', *Public Administration*, 81, 575–606.

Rivera, J. (2002), 'Assessing a Voluntary Environmental Initiative in the Developing World: The Costa Rican Certification for Sustainable Tourism', *Policy Sciences*, 35, 333–60.

Rodrik, D. (1997), *Has Globalisation Gone too Far?* (Washington, DC: Institute for International Studies).

—— (1998), 'Globalisation, Social Conflict and Economic Growth', *World Economy*, 21, 143–58.

Rosenau, J. (1992), 'Governance, Order and Change in World Politics', in J. Rosenau and E. Czempiel (eds), *Governance Without Government: Order and Change in World Politics* (Cambridge University Press).

—— and Czempiel, E. (eds) (1992), *Governance Without Government: Order and Change in World Politics* (Cambridge University Press).

Rothstein, B. (2005), *Social Traps and the Problem of Trust* (Cambridge University Press).

Rowley, C., Tollison, R. and Tullock, G. (eds) (1988), *The Political Economy of Rent-Seeking* (London: Kluwer).

Sabatier, P. (1986), 'Top-Down and Bottom-Up Approaches to Implementation Research', *Journal of Public Policy*, 6, 21–48.

Salamon, L. (ed.) (2002), *The Tools of Government: A Guide to the New Governance* (Oxford University Press).

Salamon, L., Sokolowski, S., and List, R. (2003), *Global Civil Society: An Overview* (Johns Hopkins University: Centre for Civil Society Studies).

Samuels, R. (1987), *The Business of the Japanese State: Energy Markets in Comparative and Historical Perspective* (Ithaca: Cornell University Press).

Sandler, T. (2004), *Global Collective Action* (Cambridge University Press).

Saward, M. (1997), 'In Search of the Hollow Crown', in P. Weller, et al. (eds), *The Hollow Crown: Countervailing Trends in Core Executives* (Basingstoke: Macmillan).

Sbragia, A. (2000), 'Governance, the State, and the Market: What is Going On?', *Governance*, 13, 243–50.

Scahill, J. (2007), *Blackwater: The Rise of the World's Most Powerful Mercenary Army* (New York: Nation Books).

Scanlon, C. (2004), *What's Wrong with Social Capital* (Melbourne: Australian Fabian Society).

Scharpf, F. (1994), 'Games Real Actors Could Play: Positive and Negative Coordination in Embedded Negotiations', *Journal of Theoretical Politics*, 6, 27–53.

—— (1997), *Games Real Actors Play: Actor-Centered Institutionalism in Policy Research* (Boulder: Westview Press).

—— (1999), *Governing in Europe: Effective and Democratic?* (Oxford University Press).

Schmidt, V. A. (2000), 'Values and Discourse in the Politics of Adjustment', in F. Scharpf and V. A. Schmidt (eds), *Welfare and Work in the Open Economy*, vol. 1 (Oxford University Press).

Schmitter, P. C. and Streeck, W. (1985), 'Community, Market, State and Associations?', in W. Streeck and P. C. Schmitter (eds), *Private Interest Government* (London: Sage).

Schmitter, W. (1974), 'Still the Century of Corporatism', *Review of Politics*, 36, 85–131.

Schumpeter, J. (1942), *Capitalism, Socialism and Democracy* (London: George Allen & Unwin).

Seabrooke, L. (2006), 'Why We Need Legitimacy in Political Economy and Institutional Theory', Paper presented at the annual meeting of the International Studies Association, San Diego, California, USA, 22 March <http://www.allacademic.com/meta/p99299_index.html>.

Self, P. (1993), *Government by the Market? The Politics of Public Choice* (Basingstoke: Macmillan).

Sellers, M. (2003), 'Privatization Morphs Into "Publicization": Businesses Look a Lot Like Government', *Public Administration*, 81, 607–20.

Singer, P. (2001), 'Corporate Warriors: The Rise of the Privatised Military Industry and its Ramifications for International Security', *International Security*, 26, 186–220.

Singleton, S. (2000), 'Co-operation or Capture? The Paradox of Co-management and Community Participation in Natural Resource Management and Environmental Policy Making', *Environmental Politics*, 9, 1–21.

Skocpol, T. (1980), 'Political Responses to Capitalist Crisis: Neo-Marxist Theories of the State and the Case of the new Deal', *Politics and Society*, 10, 155–201.

—— (1985), 'Bringing the State Back In: Strategies of Analysis in Current Research', in P. B. Evans, D. Rueschemeyer and T. Skocpol (eds), *Bringing the State Back In* (Cambridge University Press).

—— (1996), 'Unravelling From Above', *American Prospect*, 25, 20–6.

Skogstad, G. (2003), 'Who Governs, Who Should Govern? Political Authority and Legitimacy in Canada in the Twenty-First Century', *Canadian Journal of Political Science*, 36, 955–73.

Smart, H. (1991), *Criticism and Public Rationality: Professional Rigidity and the Search for Caring Government* (London: Routledge).

Smith, G. and Wales, C. (2000), 'Citizens' Juries and Deliberative Democracy', *Political Studies*, 48, 51–65.

Smith, K. (2007), *The Carbon Neutral Myth: Offset Indulgences for Your Carbon Sins* (Amsterdam: Transnational Institute).

Smith, M. (2006), 'Pluralism', in C. Hay, M. Lister and D. Marsh (eds), *The State: Theories and Issues* (Basingstoke: Palgrave Macmillan).

Smith, P. D. and McDonough, H. (2001), 'Beyond Public Participation: Fairness in Natural Resource Decision Making', *Society and Natural Resources*, 14, 239–49.

Soleille, S. (2006), 'Greenhouse Gas Emission Trading Schemes: A New Tool for the Environmental Regulator's Kit', *Energy Policy*, 34, 1473–7.

Sorensen, E. (2006), 'Metagovernance: The Changing Role of Politicians in Processes of Democratic Governance', *American Review of Public Administration*, 36, 98–114.

—— and Torfing, J. (2008a), 'Governance Network Research: Towards a Second Generation', in E. Sorensen and J. Torfing (eds), *Theories of Democratic Network Governance* (London: Palgrave).

—— and —— (2008b), 'Theoretical Approaches to Metagovernance', in E. Sorensen and J. Torfing (eds), *Theories of Democratic Network Governance* (London: Palgrave).

Sorensen, G. (2006), 'The Transformation of the State', in C. Hay, M. Lister and D. Marsh. (eds), *The State: Theories and Issues* (Basingstoke: Palgrave Macmillan).

Spar, D. (1999), 'Lost in (Cyber) Space: The Private Rules of Online Commerce', in C. Culter, T. Porter and V. Haufler. (eds), *Private Authority and International Affairs* (Albany: SUNY Press).

Squires, P. (1990), *Anti-Social Policy: Welfare, Ideology and the Discipline State* (Brighton: Harvester Wheatsheaf).

Stanyer, J. (2007), *Modern Political Communication* (Cambridge: Polity).

Steinzor, R. (1998), 'Reinventing Environmental Regulation: The Dangerous Journey from Command to Self-Control', *Harvard Environmental Law Review*, 22, 103–6.

Stigler, G. (1971), 'The Theory of Economic Regulation', *Bell Journal of Economics and Management Science*, 2, 3–21.

Stiglitz, J. (2002), *Globalization and its Discontents* (New York: Norton).

—— and Bilmes, L. (2008), *The Three Trillion Dollar War* (Penguin Books).

Stoker, G. (1998), 'Governance as Theory: Five Propositions', *International Social Science Journal*, 50, 17–28.

—— (2006), *Why Politics Matters: Making Democracy Work* (Basingstoke: Palgrave Macmillan).

Strange, S. (1996), *The Retreat of the State: The Diffusion of Power in the World Economy* (Cambridge University Press).

Streeck, W. (1983), 'Between Pluralism and Corporatism: German Business Associations and the State', *Journal of Public Policy*, 3, 265–84.

—— and Schmitter, P. C. (1985), *Private Interest Government* (London: Sage).

Street, J. (1988), 'British Government Policy on AIDS: Learning Not to Die of Ignorance', *Parliamentary Affairs*, 41, 490–507.

Stretton, H. and Orchard, L. (1994), *Public Goods, Public Enterprise, Public Choice* (Basingstoke: Macmillan).

Sunstein, C. R. (1990), *After the Rights Revolution: Reconceiving the Regulatory State* (Cambridge, Mass.: Harvard University Press).

Swank, D. (2002), *Global Capital, Political Institutions and Policy Change in the Developed Welfare States* (Cambridge University Press).

Szreter, S. (2002), 'The State of Social Capital: Bringing Back in Power, Politics and History', *Theory and Society*, 31, 573–621.

Tanzi, V. and Schuknecht, L. (2000), *Public Spending in the 20th Century* (Cambridge University Press).

Taylor, A. (2000), 'Hollowing Out or Filling In? Task Forces and the Management of Cross-Cutting Issues in British Government', *British Journal of Politics and International Relations*, 2, 46–71.

Taylor-Gooby, P., Sylvester, S., Calnan, M. and Graham, M. (2000), 'Knights, Knaves and Gnashers: Professional Values and Private Dentistry', *Journal of Social Policy*, 29, 375–95.

Teisman, G. R. and Klijn, E. (2002), 'Partnership Arrangements: Governmental Rhetoric or Governance Scheme?', *Public Administration Review*, 62, 197–204.

Terrence Higgins Trust (2007), *Trustees' Report and Financial Statement*, <http://www.tht.org.uk/binarylibrary/trusteesreport/trusteesreportsix.pdf>.

Thaler, R. and Sunstein, C. (2008), *Nudge: Improving Decisions About Health, Wealth and Happiness* (New Haven: Yale University Press).

Thatcher, M. (1993), *The Downing Street Years* (London: Harper Collins).

Thelen, K. (1999), 'Historical Institutionalism in Comparative Politics,' *Annual Review of Political Science*, 2, 374–77.

—— and Steinmo, S. (1992), 'Historical Institutionalism in Comparative Perspective', in K. Thelen and S. Steinmo (eds), *Structuring Politics: Historical Institutionalism in Comparative Analysis* (Cambridge University Press).

Thomas, C. W. (2003), 'Habitat Conservation Planning', in A. Fung and E. O. Wright (eds), *Deepening Democracy: Innovations in Empowered Participatory Governance* (London: Verso).

Thompson, D. (1983), 'Bureaucracy and Democracy', in G. Duncan (ed.), *Democratic Theory and Practice* (Cambridge University Press).

Thompson, G., Frances, J., Levacic, R. and Mitchell, J. (1991), *Markets, Hierarchies and Networks: The Coordination of Social Life* (London: Sage).

Toke, D. and Marsh, D. (2003), 'Policy Networks and the GM Crops Issue: Assessing the Utility of a Dialectical Model of Policy Networks', *Public Administration*, 81, 229–51.

Tollefson, C., Gale, F. and Haley, D. (2009), *Setting the Standard: Certification, Governance and the Forest Stewardship Council* (Vancouver: UBC Press).

Toohey, P. (2008), *Last Drinks? The Impact of the Northern Territory Intervention* (Melbourne: Black Inc.).

Torres, L., Pina, V., and Acerete, B. (2006), 'E-Governance Developments in European Union Cities: Reshaping Government's Relationship with Citizens', *Governance*, 19, 277–302.

Treib, O., Bahr, H. and Falkner, G. (2007), 'Modes of Governance: Toward a Conceptual Clarification', *Journal of European Public Policy*, 14, 1–20.

Truman, D. (1951), *The Governmental Process* (New York: Alfred & Knopf).

Tsebelis, G. (2002), *Veto Players: How Political Institutions Work* (Princeton University Press).

Tullock, G. (1976), *The Vote Motive* (London: Institute of Economic Affairs).

—— (1989), *The Economics of Special Privilege and Rent Seeking* (Boston: Kluwer Academic).

—— (1993), 'Rent Seeking', in C. Rowley (ed.), *Property Rights and the Limits of Democracy* (Cheltenham: Edward Elgar).

—— (2005), *Public Goods, Redistribution and Rent Seeking* (Cheltenham: Edward Elgar).

Vedung, E. and van der Doelen, C. (1998), 'The Sermon: Information Programs in the Public Policy Process: Choice, Effects and Evaluation', in M. Bemelmans-Videc, R. Rist and E. Vedung (eds), *Carrots, Sticks and Sermons: Policy Instruments and their Evaluation* (New Brunswick: Transaction Publishers).

Verba, S., Schlozman, K. and Brady, H. (1995), *Voice and Equality: Civic Voluntarism in American Politics* (Cambridge, Mass.: Harvard University Press).

Vibert, F. (2007), *The Rise of the Unelected: Democracy and the New Separation of Powers* (Cambridge University Press).

Vigoda, E. (2002), 'From Responsiveness to Collaboration: Governance, Citizens, and the Next Generation of Public Administration', *Public Administration Review*, 62, 527–40.

Visser, J. and Hemerijck, A. (1997), *A Dutch Miracle* (Amsterdam University Press).

Vogel, D. (1986), *National Styles of Regulation: Environmental Policy in Great Britain and the United States* (Ithaca: Cornell University Press).

—— (1995), *Trading Up: Consumer and Environmental Regulation in a Global Economy* (Cambridge, Mass.: Harvard University Press).

—— (2008), 'Private Global Business Regulation', *Annual Review of Political Science*, 11, 261–82.

—— and Kagan, R. (2004), *The Dynamics of Regulatory Change: How Globalisation Affects National Regulatory Policies* (Berkeley: University of California Press).

Vogel, S. (1996), *Freer Markets, More Rules: Regulatory Reform in Advanced Industrialized Countries* (Ithaca: Cornell University Press).

Wade, R. (1990), *Governing the Market* (Princeton University Press).

—— (2003), 'The Invisible Hand of the American Empire', *Ethics and International Affairs*, 17, 77–88.

—— (2005), 'Globalisation, Poverty and Inequality', in J. Ravenhill (ed.), *Global Political Economy* (Oxford University Press).

Wagschal, U. (2007), 'A Mortgage on the Future? Public Debt Expenditure and its Determinants', in F. Castles (ed.), *The Disappearing State? Retrenchment Realities in an Era of Globalisation* (Cheltenham: Edward Elgar).

Wallace, D. (1995), *Environmental Policy and Industrial Innovation: Strategies in Europe, the U.S.A. and Japan* (London: Earthscan).

Wallace, H. (2000), 'Politics and Policy in the EU: The Challenge of Governance in the EU', in H. Wallace and W. Wallace (eds), *Policy-Making in the European Union* (Oxford University Press).

Wallington, T., Lawrence, G. and Loechel, B. (2005), 'Regional Arrangements for Natural Resource Management in Queensland: Preliminary Findings from a Case Study of the Fitzroy Basin Association', Conference of the Australian Sociological Association, Hobart, 6–8 December.

——, —— and —— (2008), 'Reflections on the Legitimacy of Regional Environmental Governance: Lessons from Australia's Experiment in Natural Resource Management', *Journal of Environmental Policy and Planning*, 10, 1–30.

Walter, J. (2008), 'Can Kevin Kick the Command Culture?', Australian Political Studies Association, Presidential Address, Brisbane, 7 July.

—— and Strangio, P. (2007), *No Prime Minister: Reclaiming Politics from Leaders* (Sydney: UNSW Press).

Wanna, J. (2006), 'From Afterthought to Afterburner: Australia's Cabinet Implementation Unit', *Journal of Comparative Policy Analysis: Research and Practice*, 8, 347–369.

Ward, I. (2007), 'Mapping the Australian PR State', in S. Young (ed.), *Government Communication in Australia* (Cambridge University Press).

Warleigh, A (2001), '"Europeanisating" Civil Society: NGOs as Agents of Political Socialisation', *Journal of Common Market Studies*, 39, 619–39.

Watanabe, R. and Robinson, G. (2005), 'The European Union Emissions Trading Scheme', *Climate Policy*, 5, 10–14.

Weber, M. (1968), *Economy and Society* (New York: Bedminster Press).

Weiss, J. (2002), 'Public Information', in L. Salamon (ed.), *The Tools of Government: A Guide to the New Governance* (Oxford University Press).

Weiss, L. (1998), *The Myth of the Powerless State* (Ithaca: Cornell University Press).

—— and Hobson, J. (1995), *States and Economic Development: A Comparative Historical Analysis* (Cambridge: Polity).

Weiss, L. and Thurbon, E. (2006), 'Investing in Openness: The Evolution of FDI Strategy in Korea and Taiwan', *New Political Economy*, 11, 1–24.

Welch, E. and Hibiki, A. (2002), 'Japanese Voluntary Environmental Agreements: Bargaining Power and Reciprocity as Contributors to Effectiveness', *Policy Sciences*, 35, 401–24.

Whelan, J. and Lyons, K. (2005), 'Community Engagement or Community Action: Choosing Not to Play the Game', *Environmental Politics*, 14, 596–610.

Whitehead, M. (2003), ' "In the Shadow of Hierarchy": Metagovernance, Policy Reform and Urban Regeneration in the West Midlands', *Area*, 35, 6–14.

WHO (World Health Organisation) (2007), *Making the Most of World Blood Day* (Geneva: WHO).

Wilensky, H. (2002), *Rich Democracies: Political Economy, Public Policy and Performance* (Berkeley: University of California Press).

Williams, B. L. et al. (2001), 'Hierarchical Linear Models of Factors Associated with Public Participation Among Residents Living Near US Army Chemical Weapons Stockpiles sites', *Journal of Environmental Planning and Management*, 44, 41–65.

Williamson, O. (1985), *The Economic Institutions of Capitalism* (New York: Free Press).

Wilson, G. (1990), *Business and Politics: A Comparative Introduction* (London, Macmillan).

—— (2000), 'In a State?', *Governance*, 13, 235–42.

Winston, C. (2006), *Government Failure versus Market Failure* (Washington, DC: American Enterprise Institute).

Wiseman, J. (2006), 'Local Heroes: Learning From Recent Community Strengthening Initiatives in Victor', *Australian Journal of Public Administration*, 65, 95–107.

Wittman, D. (1995), *The Myth of Democratic Failure: Why Political Institutions are Efficient* (University of Chicago Press).

Wong, J. (2006), 'Technovation in Taiwan: Implications for Industrial Governance', *Governance*, 19, 651–72.

Woodward, B. (2002), *Bush at War* (New York: Simon & Schuster).

World Bank (1998), *The Initiative on Defining, Monitoring and Measuring Social Capital: Overview and Program Description* (Washington, DC: World Bank).

Worms, J. (2000), 'Old and New Civic and Social Ties in France', in R. Putnam (ed.), *Democracies in Flux: The Evolution of Social Capital in Contemporary Society* (Oxford University Press).

Wurzel, R., Bruckner, L., Jordan, A. and Zito, A. (2003), 'Struggling to Leave Behind a Highly Regulatory Past? New Environmental Policy Instruments in Austria', *Environmental Politics*, 12, 51–72.

Zysman, J. (1983), *Governments, Markets and Growth: Financial Systems and the Politics of Industrial Change* (Ithaca: Cornell University Press).

—— and Newman, A. (2006), 'The State in the Digital Economy', in J. Levy (ed.), *The State After Statism: New State Activities in the Age of Liberalisation* (Cambridge, Mass.: Harvard University Press).

Index